MILITARY LIFE UNDER NAPOLEON

by Elzéar Blaze

translation and notes by
John R. Elting

EMPEROR'S PRESS
Chicago, Illinois

MILTARY LIFE UNDER NAPOLEON

©Emperor's Press

Original Edition; Published in 1995

Printed and Bound in the United States of America

ISBN 1-883476-06

THE EMPEROR'S PRESS
5744 West Irving Park Road
Chicago, Il. 60634 U.S.A.
Toll Free, if calling in U.S.A: 1.800.59.EAGLE
Calling from outside U.S.A: 312.777.7307

Preface

from the original text.

Elzéar Blaze, the author of this book, belonged to a family long-established in Cavaillon (on the Durance River, southeast of Avignon), and noted for its contributions to the theater, music, literature, and journalism. He was born there in 1786 at Palais-Cardinal, his father's "splendid, ancient, and spacious" manor house.

At first he did not choose to take up writing or composing like the rest of his family. Young and dazzled by the victories and fame of Napoleon, he preferred to try the noble profession of arms — did not every soldier carry a marshal's baton in his cartridge box? Was that perhaps Elzéar Blaze's hope? To accomplish that he entered the Imperial Guard as a "velite" in 1804, later attending the Fontainebleau Military School from which he graduated in 1806 "with the epaulette" of a second lieutenant of infantry. He left immediately and took part in the campaign of Germany, then those of Poland and Spain, remaining in the Imperial Army until the final defeat of Napoleon. He then served under the Restoration, but retired early in 1819 with the grade of captain.

He thereafter lived on his wife's estate at Chennevières-sur-Marne, where at last he could devote himself to a passion he had always felt — that of hunting. He also began a series of books on that subject. The first, *Le Chasseur au Chien d'arrêt (Hunting with a Pointer)*, published in 1836, was apparently still being reissued in 1901!

His *La Vie Militaire Sous le Premier Empire (Military Life Under the First Empire)* appeared in 1837 as a 2-volume work, and at once enjoyed such success that copies became quite rare. Turned author, the onetime captain of the *Grande Armée* described his service with racy good humor. All its characters, from marshals of the Empire to buck privates, are depicted with an astonishing accuracy; the reader senses that they have really lived. The conversations are imagined — very much so, but at the end — in spite of their everyday behavior — one realizes that these soldiers, so well depicted by their former comrade at arms, had the hearts of warriors whose only thought was to do their duty. After finishing this volume, we are certain that you will feel the same inexpressible regret that comes when you turn, all too soon, the last page of a bestselling novel.

Translator's Note

Putting Blaze into English was a minor adventure. His style of writing was a rough version of the "stream of consciousness" technique — he wrote down whatever popped into his head as he went along, regardless of subject. Unrelated incidents were dropped in anywhere, like raisins in cookie dough. Consequently, there often is only a limited relationship between a chapter's title and its actual content. He wrote in paragraph-long sentences, liberally — and sometimes erratically — sprinkled with commas and semi-colons. Also he wrote in 1837 for other Frenchmen, many of whom had likewise followed the Emperor's eagles and drums, and so needed no detailed explanations. I have thought it best to provide these, either as footnotes or in brackets, since we are almost two centuries distant from the events and institutions Blaze describes. Occasionally I have found a word which modern French dictionaries define differently from Blaze's usage of it — but then word values change with the years; in our own American speech within those same almost-two centuries such descriptions of laudable soldierly qualities as "pretty," "stout," and "nervous" have metamorphosed into insults. Finally, Blaze's viewpoint was that of a junior officer, who could have only a sketchy understanding of the "big picture" — and often an erroneous one at that.

But what manner of man and soldier was Elzèar Blaze? Ten of his fourteen years of active service were years of combat. He went through the miserable, hungry months of the 1806-1807 Polish campaign, and the long, grinding, dreary war in Spain. By good fortune he did not go to Moscow in 1812, but 1813 found him again in Germany with Davout. He was obviously well educated; his book is stuffed with literary references, a good many of them now worse than obscure. Cheerful, fond of good living and hunting, he had a taste for practical jokes, some of them rather rough. More than most of his contemporaries, he made himself at home wherever he served, observing peoples and customs with a surprisingly impartial eye and mind. His blunt descriptions — which include French greed, stinginess, and spite — offer an unexpected resource for students of the social background of Napoleon's wars.

All in all, Blaze's memoirs present a clear-eyed, remarkably complete description of French Army life, as seen by a company-grade officer with both line and staff service. He wrote of his experiences with zest and humor — just possibly more of the latter than he felt while actually undergoing them. (We old soldiers typically come to see a funny side to our hardships — once they are safely past.) It may be that he threw in some of those typical old-soldier stories that reappear (and, in honesty, may really reoccur) in every war.

Fame may have overlooked him, but his promotions came rapidly enough. He apparently was considered a solid, reliable officer — undoubtedly something of a rake, but giving at least a surface observance to the contemporary standards of a "man of honor." He respected Napoleon, and gave him — until one April day in 1814 — efficient service, if no personal devotion. His little book tells of dangers and hardships safely survived and duty done - but not the discreditable ending of it all.[1]

John R. Elting

[1]　See Appendix I: Statement of Service..

Table of Contents

Dedication

To Ann,
beloved veteran of fifty-nine years as
Major General,[1]
Intendant General,[2]
Médecin-Major,
and Vivandiere.

---

[1]   Chief of Staff.
[2]   Chief of Administration and Supply

I

THE VELITES

Under the Empire, there were three different ways of entering the Army: you could enlist as a private, which was the simplest and least expensive; you could enroll as a velite;[1] or you could secure admittance as a student at the Military School at Fontainebleau.

A lady of my acquaintance, when she wished to punish her little daughter, said to her, "Mademoiselle, since you have not been well-behaved today, you may not take any lessons."[2] And the child would think herself punished, and the next day would do whatever her mother wished.

If Napoleon, in creating the velites of the Imperial Guard, had set only physical standards for admission into this new organization, he might have found few volunteers; however the decree establishing it required that the young candidates have a certain education and that they pay an annuity of 200 francs to serve with its infantry, or 300 with the cavalry — all to have the honor of being a soldier of the Guard, with the promise of an officer's commission after four years. A mass of candidates descended on the Ministry of War and all vacancies were quickly filled. Likewise, in a commercial enterprise, if you offer 500 franc shares at half-price, nobody wants them; price them at 600 francs and they are soon sold.

Philip Augustus [1165-1223] was the first of the kings of France to have a guard of picked men. He was warned one day that the sheiks of the Mountain[3] had planned to assassinate him; immediately he assembled his gallant nobility, chose a hundred gentlemen whom he armed with bronze maces and bows and arrows, and ordered them to follow him everywhere. They were called "the sergeants at arms." That was the origin of the first Guard of our Kings; from it came the *Gardes du Corps*, the Imperial Guard, and the Royal Guard.[4]

At the beginning of the 19th century warlike thoughts fermented in all our young heads; the immortal exploits of our armies made our hearts beat and filled them with an exalted enthusiasm. In ancient Greece Themistocles lost sleep thinking of the triumphs of Miltiades.[5] Ambition, that powerful stimulus of men's actions, which often mingles with patriotism, sent our twenty-year-olds towards our expanding frontiers. Perhaps also the prospect of the inevitable conscription encouraged them to join up ahead of time — like a swimmer who, seeing a storm approaching, puts his clothes under shelter and leaps into the river.

---

[1] Velites: A borrowing from early Rome, where velites were light-armed young men who skirmished to the front and flanks of the heavy infantry of the legions.

[2] Young girls of good family in Blaze's day were educated at home.

[3] This was the aberrant Ismailite sect of Moslems, known to the crusaders as the "Assassins". Their chief, the "Old Man of the Mountain", terrorized Persia and Asia Minor by his hashish-and-religion crazed daggermen during the 12th century.

[4] *"Gardes du Corps"* were the cavalry bodyguard of the King before the French Revolution; the "Royal Guard" was formed by the restored Bourbons during 1814-1816.

[5] Rival Athenian generals of the First Persian War.

The Army's ranks were always ready to receive a new recruit. From time to time the cannon thinned them; there were always vacant places. However, the pack, the musket, and barracks life frightened gently reared young men, much more than the cannon balls and bullets. That novitiate might be very long; it might not ever end.[6] You had to be confident of withstanding the hardships, of being a better soldier than your comrades — such were the essential requirements to be commissioned out of the ranks.

The Military School of Fontainebleau's gates were open for 1,200 francs a year, but the crowd of young men applying for admission was greater than could be accommodated. Those who did not have time to await their turn for admission[7] entered the velites; this service was harder, it was more difficult to win your epaulet,[8] but you were in uniform sooner — and, at eighteen years, that was *really* important. Only if you had been a soldier at that epoch can you imagine the magic of a uniform. What hope surged in all those young heads topped for the first time with a plume! Every French soldier carried the baton of a Marshal of France in his cartridge box; it was only a question of getting it out. We foresaw no difficulty in that; even today I think that there was no limit to our ambitious daydreams.

One thing worried us: What if Napoleon halted in his successful career? If by chance he should decide to make peace, good-bye to all our hopes. Fortunately our fears were not realized, for he cut out more work for us than we were able to handle.

The velites were soldiers in the Imperial Guard; the annuity that they paid gave them the honor to learn their trade with the elite of the army. They arrived full of zeal, decided at first that they were not drilled sufficiently — and soon were complaining that the drills lasted too long; their early fervor was calmed. Having passed through those different phases, I remember it well.

Fifteen days after my arrival I had worked hard enough to be thought qualified to mount my first guard.[9] Once on that service, the veteran chasseurs[10] who had been assigned with me discussed all the young velites who, in my position, had paid their *"bienvenue"*[11] by buying their comrades a meal from a neighboring restaurant. This one had done it properly; that one had conducted himself like a *pékin*,[12] hardly even providing free drinks; another had done it magnificently — fresh pork chops, vintage wine, coffee, liqueurs. I said that, in that case, I would do as much. With one voice they all proclaimed me a good fellow. (The word "fellow" was not exactly the one those chasseurs used, but I cannot employ the one they did[13] — my bashful pen refuses. Content yourselves with "fellow".)

During the dinner I was loaded with compliments; they insisted largely on the aptitude which I had shown since my arrival, in the extraordinary success I had demonstrated in handling my weapons. Nobody, said these old "grumblers", had

---

[6] Voluntary enlistment as a private.

[7] Because they would soon face conscription.

[8] Become an officer. A *sous* (second) lieutenant wore his single epaulet on his left shoulder, and a fringeless *contre-epaulette* on his right.

[9] To be a member of the guard detail, competent to stand sentry duty.

[10] Blaze had been assigned to the famous Regiment of Chasseurs à Cheval of the Guard.

[11] "Welcome"— the customary treat given by new comers, to pay for their "footing."

[12] A mere 105% civilian.

[13] Possibly *"bougre,"* which has various scatological connotations.

mounted guard so soon; all other velites had required two months after their admission to reach that excessive honor. Each of them predicted high destinies for me; I would go far. (Looking at it matter-of-factly, it is plain that those gentlemen were not mistaken, for I have done well indeed.)

Although a greenhorn, I was not fool enough to take at face value the praises they showered on their host; I knew very well that they were speaking to my dinner. However, all that pleased me: I had my flatterers — me, a buck private — and these flatterers were the conquerors of Egypt and Italy. These mustachioed old foxes praised a young *blanc-bec*[14] whose virgin chin still had not felt a barber's hands. For all that, in higher classes you find courtiers and men who believe what they say. Everyone in that world has a little group who praise him; the people who compose it move around him as the planets do around the sun. Returning home, such persons become center and sun in their turn; thus the courtier who leaves the king's presence finds courtiers who wait upon him; those similarly have still others, on down to the lowest levels.

That day then I carved my name with my bayonet[15] on the wall behind the sentry-box. Chance having brought me many years later to the gate of that parade ground, I wanted to see if I could still read it; after having searched long and hard, I found it all covered with moss. That dinner in the guard room came back into my memory with all its happy details. I asked myself if any other guest might remain alive, thinking of all the events which had taken place in the thirty year interval. If some old chasseur had shown his face, darkened by the sun of the pyramids, I would have embraced him joyfully — and oh the fine dinner we would have had together!

In garrison, the soldiers of the Imperial Guard were, as compared to those of the line,[16] little Sardanapaluses.[17] In each barracks room they had a cook, a Sybaritic[18] luxury which the rest of the army ridiculed — while envying it.

I shall explain to you here the process by which military pay furnishes all the needs of a soldier. That of the Guard being an exception, we will take that of the line as it is today.[19]

When a soldier enters a regiment, he is clothed at the expense of the state. He receives, in addition, a 40-franc clothing allowance which serves to purchase the shirts, shoes, and leggings for which he is personally responsible. That sum, increased every day by a stoppage of ten *centimes* from his pay, is reduced every time he does not have a "full pack" (the regulation three shirts and three pairs of shoes). The regimental supply room will then issue whatever he lacks. Thus his "linen and shoe fund" tends to vary constantly. At the end of each quarter, if the soldier's *livret*,[20] which shows the running account of property issued him, carries a total above 35 francs, the surplus is paid him at once, a procedure called "balancing the account." When there is a large deficit the soldier's "pocket sou"[21] is added to the usual stoppage until the account is balanced. It

---

[14] Johnny Raw/Greenhorn/Raw recruit.
[15] The chasseurs à cheval were issued bayonets for their carbines.
[16] The regular army.
[17] Sardanapalus — the mythical last king of Assyria, famous for wealth and luxury.
[18] From Sybaris, a Greek colony in southern Italy, proverbial for self-indulgence.
[19] 1837.
[20] The soldier's pocket account book.

"You have most estimable parents."
A recruit treating veterans. (Bellange)

was an honor for the soldier to maintain a surplus, showing he had a sense of order; the company commanders themselves took pride in it. I knew a captain who, congratulated by the ladies on the fine appearance of his soldiers, enthusiastically responded, "They all have their accounts in order!"

This worthy officer had the ambition to be considered the oldest soldier in the army. He would have been pleased to have been a hundred years old and to show eighty years of service, not counting campaigns. You can easily see that all his tastes were of that nature.

By habit, he always lodged in a house on the edge of the parade ground, opposite the guard room.[22] "This is not for my sake," he said. "It is for my old soldiers. In the morning they watch my windows. 'Good, there is our Captain getting up. Look — now he is getting dressed. See, to be sure he is shaving.' Since that gives them pleasure, why should I not indulge them?"

The soldier's pay is 52 centimes a day; 10 centimes go to that linen and shoe fund; 32 or 35 centimes to the mess fund [for food]. The 7 or 10 centimes remaining serve to play the boy[23] after the laundress and hairdresser have been paid. Every five days the soldier receives the *"pret"*; that is to say five days pay in advance, as a loan.[24] He therefor receives 25 centimes of "new silver." That modest sum pays for tobacco and a small drink; there remains enough to promenade Perrette on Sunday. But he certainly does not take her to dine at Very's.[25] But what does that matter? One enjoys oneself more sometimes in the stalls than in the dress circle.[26] The great restaurants have killed more people than army ration bread. Those who eat it are cheerful, without cares, fearing neither bankruptcy nor thieves; every day brings them their necessities. What should I say? The soldiers have a surplus. The poor always can find a morsel of bread at the barracks' gates. When they ask at the fine residences, they often get only a "God bless you."

A high aristocracy exists in the regiments: the grenadiers and voltigeurs[27] received twice as much as the fusiliers — that is to say that their "sou of the grenade"[28] added to their "pocket sou," raised their *pret* for five days to the round sum of 50 centimes. Thus it is the elite companies who drink the better wine; the soldiers of the center[29] are not able to come up with the sealed bottles.[30] "That's fine for the grenadiers, who can afford it," the fusilier Pechemafou said to me one day.

In Paris the soldiers receive a supplement of 7½ centimes a day, but this goes to the mess fund. The stomach gets it all. The pocket sou is never more than 5 centimes.

---

[21] His pret. See note 24. A sou equaled 5 centimes.
[22] This normally was next to the main gate of the barracks area.
[23] Have fun.
[24] *"Pret"* meant both "ready cash" and "loan."
[25] A famous Paris restaurant.
[26] Of a theater.
[27] Respectively, the pick of the regiment's bigger and smaller men. These companies (one of each in every battalion) were classed as elite troops and therefore drew "high pay".
[28] Soldier slang for the extra sou of high pay. A flaming grenade was the grenadiers' traditional insignia.
[29] Non-elite. In line infantry, the four "fusilier" companies in each battalion.
[30] Apparently Blaze means that they could only afford to buy their wine by the glass, not by whole bottles.

The government furnishes firewood and bread to the soldier who must pay for all the rest of his food. Those 32 centimes deducted from his pay for the mess fund, when combined with those of his comrades, furnish money enough to have a piece of beef or mutton, flanked with vegetables. "When you are in the regiment, you will eat like a crazy cow,"[31] people frequently tell the young conscripts.[32] That is nonsense: In the regiment the food is good, healthful, sufficient, and better than that of three-fourths of the French peasants.

The need to eat, which returns several times a day, is a pleasure for a man. Recruiting sergeants know that well; it is always the means by which they catch the attention of prospective recruits. "Do you like roast chicken? Please tell me if you like roast chickens? For, if you don't like them, I'll tell you frankly not to enlist. You know very well that in the army we don't always have time to prepare a regular meal. In that case we do what we can — a chicken, a 2-pound loaf of bread, a bottle of wine, and everyone handles it according to his fancy. You see, my friends, we must take things as they come." The idlers find this very much to their liking, and they enlist.

You rarely eat roast chicken in the barracks mess. The dinner, without being sumptuous, is sufficient. One does better there than in fine hotels.

There are however men whom the ration does not satisfy. I have known those whose stomach absorbed a day's nourishment in an hour. For them, you request an order from the Minister of War, and soon they are issued double rations. One soldier named Dabreuil, a living colossus, passed in review before the Emperor, carrying a 4-pounder gun like a musket.[33]

"You are really strong," Napoleon said to him.

"Yes, Sire, fairly so. I could do much better if I were better nourished, but I do not eat enough, my rations do not suffice me."

"I accord you two rations."

"I have those already."

"Very well, go for four."

"*Vive l'Empereur!*"

Each time a soldier receives a shirt or a pair of shoes from the supply room, the first sergeant enters the resulting balance in his *livret*. One day I was with a veteran captain who had never won a prize in school. (You will soon comprehend why.) A soldier of his company came to complain that his clothing account had not been correctly done. The company *fourrier*[34] was immediately called in; to justify himself, he first laid out the receipts, showing the plaintiff what sums had been due him, then passing to the debits against them. After having enumerated the number of shirts, pairs of shoes, and leggings furnished, the *fourrier* went through the additions and subtractions in each column to check the balance. In doing so, he repeated softly the numerals that he entered and those he retained.[35] We heard him murmur between his teeth, "I enter two and retain one; I enter six and retain two; I enter three and retain nine." At that last number the captain stopped the fourrier. "The Devil," he said, "If I let you keep that up, you'd

---

[31] A quaint Gallic expression meaning "have it rough."
[32] Recruit brought in by the annual conscription — a draftee.
[33] Obviously, just the gun tube and *not* tube and carriage!
[34] Combination company clerk and supply sergeant.
[35] Americans would say "carry/carried."

soon be rich. How can you expect that no one will complain, when you are always retaining. I know very well that the *fourrier's* assignment is a *benefice*,[36] but you should pluck the chicken without making it squawk. As long as you said 'I retain one; I retain two' I have let you go, because everyone must live — but, profiting from my weakness, you want to retain nine! I won't stand for that; also, for you punishment, you will settle that man's account without retaining anything."

The *fourrier* appealed to me; I was obliged to intervene to explain the mechanism of addition to the brave captain. It took a long time to get him to comprehend the basics of arithmetic, and I am not certain that I succeeded. However struck by the profundity of my reasoning, which he did not understand, he took me from that day on for a genius. "That young fellow," he would say in speaking of me, "knows more that we do. I'll bet that he studied to become a priest." Among the soldiers, to study to become a priest is the *ne plus ultra* of education; they cannot find more expressive words to describe a learned man; those completely express their thought.

A good many velites wearied of an enlisted man's life; to become officers more quickly, they transferred to the Fontainebleau military school. Others, after having applied for admission to the school when all places there were taken, pushed by their impatience to get into uniform as soon as possible, entered the velites, whose elastic ranks would always open for a newcomer. I was one of the latter. My turn came to go to Fontainebleau. I left to recommence my education. In the velites I had drilled on horseback, there we maneuvered on foot; from the carbine I must pass to the infantry musket. That was nothing much. In the Imperial Guard you wore your hair cut short in front with a queue behind; at the military school you had a forelock and no queue. As a result, for six months, cut before and cut behind, I was always cropped; my head remained denuded and very much resembled that of a choir boy.

---

[36] Ecclesiastic term meaning a post guaranteeing a fixed income. Here, one allowing for continual graft.

II
The Military School of Fontainebleau

The governor of the Fontainebleau Military School was General Bellavène.[1] Everyone who knew him could say that place seemed to have been created for him. We thought him severe and we were wrong; when you have 600 eighteen-year-olds to guide, it is difficult to manage them without a very firm hand. His *alter ego*, the brave Kuhman,[2] seconded him admirably. That epithet "the brave" had been given him by a man who knew what it meant, by Napoleon himself. He was a good, excellent Alsatian, who spoke a jargon of French, was an ultra-strict disciplinarian, and dreamed only of drilling. I see him still above the gate at the moment when the student battalion fell in to parade under arms, drawing himself up an extra three inches and shouting "Heads up! Heads up! Don't move! Immobility is the finest movement of the drill."

The antiquary who sees the Parthenon or the ruins of Balbeck,[3] the painter placed before the masterpieces of a Raphaël or Michael-Angelo; the dilettante seated in the pit of the *Theatre-Italien*, the hunter watching his pointer, experience less pleasure than the brave Kuhman watching a platoon maneuver according to the regulations. When a movement was well executed, when a conversion[4] took place exactly and precisely, tears would slip from his eyes, wetting his powder-blackened face.[5] He could not find a word to express his satisfaction; he contemplated his work and admired it himself. "Nothing is so fine" he would say sometimes, "as a soldier under arms. Motionless, head straight, chest out — it is superb, it is magnificent, it is impressive."

At five in the morning, the drummer awakened us. Lessons in history, geography, mathematics, drawing, and fortification kept us busy hour after hour. You relaxed by working at something different and — to vary our pleasures — four hours of ably managed drill were interspersed through our day in a very agreeable manner so that, when we went to bed, our heads were stuffed with the heroes of Greece and Rome, rivers and mountains, angles and tangents, ditches and bastions. All that got slightly muddled in our minds; the drill alone was practical: our sore knees, shoulders and hands kept us from confounding it with the rest.

Novels were prohibited at the school. One of our officers detested them. When he walked through the study halls he confiscated all books which seemed to him to be part of the "blue library."[6] He knew the titles of the books we were supposed to have; the rest were assumed to be novels, to be forbidden, seizable, and a lawful capture.

---

[1] Jacques-Nicolas Bellavene, general of brigade 1796; general of division 1807. Especially known for service as director of studies at St. Cyr.

[2] The school's adjutant.

[3] Baalbek, Ba'albek. (Originally Heliopolis). Ruined city in Lebanon.

[4] A change of direction, usually by a wheeling movement.

[5] Prolonged service with black-powder weapons would leave powder grains embedded in the skin.

[6] Apparently "invisible library" — one that did not officially exist.

The students were supposed to know Latin. It was not taught at the school — consequently Vergil was not listed on our officer's catalog. One morning in the study hall I was reading the *Aeneid*; he passed behind me and seized my book, like a vulture carrying off a nightingale.

"Another novel!" he shouted in triumph.

"You are mistaken; it is Vergil."

"What does he write about, this Vergil?"

"Of the siege of Troy, of wars, of battles —"

"Troy! Troy! That's a fable! Another novel. I'm certain. Read *The School of the Platoon* — that's the best book to educate young men. If you must have something different, imitate that student next to you. He studies; he's a young man who spends his time usefully. If he stops his reading of the interesting *Regulations of 1791* [7] it is for books of philosophy. He doesn't waste his time like you reading nonsense." (But my "neighbor" was reading *Philosopher Thérèse* .)[8]

"See how tricky these students are! To fool me, they have gotten novels printed in code." So said our gallant officer while confiscating a *Tables of Logarithms*.

Our mess at the school resembled that of soldiers in barracks — ration bread, stew, and kidney beans alternating with lentils; that, as you can see, was the essentials without superfluity. Bringing in any sort of tidbits was forbidden. Young men are gourmands, and we were always trying to invent new ways to smuggle them in. The porter,[9] like a terrible customs-officer, seized everything that was the least bit suspicious; since he could sell what he confiscated, God knows he kept a strict watch!

Once a week we went into the Forest of Fontainebleau, either to make a survey[10] or for artillery drill. The artillery officers or the professors of mathematics who were with us on those days were much more indulgent than the officers responsible for the administration of the school. They permitted us to meet with a crowd of boys from pastry shops, restaurants, and cook shops[11] with baskets full of fine things, the price of which was increased to take advantage of our need. It was, so to speak, tacitly understood that the officers would see nothing for a quarter-of-an-hour. What resulted? You ate a lot and quickly; many students came back to the school with fine cases of indigestion which, the next day, sent them to the infirmary.

Every week, the same thing happened. The school physician said that the school's cannon were as dangerous to us as those of the enemy would be.

Like men who go to get drunk outside the city gates,[12] we could smuggle in nothing except what we had in our stomachs. On reentering, we were always checked by

7 The French infantry drill regulations.
8 A novel.
9 Short for *portier-consigne* — the gate-keeper of a military installation, usually a retired NCO.
10 For mapping or to lay out a fortification.
11 These last specialized in cooked meats — the McDonalds of Napoleonic France.
12 A duty was levied on wine brought in through the city "barriers," so it was cheaper at drinking places outside them.

piercing eyes, searched sometimes by skilled hands; contrabanders were punished. However it was disagreeable, after having fowls, pates, and ham as we wished for a day, to return the next to a plate of plain cooked lentils. The difference was enormous, much too sharp; to make it disappear gradually and to prolong our gastronomic joys, I invented the "cartridge box pate." That sublimity brought the most flattering praises from my comrades, and placed my name among those of the benefactors of the school.

You know or you don't know how a cartridge box is constructed; it is a leather box containing a block of wood pierced with holes to contain the cartridges. When we left the school we had our muskets and our cartridge boxes, but they were empty. One day when, in the Forest of Fontainebleau, I bargained with appropriate seriousness with a pastry cook's boy, a bright idea went through my brain, — the most ordinary man sometimes has flashes of genius. I took out the wood I have mentioned and — showing it to the scullion — told him to make us pates in precisely that form. I told all my comrades. Eight days later, before leaving, each of us left his block of wood under his bed. We came back, drums beating, with our contraband pates, which we had the pleasure of bringing in under the noses of all the "customs officers" of the school. We did it again every week.

During the time I was at Fontainebleau, the secret was carefully kept. I don't know what happened later, but — since all things must end, even in the best of worlds, even the most useful things, the cartridge box pates were bound to have their ill-fated day.

One day General Bellavène gave a grand dinner for the officers of the school and the leading citizens of Fontainebleau. Thirty guests gathered in his drawing-room. The students, walking past the kitchen windows, inhaled a mix of aromas which caused a high degree of irritation to their salivary glands and the mucous membranes of their stomachs.

Reasoning by analogy and consulting their memories, they deduced that the general's dinner would be excellent. Certain intrepid gallants, humiliated by having to eat their bread in the kitchen smoke, resolved all at once to judge the talents of the general's cook by a more positive operation than merely smelling.

Like grenadiers storming a redoubt, they broke into the kitchen: cooks and cooks boys were seized, thrust head first into sacks. Into another sack they hurriedly stuffed woodcocks and partridges, salmon and turbot, cold and hot pates, and turkey stuffed with truffles. All that made an unusual ragout – never mind, no one was particular. It was carried off, distributed, eaten; it vanished in short order. The general and his officers arrived, red with the anger of men who had nothing left to eat. They searched, turned things over, turned them over again, interrogated — and found nothing, learned nothing. They confined us all to our barracks, which did nothing to keep them from having a very unsatisfactory meal. No one ever learned the identity of the guilty students. Although the right to punish them has expired with the passing years, I think it best not to mention their names.

The height of style[13] at the school was to smoke; first, because it was forbidden; next, because we thought it gave us a military air. The smuggling of tobacco went on night and day in small quantities, but a little brook that runs constantly finally fills the reservoir. The school drummers[14] did nothing else from morning to evening, yet had

[13] *bon ton.*
[14] Part of the school's regular army cadre.

16

difficulty filling the pretended needs of their consumers. We smoked in certain secluded areas where, during periods of recreation, some thirty intrepid smokers would brave the effluvium which the tobacco smoke could not always neutralize.[15] Had they been condemned to smoke there, they would have screamed to high Heaven, but it was forbidden, therefore it was delightful.

It appears that, for certain men, to smoke is a thing of absolute necessity, like bread or like air. One day I overheard several officers talking about the various privations that they had experienced before, during, and after the battle of Eylau; one complained of not having any bread for three days — another of having to eat horse meat – a third of having had nothing at all to eat. Then an old hussar officer said, with the greatest composure, "And there was I, who during five days was obliged to smoke hay."

Duels were frequent at the Military School. Before my arrival, they fought with bayonets but, a student having been killed, the school "suppressed" that weapon. That didn't stop the dueling; we acquired foils, bit by bit, and in a pinch we used compasses attached to the end of a stick — all that to give ourselves a dashing air.[16] When, by a duel we had won that, and could join to it the reputation of being a smoker, we had reached the apogee of glory.

One fine day, during a review, General Bellavene announced the names of those who would leave on the morrow for the army. Oh! What emotions as he read his list! Our hearts beat hard enough to crack our breasts. What joy among those chosen! What anxiety among those whose names had not yet been pronounced! To put on an officer's full-dress coat, wear an epaulet, gird on an *epée*[17] — oh, such wonderful things when one is eighteen. We were soldiers; an instant afterwards we became officers. One word had produced that blessed metamorphosis. Man is always a child; throughout his life he has a need for playthings. His self-esteem often depends upon the coat he wears. In this he perhaps is correct because the common herd does judge a man by his clothes. Be that as it may, with our second lieutenants' epaulets, we thought we really were something.[18]

A captain of the school staff was detailed to take us to the Emperor's headquarters. We were to go by post,[19] at least that's what they said, but the fact was that they bundled us, a dozen each, into 2-wheeled carts and that we moved at a walk from sunrise to sunset, covering two days' normal marches in one day. Before our departure, we had written to the best restaurant in Montereau[20] to prepare a dinner for the 127 of us, at twenty francs a head, for the day of our arrival. However, as soon as our column of carts left the school, it was surrounded by merchants offering all sorts of edibles. For three days, in preparation for our departure, it was for us that all the spits had turned, the ovens

---

[15] Obviously, they were in the latrine, which — in France — is usually a place with old and remarkable airs.

[16] "...un air crâne."

[17] An officer's light, straight dress sword.

[18] The normal course at Fontainebleau was 2 years. However Napoleon needed officer replacements for losses during his Eylau campaign.

[19] "Post" normally meant the government mail coach system, which offered a certain degree of comfort, as comfort went in those days.

[20] This must be the Montereau some 50 miles southeast of Paris.

[21] In 1808.

baked, and the cooks cooked. The town of Fontainebleau should feel the effects of the transfer of the school to St Cyr;[21] we were such terrible consumers.

If it is disagreeable to have a devouring appetite without being able to satisfy it, it is worse when you seat yourself at a magnificently spread table and find it physically impossible to swallow even a macaroon. That is precisely the state in which we all found ourselves on arriving at Montereau.[22] What to do? Not being able to eat, it was necessary to content ourselves with the sad role of spectators. After having thoroughly deplored our lack of foresight, after having paid our bill, we called together all the poor, all the street children[23] of the town, and gave ourselves the honest pleasure of seeing them eat.

In all the towns our greatest occupation was getting ourselves saluted by the sentinels. Nothing could be as ludicrous as the gravity and especially the indifference with which we returned their salutes. All the old soldiers before whom we constantly passed and repassed must have joked among themselves over our childishness.

The whole of our ambition was to have a certain rakish appearance. We smoked, we drank, thinking that these rascally habits would give us a military air. Our coats, our swords, our epaulets were all new, fresh from the store shelves. We exposed them to the rain and the sun to give them the appearance of having seen some service. However the school buttons on our coats[24] and our beardless faces betrayed us; Captain Dornier, who marched at our head, made it plain that despite our eight-day-old epaulets, we still were only scholars.

One day — it was at Cassel — we found ourselves at an inn where I ate quickly so as to be able to see something of the town before our departure, when two of our comrades suddenly quarreled and resolved to settle things immediately,[25] sword in hand. We tried vainly to get them to be reasonable; they would listen to nothing, and one of them chose me to accompany him as a witness. The weather was frightful, the snow fell in big flakes, and I did not much care to go out in the open fields to assist in their single combat.

"Wait until tomorrow," I said. "We shall have better weather, or — even better — put off the business indefinitely; if you want to prove your courage, once you are assigned to a regiment there will be plenty of opportunities."

All was useless. However I could see that the two champions were really no more anxious to fight than we two witnesses — that they were trying hard to appear angry, in continuing out of vanity a quarrel which they both regretted having started.

"Gentlemen," I told them, "since you won't listen to reason, let's go. We are ready to follow you, but understand clearly that, once you are on the ground,[26] no reconciliation will be possible — you must fight."

"That's all we want," said both adversaries at once.

"If you wish to settle the affair, the occasion is favorable. A bottle of this inn's champagne could get you to agree much better than a sword thrust. Reflect – there still is time."

"No, no," said the two together. "Let's go."

"All right! Let's go."

---

[22] They had gorged themselves sick on food picked up after leaving the school.
[23] Term used was *"polisson"* which can also mean "rascally or loose person."
[24] Worn until they were assigned to a regiment.
[25] Fight a duel.
[26] Where the duel will take place.

We took the Berlin road so that we could rejoin our column as it passed, and immediately after leaving Cassel we cut across the fields to a little woodlot near the highway. The cold, the snow, and second thoughts had markedly tempered the pugnacity of my two fine fellows.

"I responded a little hotly perhaps," said the one who had chosen me as his witness. "But why did he say such a thing to me?"

"What does it matter! That's no longer of any importance. The time has come to draw your sword."

"But —" said the other, "I don't ask anything more than to forget the whole thing, if he will agree that he was to blame."

"Not so," replied his witness. "It is necessary to fight. Come on, coats off," he added as soon as we had found a suitable spot.

"Coats off! That suits us."

They commenced to strip, but — whether because of the cold or for any other reason, that operation went very slowly on both sides. Then, seeing that he could get no help from me, the one whose witness I was turned to his adversary's witness, "I ask your judgement," he said, "what would you do if you were in my place?"

"In your place, I'd fight."

"But," said the other gallant, happy to see negotiations beginning.

"But," I interrupted, "you must fight."

"However —"

"There is no but, no however in this business. We did not come here for nothing! *En garde!*"

Our two blustering boys realized that they could no longer back out, and so their swords crossed — but at long reach.

After several thrusts back and forth, one of them — I no longer remember which – received a cat-scratch wound on his hand. We proclaimed the fight over, their honor saved; our two cavaliers embraced one another.

We traveled gaily for we were young, without worries and full of anticipation. While crossing Prussia, then Poland, and then Prussia again,[27] whether things went well or badly, we were always laughing.

It was in the homeland of Copernicus[28] at Thorn that we realized that we were nearing the *Grande Armée*. That town, encumbered with the depots of almost all of its regiments, had half its houses converted into hospitals. It was necessary to find quarters overnight in garrets and stables. We began to comprehend that war might not be exactly the finest thing in the world.

The army at that time was in the camps which it had occupied after the battle of Eylau, won by the French — and by the Russians, to hear them tell about it. Napoleon was at Finckenstein,[29] reviewing his troops, repairing his February[30] losses, communicating his extraordinary activity to everyone around him. It was there for the first time that I saw that astonishing man, whom some people would make a god, and certain imbeciles have

---

[27] East Prussia.

[28] Famous Polish astronomer (1473-1543). An example of the breadth of Blaze's education.

[29] A large castle, near Osterode in East Prussia (now Ostroda, northern Poland), approximately 85 miles southeast of Danzig.

[30] The costly campaign and battle of Eylau, 10 January – 4 March.

called a fool. He has proved that he was neither. The judgments so far made of him are too close to the events of his life to be free of partiality. It will be impossible to write a proper history of Napoleon for a long time: for that we must wait until his contemporaries and their sons are dead, until the enthusiasm has cooled and the hatreds are extinct. Then, and only then, a man without passions, consulting the thousands of written volumes and those that will be written, may be able to find the truth at the bottom of the well.[31] From these materials a monument will rise, superb, imperishable. To aid in that grand construction, I bring my grain of sand.

We maneuvered before the Emperor,[32] who appeared sufficiently pleased; the next day, they scattered us through all the regiments of the army.

At the army headquarters at Finckenstein, I met my former velite comrades again; I had the satisfaction of seeing that they all envied my epaulets. I had commenced to get used to them, and the congratulations I received had all the charm of novelty to me. Many things have no value in men's eyes except for the envy they incite among those who are not able to possess them. Thus a child happily takes back a toy he has long ago thrown away because a little friend happens to want to play with it.

A veteran training a recruit. (Bellange)

31 From the old proverb, "Truth lies at the bottom of the well."
32 Napoleon always put replacements through appropriate drills, to test their readiness.

III
Bivouacs and Marauders

Behold us on a fine plain, ploughed up by artillery wheels, trampled by the cavalry; it has rained all day. It is here that we are going to sleep. The order is given: twenty men from each company are sent into the neighboring villages to bring back wood, straw, and food. Shortly a curious spectacle comes into view.

"The market will be a good," say the soldiers. "Here come the merchants."

Indeed from all directions we see our intrepid freebooters come, loaded with sacks of poultry, baskets of eggs, loaves of bread spitted on their ramrods. Some drive sheep and cows, oxen and pigs before them; others the peasants they have impressed to haul cart loads of wood and straw. From the latters' sullen faces, the interjections they utter, it's easy to see that they are not happy, but their words are drowned out by the bawlings of the animals and the laughter of the soldiers.

Nevertheless the fires are lighted, the camp kettles begin to boil; night falls and everyone has done his best to improvise some sort of shelter — but an aide-de-camp, a real kill-joy, arrives at the gallop, and soon an order, passed along our line, stops our preparations. We must move out without drum beat or trumpet call; to camp again 1,000 paces further on. We leave our campfires burning and will light new ones at our new campsite. The enemy will believe that there are 20,000 men in the area, though there really are only 10,000. This maneuver doubtlessly is very clever, but the 10,000 do not appreciate it.

Our camp kettles are quickly emptied; the steaming meat, which has begun to cook, is taken out, wrapped in straw, and fastened on the haversacks[1] and we move out, to commence again exactly what we had been doing. We light our new fires and soon no one would have noticed any difference.

When we bivouacked in the face of the enemy, everyone slept fully clothed and — as they say — with both eyes open, ready for anything. Sometimes we went a month without being able to take off our boots which was certainly most uncomfortable. Sometimes also, when we lay down for the night, we would feel the urge to unbutton our coat, then our trousers; we would loosen one buckle, then another. Thereafter it would take longer to get straightened out again than if we had undressed completely. When it was cold, everyone slept around their campfire, but that broiled you on one side while you froze on the other; you *could* keep turning over like Saint Lawrence,[2] but that was not at all convenient.

When you were in reserve, you had fewer precautions to observe and so could undress. The officers had canvas bed sacks which they used instead of blankets, and

---

[1]   A light canvas bag carried on a cloth strip over the right shoulder, used in the field for rations and small necessities.

[2]   Patron saint of leatherworkers, martyred by being slow-roasted on a gridiron.

two bundles of straw for their mattress and feather bed. Under such conditions the sack was really preferable to blankets since its tight seams let nothing penetrate it.[3]

Reveille in a bivouac is never amusing. You have slept because you were exhausted; but when you get up, your limbs are numb; mustaches look like tufts of alfalfa with drops of dew on every hair. Teeth are clenched; you have to really rub your gums to restore the circulation.

These minor inconveniences always occur, even when the weather is fine, but when it rains or turns cold the situation greatly complicates itself, and that is why heroes have the gout[4] and rheumatism.

Those who have not made war never can have an idea of the evils which it brings with it. I shall not give a complete description; that would exceed the limits I have set myself. I shall say only two words on our life in bivouacs and on the waste that it made. We lived on what our soldiers "found;" our swift marches made it impossible for our supplies to keep up with us — even when we had a functioning supply system. In rich areas, our foragers brought in twenty times as much food as we could consume; the rest went to waste. The soldier lives from day to day; today, he lacks everything; tomorrow, if he eats well, he forgets yesterday's privations and doesn't worry about tomorrow. Neither does he think of the days to come, of other regiments which will arrive at the area he is leaving, or that, while taking what he needs, that it would be wise to leave something for those who will be following him. Not at all! A company of 100 men has already killed two oxen, which is enough — but then they find four cows, six calves, and twelve sheep, and kill them all without pity, so that they can eat their tongues, kidneys, and brains. They go into a wine cellar where twenty tuns present a majestic and imposing battle-front; they have no tool to tap them, but that doesn't trouble soldiers — they shoot holes in them and at once twenty fountains of wine spray on all sides amid great shouts of laughter. If there were 100 tuns in the cellar, they would pierce them all at the same time because, after all, that would make it easier for them all to drink at once. All the wine runs out, all is wasted, and frequently the drunkards, swallowing too much, fall and drown themselves in the floods of wine which fill the cellar.

Austria is a rich, productive country; at each bivouac we abandoned enough food to nourish a regiment for fifteen days. The soldiers, after having marched all day, spent part of the night finding food, then cooking and eating it.

They slept as little as possible; spending their time making hashes, pancakes, and fritters. Since some stomachs aren't strong enough to handle such sustained eating and drinking, the result was numerous cases of indigestion which filled the hospitals. In the army, abundance is sometimes more damaging than scarcity.

The soldier's supreme happiness is to "*godailler.*" I do not know if that is a French word but, no problem, it expresses my thought and I shall use it.[5] In general they prefer to cook and fry for themselves, rather than have good meals properly served to them at regular hours. Near Linz, I was billeted on a very rich farmer with all my company; our host had entreated me to maintain strict discipline in his farm yard, promising to provide my men with everything they needed. They were bedded down in straw in a big barn, and three times a day they were served a very well prepared and plentiful meal. While making my rounds, I decided to ask these characters if they were satisfied with their treatment.

---

[3] Probably, like shako covers, the canvas was waxed or oiled to make it waterproof.
[4] Susceptible people *can* develop gout after overexertion and stress.
[5] In modern French "stuff and swill."

"So-so," they said. "Not too well."

"I intend that your meals are good and plentiful. It is only fair, after so much hardship, to have a little compensation."

"We don't have too much to complain about, but..."

"Has your food been bad?"

"No — but —"

"Has the quantity been insufficient?"

"No — but—"

"But! but! Explain yourselves. What were given today for dinner?"

"Soup, boiled beef, a plate of vegetables, roast mutton, a salad, cheese, a bottle of wine apiece and a little glass of brandy.

"The devil! And you aren't content?"

"Excuse me, my lieutenant — but —"

"I hope that you never are worse off."

Later, an old corporal told me, "By God, you try too hard to satisfy those parishioners.[6] Give them toasted angels and they'd still complain!"

They would have preferred, without any doubt, to have had less and to have prepared their own meals. It angered them to see cattle, sheep, pigeons, and chickens existing peacefully in the barnyard and trusting to the faith of my agreement. They would rather have hunted them down with musket and saber, killed them all, cooked them up in one day, and then gone on doing the same thing in neighboring villages.

In each regiment, in every company, there were marauders, determined men who traveled along the side roads, from one to three leagues[7] distant from their column. Sometimes they were attacked by the enemy, but one can say that the French soldier's intelligence equals his bravery. These gentlemen chose a leader among themselves who commanded like a dictator, and often these improvised generals fought serious engagements and reported victories.

When General [Sir John] Moore's English army made its retreat to Corunna, our advance guard which pursued it was very surprised to encounter a palisaded village. The French tricolor floated from the clock tower, the sentinels wore French uniforms. The officers who investigated it soon learned that 200 marauders held the village. Cut off from our army they had established themselves in the village and fortified it. Often attacked, they had always repulsed the enemy. Their commanding general was a corporal; they obeyed his orders as if he had been the Emperor. Entering the village the officers headed for his headquarters, but learned that he and his staff had gone hunting. Shortly thereafter he returned and made his report, showing what could be accomplished by bravery aided by intelligence.

The corporal, with his old-soldier experience, had fortified the village as well as an engineer officer could have done and — a remarkable thing — had gained the perfect friendship of the inhabitants. On his departure he received from the mayor the most honorable certificates.[8] We have known quite a few generals who would not be able to show the like.

---

[6] Apparently an Army term of mild contempt — "fellow", "jerk."

[7] A league was roughly 3 miles. Compare these men with Sherman's "bummers" during the Atlanta/Carolinas campaigns.

[8] Of good behavior, commonly given the commander of troops leaving a locality.

A French marauder. (Knötel)

From time to time, the army would make distributions of rations. Thereafter pillage would be strictly forbidden; often terrible "examples" would be made if it continued. However this happened only periodically, and nothing much came of it.

When we remained several days in or near a town, all the marauders had no other worry than to spend the money "earned" in their nocturnal excursions. They feared only one thing — to die with a full purse. They obtained leave for one day, and then took three. One hour before the third day ended, they arrived at their regiment's bivouac, for they knew very well that they would be charged with desertion if they came any later. At Vienna, Berlin, and Warsaw, you could see them come in elegant carriages which they had hired. Women accompanied them, their tendernesses directed at the last few coins remaining in these gentlemen's pockets; they left them only at the last possible moment.

Knowing in advance the punishment that they faced, they would order the coachman to drive them to their regiment's camp guard,[9] which served as a prison on campaign. The carriage would proceed amid the shouts and envious applause of their comrades. Once "installed" there, they would send word to their captain and first sergeant and, while awaiting their release, console themselves by long tales about the games of billiards they had played, the fancy meals they had eaten, the bottles drunk, and the rest.

"My lieutenant," said Dieudonne, the most intrepid marauder in the army, "if you will give me permission, I'll go to a village which should be on the other side of that wood — I've heard roosters crowing, and probably I could find some hens."

"You know that it is forbidden."

"Yes, but if you would—"

"What?"

"Do not notice that I am absent for roll call."

"OK, go — and do it so that I know nothing about it."

Dieudonne returned with a wagon loaded with provisions, part of which he gave to his officers to keep on their good side. Thanks to him our bivouac table was always well supplied. Note also that, along the way, several rabbits and several young partridges had gone into our game bag during the day.[10] That evening all these precious items, placed in the skilled hands of a former assistant chef of the *Frères Provencaux*,[11] whom the conscription had plucked from their famous kitchen, became a masterful creation. Its aroma spread far and wide, even to the enemy's outposts, and if you keep in mind that we had marched all day, you can easily realize that we dined very well. A good dinner is always a good thing, but in war — as in hunting — no superlative is strong enough to describe it. You might say that it is bad to authorize pillage — I answer that my conscience has never troubled me for the pigeons, chickens, and ducks which I procured by that means.

Whenever a detachment of conscripts reached the regiment we questioned them as to what their civilian profession had been; when a young man held the glorious title of "cook", we argued as to which of us would get him in our company. A cook is a man of high importance in a bivouac; it fact, it is not so much to have the raw materials as to know what to do with them. An able cook can do all sorts of things; a chicken cooked in a wayside tavern and one which is served to the habitues of the *Rocher de Cancale*[12] are as different as the moon and the sun.

These cooks did not fight; not wanting to risk their precious lives, we left them behind our battle line. If a captain is killed, his lieutenant takes his place, but how do you replace a good cook? "To be or not to be," said Shakespeare, "that is the question." And I say, "To dine well or dine badly," that is what one always ought to consider. Throughout history a cook's work has been highly appreciated by kings and by the wealthy. Henry

[9] A guard posted in front of each regiment to control its local security, discipline, etc. Also called "quarterguard."
[10] Blaze probably had been at his favorite sport — hunting.
[11] Famous Paris restaurant.
[12] Another famous restaurant. Incidentally, we wonder how Blaze would have reacted to an issue of World War II "C" or "K" rations. As we recall, German prisoners refused to believe we ate them regularly.

VIII, who was not a man to be trifled with, raised his cook to one of the highest dignities in England for having roasted a young wild boar to perfection.[13]

The Emperor Wencelas had a kitchen scullion spitted and roasted for having allowed a suckling pig to overcook.[14] This is dealing out justice, if I know anything about it — behold, two sovereigns who knew how to punish and reward fittingly.

Every captain had a man like Dieudonne; each of these jolly fellows was the leader of three or four others who worked with him. To follow their trade, you had to be indefatigable, because — having marched all day with the regiment, the marauders roamed almost all night; coming into camp in the morning, they moved out again with us and almost never slept.

"My lieutenant," said one of these fellows, "I have some famous wine, wine we found packed in a case. I have set several bottles aside for the company officers. We have tasted it, and I can assure you that one could drink nothing better; what's more, I need only tell you that it is the wine of *Posa-Piano!*" The marauder had mistaken a label on the packing around the bottles for the name of the district which produced that wine. As far as I can remember, a jury of wine tasters found the *Posa-Piano* delicious.

Several days before the battle of Friedland[15], close to 50,000 of us massed on the plains near Guttstadt. Everyone had made their preparations to spend the night with the least possible discomfort when shooting broke out in a small nearby woods. The shout "To arms" rang out and we thought the enemy was attacking. Instantly, the camp kettles were overturned;[16] the meat, which had been cooking for two hours, was tied onto the packs, the regiments formed into line. In an instant everyone was at his post.

We waited to see a Russian column debouch from the woods. Bah! The Russians had something better to do — they were dining, and we set about learning what had kept us from doing the same. An enormous bull, which had broken loose from the army slaughter house, had caused all that disturbance; running wild, he knocked over everything that got in his way, scattering entire squads that tried to halt him with their bayonets. At last, however, he fell pierced with many wounds; the soldiers recommenced preparing their supper, but their meat — already almost cooked — had lost half its juice and produced only a thin, flavorless broth. For a long time afterwards, whenever their soup was unsatisfying, we heard the soldiers say that it resembled that from the Guttstadt bull.

This happened near the battle field of Eylau which we crossed the following day. Everyone recognized the position which he had occupied four months before and that of the enemy. Like the Trojans after the retreat of the Greeks, our soldiers were happy to go over the scenes of their high deeds and their dangers.

Hic Dolopem manus, hic saevus tendebat Achilles;
Classibus hic locus: hic acie certare solebant.[17]

Which signifies when translated: Here were the Russian columns; there, we saw Napoleon; here we charged with the bayonet; there we got a good drubbing. For that

---

13 Henry VIII, of England and six wives. But we've never seen *this* story.
14 Holy Roman Emperor Wenceslaus (1361-1419), *not* "Good King Wencelas" of the carol.
15 1807. Friedland and Guttstadt were in former East Prussia, now part of northeast Poland.
16 Their liquid contents would put out the campfires, which would otherwise hinder the units forming up.
17 "Here Dolopum yielded, there Achilles raged."

famous battle, *Te Deums*[18] were chanted in Paris and in Saint Petersburg. The Good Lord must have been really astonished to be thanked by both sides.

Pantagruel[19] heard the cries of fighting men and the wounded on a battlefield where he could see no one, and naturally was most astonished. Panurge then explained the mystery — those cries had been uttered during the winter and the extreme cold had frozen them in the air; the sun was melting them little by little, so what could be simpler than to hear them without seeing anyone. If a similar thing had happened the day of the battle of Eylau, if the roar of cannon and muskets had been frozen, what a splendid racket we would have heard that day!

We were in bivouac one fine night; not being able to sleep I sat near the fire smoking my pipe by the side of the soldier detailed to cook the breakfast soup.[20] While watching the kettle boil vigorously, I noticed a black object that came to the surface from time to time and promptly vanished into the depths of the big pot. That black "something" roused my curiosity, appearing at such short intervals that I began to suspect there were several of them. I bravely drew my sword and watched for a passing speck of black; after several misses, I finally caught it. It was a mouse — two mice — three mice — four mice. I woke up our cook.

"Well, comrade, it appears that today the soup is unusually seasoned!"

"Like it is everyday, my lieutenant: potatoes and cabbage — that's all I have."

"And all that cooked in a decoction of mice. Here, look at the fine vegetables which I fished out of your kettle."

"That's not possible, my lieutenant."

"It is so possible that it's a fact. Where in the devil did you get your water?"

"In a tub in that village over there."

"Didn't you see what its contents were?"

"It was dark; It smelled like water and so I took some of it to make my soup. Besides, who could imagine that in a peasant's tub you'd find a squadron of mice?"

"You could poison all the company, for if that is a copper tub..."[21]

"It was wooden, I'm certain. Don't worry."

"Just the same, you'll have to throw out that soup and start making another batch."

"Impossible, my lieutenant, I won't have time. These characters who are snoring all around us will be getting up in a few minutes; their appetites will be open before their eyes are, and if by misfortune the soup isn't ready, they'll balance my quarterly accounts[22] by giving me fifty *savate* whacks[23] — and you know where! I beg you, lieutenant, now that the mice have been removed, to say nothing to anyone. The soup will be good just the same, and you can eat with another company."

---

[18] Services of thanksgiving for a victory. General Levin Bennigsen, the Russian commander always reported, as here, his defeats as mighty victories.

[19] The giant hero of Francois Rabelais satirical *Gargantua and Pantagruel*. Panurge was his somewhat rascally companion.

[20] *Soupe* was the general term for a meal — almost always a soup or stew, made up of whatever was available.

[21] Copper readily forms poisonous compounds, especially with ammonia products which are plentiful around a barnyard.

[22] See page 9.

[23] A paddy whacking with issue shoes.

"And you?"

"Me — I'll eat it."

He ate it. Later he told me that he had never had such good soup.

Now, see how this came about. In many German farms, to get rid of mice, they use a tub half full of water. Some little planks on which they put lard, flour, or some other bait, are balanced above it. As soon as the mouse runs out on this bridge, it tips under its weight; the mouse falls into the tub and drowns. The plank rises back into its original position and is always ready to do its job. It was from a similar reservoir that our bivouac chef got the water with which he made his odd bouillon. Yet no one was aware of that fact; the soup was considered delicious.

Between the camp and the bivouac, strictly speaking, there is something that is neither bivouac nor camp. In the bivouac, you sleep entirely under the open sky; in camp, you are in carefully aligned huts. But in the something-in-between, you find yourself under little shelters which protect you from the rain.

You construct these only when you expect to remain in the same place for several days; for a single night, it is too much trouble. A shelter is simply a roof of straw on three walls of straw; its open end is the highest, the closed end is on the windward side. Everyone builds his as he wishes, on ground of his own choosing, and the general effect makes a very pleasant picture.

In such huts, you cannot stand erect except near the entrance. You sleep very comfortably, but in the morning, you must get dressed outside, which saves you the trouble of opening the windows.[24] What varied scenes a skilled artist could sketch in passing! But none of them would be accepted for display at the Louvre.[25]

On the day we arrived at Tilsit there was talk of an armistice, of peace; therefore the shelters were built solidly enough to outlast eight days of bad weather. I was resting that evening beside Laborie, my lieutenant[26] when we were visited by a 2nd Lieutenant Héméré of our regiment. I had been almost asleep and his arrival awakened me; but the turn their conversation took made me think it best to pretend to be still asleep. Here is their dialogue, word for word, which I never shall forget:

"Good evening, Laborie."

"Good evening. Well — aren't you going to bed?"

"Ah yes, to bed — I certainly have something else to do, for sure. I'll have to be on the run all night."

"They say that they'll be making peace, that they have even signed an armistice, and I believe it because our quartermaster and our band have joined us." [27]

"Whether they make peace or war, it doesn't keep me — after having marched all day — from still getting a whopping fatigue detail tonight."

"Tell me about it."

---

[24] Most Europeans of this period considered night air unhealthy — which, in a sense, it could be in swampy areas where the malaria-carrying Anopheles mosquitoes bred in great numbers.

[25] Blaze should see our modern "art."

[26] In US terms, the 1st lieutenant of 2nd Lieutenant Blaze's company.

[27] The "quartermaster" was the regimental supply officer (U.S. S-4). He, the band, and the regimental artisans (master tailor, armorer, etc) usually stayed in the rear with the divisional trains. When they showed up, the soldiers would shout "Peace has been made, here comes our band!"

"The colonel has sent me to locate a mill some six leagues from here, and I can't find anyone who can show me how to get there. The villages are deserted, not one peasant left to guide me. All that anyone can tell me is that the place is called Brünsmuhl. I have four wagons loaded with grain which is to be ground; I'm taking our bakers to make bread; and I'm to bring it back here.

"That's good news, my dear fellow. Get going, and do manage to put aside several nice loaves for me."

"That goes without saying, but I have come to look at your map — someone told me you had one.

"Yes, I do have one, and a fine one too."

"Could we find the mill on it?"

"By Jove! Could we find it? Everything is on my map."

Now you should know that Laborie's "map" was a map of the world, which he had picked up in a bivouac among the miscellaneous stuff our marauders had "found". To give himself an important air, Laborie spread out his map every chance he had. We often[28] got him to do so; then, as soon as he rolled it up again, an apparent late-comer would get him to display it again.

"Here, behold my map," said he, spreading it out on the ground. "What's the name of your mill?"

"Brünsmuhl."

"Let's see—let's look. Here is Berlin, here is Saint Petersburg. — It should be between the two of them."

"That's true, you are right — all the same however I don't see the mill. Perhaps they forgot it."

"Forgot! I tell you everything is on my map."

"And I — I tell you that I don't see it."

"It is however, and big enough. Look here." And Laborie showed Hémére the compass rose printed on the margin of the map, the four principal points of which did rather resemble the sails of a windmill.

"Well, it is really quite the same," said Héméré, admiring Laborie's superior knowledge. "Do you think it is very far from here?"

"Eh — no. You can get there easily."

And Laborie measured with his hand the distance from his "windmill" to a point halfway between Berlin and St. Petersburg. It was a foot at most.

"But what road do I take to get there?"

"You'll have to admit that you are really stupid — the least thing confounds you. Here is your road - look at the map: the mill is there, is it not? When you leave here, turn right, keep moving straight ahead, and if you march rapidly, you will soon be there."

My conscience reproached me somewhat for letting the poor devil wander all night looking for a compass rose. I was on the verge of getting up, but Héméré was an annoying person, something of a backbiter, ranting against the young men who became officers without having served, as he had, in the *Armée de Sambre-et-Meuse*.[29] So I decided to leave him to his fate, to tease him when he returned. I assure you that he heard plenty

[28] Undoubtedly a game got up by the honorable Society of *Sous-lieutenants* — Blaze's term for the highly unofficial, but instinctive, mutual protection society of shavetails.

[29] One of the famous armies of the French Revolution, inspiration for the stirring military march named after it.

of jests when he arrived, three days later, with his wagons still loaded with grain, not having been able to find the mill.

Héméré was an odd fish; five feet tall, more or less.[30] He greatly loved physical pleasures; I think he died without suspecting that there could be any other sort. His greatest - what am I saying, his only pleasure was to drink while he smoked; for variety (I use his own expression) he smoked while he drank. One day while complaining to me concerning the privations he suffered in the field because of the lack of wine, brandy, and tobacco, his imagination suddenly recalled some happy memories.

"Oh, how well off we were," he said to me, "around Anspach and Elwangen, where we were billeted for six months! We had wine whenever we wanted it; the peasants furnished everything we demanded."

I said to him, "If you need nothing but wine whenever you want it to be happy, that's not so difficult.

"And what the devil more would you want?" he demanded. "In the morning after drill, I ate and drank my two bottles which quickly put me to sleep. When I had snored two or three hours, I took a third bottle which I had under my bed and went back to sleep until dinner. That evening, a short walk, hot wine on my return, and I went to bed, and began all over the next day. Never have I been so well entertained as there around Elwangen."

But let us leave Monsieur Héméré; we shall return to him later.

The finest of all the bivouacs, past, present, and future was that of 4 July 1809.[31] Never was there such a grand reunion of men in such a small area. All the French army had crossed the Danube on three bridges, and found itself on Lobau island under a rain which, for six hours, never stopped falling in torrents. Two hundred thousand men bivouacked together by regiment in closed columns.[32] We hardly had room enough to turn around. There remained one branch of the river to cross. The cannon roared all night long, the shells rained down [on the Austrians]. The battle for tomorrow, the victory which was certain to follow - all that presented a superb tableau, of magnificent hopes.

Never had the *Grand Armée* been so reunited; everyone recognized a friend in the veteran regiments arriving from Spain or from Italy. Not only individuals shouted their joy, but entire regiments demonstrated a lively happiness in meeting other regiments with which they had shared the glory and dangers at the bridge of Arcola, the Pyramids, Marengo, and Hohenlinden. That fraternity of peril had augmented the friendship between some, had initiated it among others. It was a long-lasting friendship, formed on the battlefield. Those who had parted on the banks of the Nile or of the Guadalquivir, rejoiced to meet again on an island in the Danube.

The sutlers' booths were besieged by all these gallants who, drinks in hand, rejoiced to have met again. Everyone vaunted his regiment's high feats of arms since the time of their separation, and the talk was endless. Everyone, satisfied with himself, proud of his comrade, had no doubt at all of victory. Like the soldiers of Casimir[33] all of them

---

[30] Approximately 5 foot 6 inches.
[31] Blaze's account is only slightly exaggerated. See Esposito and Elting, *A Military History and Atlas of the Napoleonic Wars*, Maps 103-106.
[32] Men elbow to elbow, reduced space between companies and battalions.
[33] Probably Casimir III (1300-1370), "The Great" of Poland.

could say to Napoleon, "Don't worry, count on us. If the sky falls, we'll hold it up on the points of our lances."

An instant later, they shook hands and parted. Alas, for many of them that adieu was forever, for that day was the day before Wagram.

All the nations were represented on Lobau, speaking all the languages of Europe. Italians and Poles, Mamelukes and Portugese, Spaniards and Bavarians, all wondered to find themselves marching under the Imperial eagle. We saw also the Saxons, Westphalians, Badeners and Wurttembergers.

"Who, since then...
but then they were our friends."[34]

We wandered, we searched without finding, we talked without making ourselves understood. That was a moving swarm, the Tower of Babel, the Valley of Jehoshapat[35] where, as everyone knows, we shall all meet again one day.

[34] I have not been able to identify the source of this quotation, but Blaze is referring to 1813 when these German states turned against France.
[35] This reference, so far, has defeated me. Is Blaze referring to the "Valley of Dry Bones?"

IV
The Marches

We marched to the right, to the left, to the front, sometimes to the rear, we always marched. Very often we didn't know why; the bobbin that turns while unwinding its cable never asks the engine driver the reason for its movements; it turns, that's all. We did like the bobbin. That was not always amusing, but we developed the habit. That and the necessity to obey orders, the example which each of us set and received — all that made us moving machines; they marched, we marched. When we halted, the soldiers, quite astonished, asked each other why. "It is odd," they said, "the clock has stopped."

A naturalist, tired of seeing the world's marvels only in his books, resolved to leave Paris and wander across the countryside to study botany, mineralogy, and the like. He approached the driver of a hackney-coach.[1]

"Are you available?"

"At your orders, monsieur."

"We will travel in the country, by short stages. Your vehicle remains on the road, and when I am weary I wish to be able to rest in it at my ease."

"As it pleases you."

"What do you charge?"

"Twenty francs a day."

"Agreed."

"When do we leave?"

"Tomorrow morning."

The next day they started off toward the east, leaving Paris through the Trone gateway. At Saint-Mande, the master ordered the cab halted and told the driver, "You can feed your horses. I'm going over there in that fine meadow and collect plants."

He collected, searched, turned and returned petals and stamens; three hours later, he returned with a fine bundle of hay, "Let's go," he said.

A little further on, masons were at work, and behold my savant closely examining the hewn stones and the mill stones; he reflected on their antediluvian formations; then having taken some notes and samples, he went on. That night they slept in Vincennes. The following days were spent in the Forest of Vincennes. What fine things there were to see there, from the daisy to the ancient oaks! Finally, at the end of the week, they reached St. Maur.

There, it was something else; he traced the course of the Marne River, measured the length and depth of its channel — and for each of these operations the horses went another hundred yards forward.

Fifteen days had passed when our travellers reached the neighborhood of Champigny. The opportunity for further observations was vast. To begin with, the view was

---

[1] A two-horse cab, ancestor of the modern taxi.

magnificent, the panorama superb. Furthermore, just scratching the ground revealed chalk deposits and banded onyx. There was work for a month.

"Oh, that," said the driver, "all that bores me. I'll die if I go on. Three leagues in fifteen days!"

"What does that matter if I pay you?"

"It matters that you are an idiot to spend your days on such nonsense."

"That's possible, but it doesn't concern you."

"Fifteen days to look at rocks and grass!"

"Is that why you want to leave me?"

"Yes, monsieur,"

"I owe you fifteen louis. Here they are."

"Take care of yourself. I'm leaving."

"Where are you going?"

"To Paris."

"Very well, my friend, I'll leave with you: if you wish you'll earn as much in returning as in coming here."

"Haven't you yet counted all the pebbles along the road?"

"There are still a good many things I want to see."

"Let's go," said the driver, slamming the cab door, "I'll do a lot better to drive him to Charenton."[2]

---

[2] An eastern suburb of Paris, site of a famous insane asylum.

That honest coachman could not appreciate the naturalist's researches; in a blade of grass, he saw nothing but food for his horse; an onyx was only a pebble to him. Plenty of men in the army resembled him; when we had advanced ten leagues and two days later went back ten leagues, they stupidly said, "This is a lot of trouble, because we'll just have to return."

A young man from Hamburg spoke to us often of his extreme desire to see Paris; he listened avidly to our talk about it. All his plans had the single object of one day making the journey to our capital.

"Very well," said a French courier,[3] "I'm willing to satisfy your longing — I'll take you there."

"But I couldn't afford it."

"It won't cost you a sou, either going or returning. Be ready to leave at any hour of the day or night; at any instant the marshal could give me the order to depart."

"I won't delay you."

They left, travelling by post[4] without stopping; soon they arrived at the Ministry of War in Paris. It was eleven o'clock in the evening.

"You arrive very opportunely," said the secretary. "Here are dispatches for Marshal Davout; we were about to send off a courier. Don't lose an instant — get back in your carriage and be out of Paris in an hour."

A few days later we saw them arrive in Hamburg. The young man was heart-broken to have gone all that way and yet seen nothing of Paris except the gleam of its street lamps.

Sometimes we went like that naturalist, fourteen leagues in fifteen days; sometimes, like the young Hamburger, we went and we went without seeing anything but the light of the street lamps — that is, every time we encountered street lamps, which didn't happen very often.

The day after the first bivouac of a campaign saw an enormous quantity of breeches; black and white gaiters;[5] collars; and stockings which littered the ground where we had slept — making it look as if the enemy had surprised us during the night, and we had fled clad only in our shirts. Perhaps you would not be offended to learn why all those breeches remained there, forsaken and forlorn.

Formerly the soldier was issued a pair of breeches free, and very seldom wore them; he had to pay for a pair of trousers which he wore all the time. The manufacturers of linen and shoes, being speculators, saw to this waste, stuffing our packs with high gaiters, white and black; stockings; white and black collars[6] — all things useful only to those who sold them. In garrison, soldiers had to keep all these effects or pay to have them replaced. But at the first bivouac at the start of a campaign, everyone emptied his pack of everything but the bare essentials, discarding everything else. The colonels and

---

[3] A government messenger, probably from the *Service d'Estafettes de l'Empereur et Roi*; which carried important dispatches between the army and Paris.

[4] Government postal systems, which provided relays of fresh horses and drivers. Passengers snatched food while their horses were being changed.

[5] *Grandes guetres* - which reached above the knee to mid-thigh — black for everyday wear, white for dress.

[6] These were really handkerchiefs. Blaze exaggerates here, since these articles could be useful. As for stockings, soldiers often did discard them and tallow their feet and shoes.

the supply officers[7] laughed up their sleeves; knowing that as soon as the campaign was over, they would be charging the soldiers for new breeches. So the book dealers rejoice in seeing the works of Voltaire and Rousseau burned by the missionaries.

Anyone who, in those days, could follow the army with vehicles could pick up a complete load at the first bivouac and would come back the next with as many pairs of breeches as there were men in the ranks. The military administration has made great progress since the peace.[8] Today, the soldier is issued trousers, which is a great improvement: breeches have been abolished. I have never understood why under Napoleon, when we were always at war, the soldier was clothed in those ignoble breeches which, squeezing his thighs, kept him from marching easily. What's more, his knee, also covered by the high gaiter which buttoned over the breeches, was again squeezed by the gaiter-strap which squeezed the garter of the breeches. Underneath, a pair of drawers, closed by a cord, further constricted the thighs. Behold, altogether, three layers of cloth, two layers of superimposed buttons, and three garters, destined to paralyze the efforts of the most intrepid marchers.[9]

Now, I say, if you had *wanted* to find a very inconvenient method of dressing a soldier, how could you have done better? That one was used during all the wars of the Revolution and the Empire. Also you should have seen the grotesque appearance of most of the young conscripts with those breeches and those gaiters, which — since they didn't have calves well enough developed to hold them up — drooped down around their heels. To wear that costume, it was necessary to be well built and mature; you must have legs with fine protuberances,[10] while almost everyone looks well in roomy trousers. A man of twenty years is not yet fully formed; we received conscripts who were not even yet nineteen. The regulation uniform really made them look like clumsy bumpkins. By contrast it looked very well on the Imperial Guard, which fought always in full dress, but which very rarely fought.

Moreover, the Guard was composed of picked men who could easily carry heavier packs. It always marched on the main road with the army headquarters; it received all of the army administration's attention,[11] and one might say that the rest of the army never received distributions of rations except when the Guard did not need them. Our conscripts bent under the weight of a pack, musket, and cartridge box; add to that fifty cartridges, bread, meat, a camp kettle or a hatchet[12] and you will have an idea of the appearance of those poor devils, especially in hot weather. Sweat streamed down their face, and usually three days of marching put them into the hospital. Our marches were much harder than those of the Imperial Guard; we went on much worse roads, and I risk nothing by guessing that hardship killed more young conscripts than the enemy's cannon.

[7] Properly "clothing captains" *(capitaines d'habillement)*, responsible for their regiment's clothing. Blaze is insinuating that they got a rake-off on every issue — which some did.

[8] In other words, since the end of the Napoleonic Wars, 1815.

[9] Breeches fastened just below the knee by a band and one or two buttons; high gaiters usually had a strap below the knee/above the calf to keep them from working down. Drawers came well down the lower leg and were tied at the bottom.

[10] Calves.

[11] The supply, medical, and related services.

[12] Each "squad" (a fourth of a company) formed a "mess" *(ordinaire)* of 15 to 30 men, headed by a corporal. It was issued a *bidon* (5 ½ liter canteen), a camp kettle, several mess tins, and a hatchet, which were carried turn-and-turn about, by its members.

In 1806, Napoleon had adopted a white uniform for the infantry. All the conscript replacements coming from France were clothed accordingly, which made a really unsightly mixture when they were put into units still dressed in blue. It was a really odd idea to give white uniforms to troops destined to pass their lives in bivouac. You should have seen how dirty those young recruits were! Therefore the first time the Emperor saw them he ordered the white uniforms replaced. That did not stop the fashion-mongers of the Restoration from doing it all over again in 1815. They at least had an excuse; they wanted their soldiers to look as they had before the Revolution. But the Emperor, who had us always sleeping in the open — how could he have expected to have a fine-looking army with soldiers dressed like clowns.[13]

The Imperial Guard was magnificent and rendered great services whenever it appeared. That should not be astonishing since it was recruited from the elite companies of our regiments.[14] Only the strongest and bravest soldiers, who already had four years of service and had made two campaigns, were taken for it. What could one but expect of force so composed — it was the elite of the elite. The soldiers of the line called those of the Guard, *"The Immortals"* because they rarely were in combat. They were reserved for crucial moments, and that doubtlessly was wise, for the arrival of the Guard on the battlefield nearly always was the decisive blow. Between the line and the Guard there was a jealousy that caused many quarrels. Every grade in the Guard was equivalent to the next higher one in the line.[15] We complained about that privilege in the line, and all of us did our best to acquire it.[16] Those who succeeded found it quite natural; they no longer could comprehend why those little officers of the line could have the rank pretension to be treated as equal to those of the Guard. That's the way men are, and they will be the same to the end of the world. When Frenchmen talk of equality, they mean with those placed above them, but not with the rest. "I am the equal of the Montmorencys;[17] the street sweeper is not my equal" — that is what many men have told themselves. We have protested against titles and decorations; once we have wrenched them from those who had them, we have bedecked ourselves with them. How many austere republicans have we seen become chamberlains, tribunes become peers of France — who, without ceremony, exchanged the title of "citizen" for that of "Monsieur the Duke" or "Serene Highness."[18]

We were on the march; a baggage wagon, drawn by four mules, attempted to cross our column. The soldiers, passing in succession before the noses of the poor beasts, took a malicious pleasure in blocking their progress because they belonged to the Imperial Guard; one soldier called out in a jeering way:

"Come on, soldiers of the line, make way for the mules of the Guard."

"Bah," responded another, "those are donkeys."

"I tell you those are mules."

"And I say they are donkeys."

---

[13] Literally, *"en pierrot"* — Pierrot was a clown-lover in the Italian drama/pantomime, who wore a baggy white costume.

[14] Every French infantry battalion had a grenadier (carabinier in the light infantry) and a voltigeur company of picked men. Every Cavalry regiment had a single "elite company."

[15] A Guard private was equal to a line corporal — and so on up.

[16] By winning transfer to the Guard.

[17] An ancient and powerful French noble family. "The foremost barons of Christendom."

[18] Blaze refers to Napoleon's conversion of the French Republic into the French Empire.

"Well even if they are donkeys, what's the difference. Don't you know that the Guards' donkeys have the rank of mules?"

The Imperial Guard, formed originally of veteran regiments of grenadiers and chasseurs, had been reinforced by regiments of fusiliers, and later tirailleurs, voltigeurs, flankers, and pupils.[19] The organization of these corps were quite exceptional. The original regiments formed the Old Guard, the others the Young Guard. The field grade officers[20] and captains for the latter were taken from the Old Guard; they kept their rank and prerogatives, while their lieutenants and noncommissioned officers were treated almost the same as their equivalents in the line, except that they had the honor to wear the Guard's uniform. Consequently there was a great disproportion as to army rank and pay and allowances between these captains and their lieutenants. As a minor difference, in the flanker regiments, which were uniformed in green, the captains and field-grade officers retained the blue coats of the Old Guard, which produced an odd mixture.

In creating the new regiments, they had exhausted all the possible titles, even having two of "Conscript-Grenadiers of the Imperial Guard." The words "Imperial Guard" and "Conscript" harmonized poorly; they seemed astonished to find themselves coupled. The officers of these regiments gloried in the "grenadiers" part of the title, but admitted difficulty over the rest of it.

On their regimental supply wagons you could read, in letters two feet high "GARDE IMPERIAL — Regiment of GRENADIERS" and then in very small print the word "Conscript," abbreviated "Cts." looking very abashed to find itself in such fine company. After that, we called these young grenadiers nothing but "CTS." That title became proverbial. "CTS" was the synonym for "conscript" or "raw recruit." "Thou are nothing but a CTS," the quarreling soldiers would say, and I likewise have heard officers say seriously, "We are going to get a detachment of CTS from France."

One way or another there were several sword thrusts given and received over that subject, which did not keep those grenadiers from still being called "CTS" — for when did the fear of a duel close the mouth of a Frenchman who was ready to crack a joke.

Among all these new names, one was missing; I have always been surprised that the Emperor never thought to create some regiments of "marchers." I have known in all the army corps tireless soldiers who could march thirty to forty hours at a time, without taking a moment's rest. By uniting these strong-legged men you could form an excellent regiment.

Picture two or three thousand picked men, able to march two days and two nights without stopping, lightly equipped, without any baggage or horses to slow their march or keep them for scaling mountains — and consider what missions such a regiment could accomplish in certain situations. I entrust that idea to the gentlemen of the Ministry of War; perhaps it merits their attention.

Napoleon is the man who best understood the art of marching an army. Those marches often were very difficult; sometimes half the soldiers were left behind, but — since they did not lack good will — they arrived later, but they did arrive. Nothing annoyed them like an order poorly worded or poorly understood, which kept them marching unnecessarily; they called that "marching for the capuchins."[21]

---

[19] See my *Swords Around a Throne*, New York: Free Press, 1988, pp: 183-205.

[20] Colonel, major, and battalion commanders.

[21] "Capuchin" seems to have implied stupidity or sanctimoniousness.

Also, when a commander's hesitation kept them waiting for some time in the same location, without knowing whether they would stay or go, they termed it *"drogeur."*[22] A French army is always in good humor when it fights, but its best soldiers are worthless when they *drogeur* or march for the capuchins.

Demand their best possible efforts and they obey without a murmur, but be certain that your orders are positive, brief, and plainly expressed. If they aren't, the soldiers will wish the general to all the devils. Frederick II[23] said one day (Monsieur de Montazet, an Austrian general then a prisoner in Berlin, heard it and recorded it in his *Memoires*), "If I commanded Frenchmen, I would make them the finest troops in the four quarters of the world. Disregard their minor foolishnesses, never disturb them for no good reason, nourish their natural gaiety, be scrupulously just with them, and do not afflict them with trifles — such would be my secret for making them invincible."

After the campaign of 1809, we were billeted[24] in the neighborhood of Passau, among mountains covered by six feet of snow. That was another universe, a new Siberia; we could say, like that soldier who wrote his parents from the highlands of the Tyrol: "We have arrived at the edge of the world; a hundred paces from our camp, the earth ends; you can reach up and touch the sun." However, it would have been somewhat more difficult for us to touch the sun because we never saw it. In that charming country of wolves, snow banks piled one upon the other, becoming so hard that it was impossible to bury the dead during the winter. They were placed on the roofs until the thaw. And Good God, what a thaw! What an ocean of mud! Every stream became a river, every road a torrent!

We were very contented in our villages when we received one fine night, an order to move out immediately to concentrate in Passau. The noon wind had melted the snow for several days; you can have no idea of the difficulty we had climbing and descending the flooded mountains. A painter who wishes to depict the Deluge should visit that area during similar weather. Aides-de-camp, dispatch riders, orderlies horse and foot, passed each other in every direction to hurry up all the detachments they could find. We had to be in Passau, dead or alive, at daybreak. Officers and soldiers alike thought that war was imminent — what other reason could there be for that breakneck march in time of peace!

As a company or part of a company reached Passau, the general's staff officers loaded them onto ferries to cross the Danube, which rolled along in huge waves. The melting snow had so increased its flow that we were carried downstream several leagues before we could reach the further bank. Artillery horses fell into the water, boats capsized, men drowned. Once across the Danube we continued our march without a moment's rest; we marched for forty hours. "But why are we rushing like this?" the soldiers asked. "Whatever has happened?" For nothing was allowed to stop us, neither night, torrents, nor rivers. At the end we learned the reason for that forced march, the most difficult I have ever made, even in time of war. It was necessary to get to Braunau to render military honors to Marie Louise who was traveling to France to marry Napoleon. From the way we were pushed along, you would have thought that the empress was waiting for us. We arrived fifteen days too soon.

---

[22] To wait impatiently, or to play an Army/Navy card game, the looser at which had to wear clothespins on his nose. Also to physic oneself. Take your choice.
[23] Frederick "The Great."
[24] Living with the inhabitants — in peace time, as here, usually one soldier to a family.

On the frontier between Bavaria and Austria, near the village of St. Peter, not far from Braunau, architects sent from Paris had constructed a superb pavilion. It was there that the representatives of the Emperor Francis of Austria delivered Marie Louise to those who Napoleon had designated to receive her. The Queen of Naples[25] and the Prince of Neuchâtel[26] had arrived with an army of chamberlains; dames of the bedchamber, equerries; servants of every color, grade, and species; in short the whole "boots off."[27] These people are doubtlessly indispensable, for one finds such swarms under all governments and in all countries: you could maintain an army of 50,000 men with what it costs to take off a sovereign's boots. When Her Majesty appeared the artillery made an infernal uproar, the regimental bands played out of tune, the drums beat dully, for it was raining in torrents, we were up to our knees in mud — and the Paris newspapers went into ecstasy over our good fortune in having been the first to salute our august and gracious ruler.

That, however, is how history is written. The next day the Empress left for Paris; we took the road back to our mountains by short marches, while endeavoring to convince ourselves that we had had a good time.

To reach the area of Austerlitz the III Corps covered forty leagues in thirty-six hours. One man in twenty arrived initially, the rest rejoined every hour; officers left along the road gathered up the stragglers and, after letting them rest a little while, sent them on to their regiments. That rapid march was very hard on the soldiers, but they did not complain because they sensed it was necessary and that it had a great influence on the outcome of the battle. By comparison, our trip to Braunau became a perpetual source of complaints and grousing. It became a horrible example: every time they apprehended having to "drogeur" uselessly or to "march for the capuchins," they growled, "This is what it was like when we went to Braunau."

That march of thirty-six hours to Austerlitz without a minute's rest was of major importance. A captured French officer was interrogated by the Emperor Alexander of Russia.

"Of which army corps are you?"

"The third."

"Marshal Davout's corps?"

"Yes, sire."

"That can't be true — that corps is in Vienna."

"It was there yesterday; today, it's here."

Alexander was stunned by that news.

Night marches are the most fatiguing of all; sleep is man's greatest need. Pichegru[28] paid 20,000 francs for a night of uninterrupted sleep while he was under arrest. Sometimes soldiers fall asleep on their feet while marching; one false step sends them tumbling one over another, like a house of cards, into the ditch.

---

25 Caroline Bonaparte, Napoleon's treacherous sister, wife of Murat.
26 Marshal Berthier, Napoleon's chief of staff.
27 From pre-Revolutionary France, when removing the King's boots (Debotter) after he had been hunting was a major ceremony, apparently requiring everything except the archbishop of Paris and a brass band.
28 French general during the Revolution, who turned traitor, and apparently committed suicide in prison.

In Bavaria and Austria bees are plentiful, and consequently there are large harvests of wax. The soldiers found great quantities of it with the peasants. During night marches in calm weather each one would light two, three, or four candles; some carried as many as fifteen or twenty. Nothing is as pleasing as the sight of a division thus illuminated while it climbs a hillside by a winding road, all those thousands of moving lights making a delightful picture. The company *lustig* [29] sang a sentimental song and everyone joined in with the chorus. Later, another soldier would recite the interminable story of La Ramée, who, after having been discharged, left his home and hiked 200 leagues to reclaim a ration of bread from his first sergeant. All the old-soldier stories became part of the history of La Ramée; he was the personification of the French soldier. You can easily conceive that his story would have to be somewhat long — also that no one ever finished it.

No soldier of any nation can make the best of things like the French soldier. Amid the most difficult circumstances, a joke makes him forget them. Right away, that joke inspires another one, little by little the air sparkles with joyful talk and the restored spirit acquires a new energy.

Moreover you see new places; every day your head is filled with memories.
"You see many a republic,
Many kingdoms, many people, and you profit
From the different customs which you notice."
That which the duck said to the tortoise, I frequently told myself: Note that, don't forget this — later on, they will amuse our children, if we have children, and the long winter evenings will be shortened. The lining of my shako held a little notebook in which, every day, the remarkable things were carefully recorded. A custom, a building, an inscription — such are the things that enable you to understand a people. Certainly I am not going to describe to you all the monuments which I found on my way — ten volumes would not be enough for that. But when, along the way, we encounter something extraordinary, I won't miss telling you about it. For example on the summit of the Ulm cathedral there is the most singular inscription you can find in this world. At 412 steps[30] above the ground, there is a balustrade, eight or ten inches wide, around the clock tower. In 1592, the Emperor Maximilian jumped on its railing, stood there several moments, made a pirouette (doubtlessly very gracefully), and jumped back down onto the balcony. You can read that on a plaque; the custodian of the tower never fails to show it to travelers. It's worth the trouble to tell posterity that on a certain year an Emperor of Germany played the clown, at the risk of breaking his neck.

While marching from Ratisbon to Neustadt the regiment was astonished to see, on the main road, a very fine monument. Two huge stone lions are placed there, far from any habitation: one watches the Danube which flows at its feet; the other has its eyes fixed on an enormous mass of rock cut perpendicularly. It was a surprise to find such a thing on a main highway; it made a strange sight. The whole was as well executed as conceived.[31]

---

[29] Borrowed from the German — a happy man/joker. A company character, usually a professional "high private," always ready for a fight or a frolic.
[30] Steps up the clock tower stairs.
[31] This was a monument to Charles Theodore, Elector (1777-94) of Bavaria. It's long Latin inscription has been omitted.

Further on, two leagues from Neuburg, the regiments which were marching at route step, muskets every which way, would suddenly close up their ranks; the drummers beat *"Aux Champs;"*[32] the soldiers got into cadenced, solemn step; the officers saluted with their swords. For whom were these honors? They were rendered to the "first grenadier of the Republic," to La Tour d'Auvergne![33] His tomb, placed close to the roadway is always saluted by the regiments of all nations; it is known as the "Tomb of the Brave." Constructed of stone, it bears the following inscription:

"To the Memory
of Latour-d'Auvergne
Premier Grenadier of the Army
Killed the VIII Messidor An VIII
of the Republican Era."

On the opposite surface, you read:

"To the Memory
of Fortis of the 46th Demi-Brigade.
Killed the VIII Messidor An VIII
of the Republican Era."

Fortis was La Tour d'Auvergne's colonel; they died together at the point where their tomb stands. While we protected the Confederation of the Rhine,[34] this modest monument, respected by everyone, was maintained by the town of Neuburg. The bravest of the brave should be honored in all the nations of the world.

When you see a regiment move out on a main highway, you may think that nothing is easier than controlling it. At the command "March," it departs — you say — and if it marches long enough along its route, it will finally arrive at its destination. In fact, a colonel who took no more care than that would leave half of his regiment behind. The non- commissioned officer who marches at the head of the column should have a short and regular step. The least obstacle encountered, even if it's only a rut to cross, will have all the soldiers of the rear-most battalion running as they try to recover their intervals. If the first soldier who discovers that obstacle slows his march for a half-second, the last men will have to run for a quarter-hour.[35] An experienced commander sees these things at a glance; he will order a short halt, and everyone will close up properly. After we had marched for an hour, we halted for five minutes to light our pipes — that was called "The halt of the pipes." You should not deprive the soldier of any pleasures, and for many this pleasure is a necessity. At mid-day we made the "big halt" which lasted for an hour. Everyone dined on what he had with him. Then we moved on, ending each league with a 5-minute halt.

---

[32] The drum salute.
[33] See Elting, *Swords*, pp 165 and 613.
[34] A league of German states, including Saxony, Bavaria, and Wurttemberg, allied 1806-1813 with France.
[35] What Americans call the "accordion effect."

Little causes often produce great results. Sometimes regiments have been beaten because their soldiers did not have straps on their gaiters.[36] Since that at first would seem to be a mere trifle, let me explain. When the roads are bad and the soldier's shoes are in poor condition, if the gaiter does not fit snugly over the shoe, mud gets into the shoe; contact with particles of dirt injures the foot, raising blisters. Men fall out, the ranks are thinned, and the regiment, reduced by half, cannot do what it could at full strength.

It is very important for an officer to see that his soldiers are well shod, that each one has extra *sous-pieds*, an awl, and coarse thread to sew them on when necessary. Neglecting that precaution could result in the loss of a battle. The captains, the battalion commanders,[37] the colonels have a very great interest in keeping the greatest possible number of men in the ranks. In fact, if they have a mission to carry out, if they receive an order to capture a position or to attack a post, the officer issuing the order doesn't concern himself with the number of men which they have available; he simply orders the regiment, battalion, or company forward—and so much the better for its commander if he has most of his men with him; the job will be that much easier. Thus glory, honor, and the personal interest of the officer absolutely require that he constantly occupy himself with these minor details of his unit's administration. This can give the most advantageous results. I have seen captains who, taking these precautions and plenty of others too, have succeeded in keeping their companies a fourth stronger than the average.

When you march in hot weather, the soldiers raise a great deal of dust; they stop at all the wells and streams to drink. What happens? Thirst begets thirst; the water they drInk in such immoderate quantities often causes fevers, and the hospitals fill up to the detriment of the army. You can avoid this serious inconvenience by a very simple measure — make the soldiers carry a straw in their mouth; their lips remain closed, the dust doesn't enter their mouth, they aren't thirsty, they don't drink. I recommend that recipe to everyone who travels on foot, and especially to hunters.

To appreciate all these things, you must live with the soldier, see him throughout the day, be with him under all conditions. The officers of the *ancien regime* [38] were as brave as those of today, but they never saw their soldiers except on a day of battle or a royal review, returning promptly thereafter to Versailles. They were completely ignorant of these important minutiae; had they known of them I very much doubt that they would have taken the trouble to see to them. Their concern was to join the army the evening of the day before a battle; none of them missed that rendezvous.

When we marched in times of peace, the evening halting place seldom was large enough to accommodate an entire regiment; a certain number of companies would be detached to the right and left to spend the night in nearby villages. The next morning these detachments would move by the shortest road to a predesignated point on the highway where the regiment would reassemble, to continue its march to the next town. It was essential not to arrive more than a quarter hour early or late at this point; our colonel, very rigid in this matter, would really chew out those captains who failed to do so. The soldiers certainly understood and appreciated that solicitude.

[36] *"Sous-pieds"* — straps that went under the instep to hold the gaiters down.
[37] *"Chefs de bataillon"* — Battalion commanders (equals US majors.)
[38] France before the Revolution.

At the noon halts, those officers who were the most intimate would pool their provisions and eat together; at that time we told of our *adventures galantes*,[39] and sometimes we heard some very funny tales. But, you say, what adventure could you have in a village where you arrive in the evening, to depart in the morning? Isn't that nothing more than one night? You should learn that a man who will leave the next day can be very useful the evening before, according to many women. Their secret will be kept, they do not have to blush over giving in quickly; moreover, the desire for a change or a whim can sometimes resemble love.

One of our comrades was a complete egoist. When, during a halt of the regiment, he had his haversack well filled with good things, he would find a nook and there, all alone with himself, he dined, forgetting that his comrades were not as well favored as he was by the god whom Rabelais termed the god *"ventripotent."*[40] When he was reduced to black bread and a bit of cheese, he would approach our groups, where his hawk's eye picked out the gastronomes seated in a circle and enjoying themselves, and seek an invitation to join them. One day I had a superb chicken, escorted by several good bottles, which I planned to attack unhesitatingly with several friends, when Montro__ appeared maneuvering in the vicinity. He circled around us like a planet around the sun; he heard the loud praise with which we saluted the estimable bird, and the exclamations of each of us over the pleasure we promised ourselves from devouring a part of it. The west wind carried a delicious scent to his nostrils; saliva moistened his tongue; soon all of his digestive apparatus was under arms and awaiting only the word to begin functioning. He resembled, feature by feature, the caricature of a penniless gastronome. The day before I had seen him alone, devouring a splendid pate without offering me any, and I had resolved to take vengeance for the morsel of dry bread which he had left me to eat without having pity for my distress.

"Montro__," I called to him — for he had not ventured to approach us, though making the circumference of a circle, of which we — or more probably my pullet — was the center, around us. "Montro__, do you like cold chicken?"

"Certainly," he responded, coming toward us like a buzzard jumping on a carcass, "It's excellent, especially at lunch."

"Well, my dear fellow," I said to him, "when you want to eat one, you should have the prudence to have it cooked the day before."

One of the finest regimental halts was that the 21st Light Infantry made near Lodève.[41] The worthy Colonel Taraire, en route through that village, where his father still lived, halted his command before the paternal mansion. After forming his regiment in a circle, he made them this noble and fine speech: "My comrades, I present to you my father; he is an old ploughman. My father, I present to you my regiment, composed of excellent soldiers."

The barn, the stables, the granaries had been converted into festival halls; sheets hung before their doors concealed a pleasing surprise. Quickly the colonel gave the signal; to the sound of music, the screens which concealed such a fine decoration disappeared, to the great pleasure of the travelers. At the sight of that prodigious luncheon, the *vivats*, the *bravos* rose from every rank. These magnificently served tables seemed to rise out

---

[39] "Gallant adventures," which a crude American might define as attempts to find horizontal female companionship.

[40] Apparently "Full Belly."

[41] South Central France, just north of Montpellier.

of the ground, as at the opera. Everyone took his place, and God knows with what bravery those old campaigners did their duty. How many hams, how many legs of mutton, how many turkeys were swallowed that day — how many casks were emptied! The 21st always remembered it; the veterans told the conscripts of the marvels of the lunch at Lodève, and those, much later, passed them on to newcomers as if they themselves had seen it.

When a regiment traveled in Germany, the towns it passed through furnished it requisitioned vehicles to carry its baggage, sick, and crippled. When an officer traveled singly, whether on a particular mission or to rejoin his corps, he got a new vehicle at every post station and, without opening our purses, we all have sped through Germany in all directions. In the towns along the line of communications, there you could find harnessed vehicles[42] waiting, day and night. That was very convenient for us, but a terrible expense for the Germans.

As you have seen, we traveled by *poste*[43] at small cost. At the risk of getting myself into a bad quarrel with the French postilions,[44] I'm going to tell you of an economical method which an original character whom I knew used one day. You know that regulations allow seventy-five centimes to the postilion for every post station he passes; however when you give them no more than twice as much, they aren't satisfied. My man said in departing, "I don't want to pay more than the fixed rate, and I shall go at full gallop." His inventive genius had discovered the following system:

"My friend," he said to the postilion of his first vehicle, "I am sick, crippled by pains and rheumatisms; the least jolt makes me scream loudly. It is necessary that you drive as gently as possible — otherwise I shall be dead when you reach the next relay station." They departed. The postilion kept off the pavement, chose the best roads, and was careful to keep the coach from rocking — and, at the end of his journey received a 15-sous coin as his reward for so much care.

"But, monsieur, you don't think!"

"That is precisely because of what I think."

"But everyone gives at least double."

"Everyone may do as they please. Myself, I give the legal fee."

"But, monsieur—"

"Read the law concerning—"

"That law doesn't make sense."

"I find it very intelligent."

"Because it favors you."

"It is for everyone."

"You at least will give me a tip."[45]

"The law does not mention that."

"Oh! That bitch of a law!"

"Leave me undisturbed — oaf! My pains are coming back."

Grumbling heartily, the postilion went to find the one who would replace him for the next stage of the trip, and showed him the seventy-five centime coin. "You're going to have a fine day's work," he said. "The legal rate and nothing more. No tip. Fifteen sous,

---

[42]   Vehicles with horses harnessed and ready.
[43]   See Elting, *Swords*, pp. 106-107.
[44]   Drivers of *poste* vehicles.
[45]   A *"pourboire"* — "for drinking."

44

that's all. He knows the law by heart, but, in return, you can drive him crazy. That miserly villain is ill, the least bump makes him scream as if you are skinning him alive. He'll want you to go at a walk, and moreover on dirt roads. I was stupid enough to listen to him because I expected that he would pay generously, but he gave me just the legal fee. Take him on the pavement, whip up your horses, go at full gallop — and if he croaks in his carriage, so much the better."

The comrade passed the word from relay to relay; the horses went like the wind, our sly traveler laughed up his sleeve. From time to time, to encourage the postilion, he yelled for him to stop, to let him get out, to slow down, but his words were lost in the wind. The postilions pretended to hear nothing, and the carriage burned up the pavement. The first postilion's instructions accompanied him from Paris to Marseilles; the miser was carried along like a prince. Fortunately the carriage was well-built.

I was en route from Warsaw to Posen, after having spent several days too many in the capital attending the carnival, and I had only the time absolutely necessary, traveling day and night, to reach Posen by the date indicated on my orders. Along the way I had missed being eaten by the wolves; that really would have been a great pity, had it happened — I wouldn't have the pleasure of chatting with you today. Three feet of snow covered the ground; the cold was excessive. At Lowics,[46] the post commander, an officer of the 115th Regiment whom I knew, tried to dissuade me from leaving early in the night, saying the twelve leagues of forest through which I must pass to reach Kutno, was full of wolves — that imprudent travelers faced great danger, especially in winter; and that those animals had often devoured horses and men.[47] I replied that if the forest were populated by lions and tigers, I would not hesitate to go on. I had committed a mistake and I wanted at all costs to keep it from being known. The commander then offered me a musket and cartridges for my soldier[48] and me. His foresight saved our lives.

We had hardly gone a short league before our sleigh was escorted by a regiment of wolves; you could see their eyes gleam like glowing coals, and you could see the wolves themselves quite clearly against the snow. The situation was critical, but I thought that composure and presence of mind would get us through. What worried me the most was the fear that had seized the peasant who drove our sleigh. I spoke several words of Polish to him to reassure him, but — being ignorant of his language — I could not harangue him like one of Homer's heroes.[49] The poor devil shook with cold and fear; he whipped his horses and we went like the wind.

I knew that wolves feared fire; my orderly and I fired our muskets at them as often as possible. We must have killed many of them — our shots struck into the mass of their pack and always hit several of them. However, we felt no desire to pick up the dead ones to fill our game bag. Several times wolves got within ten yards, which was certainly close, but two musket shots relieved us of their presence for several minutes. If they had

---

[46] Now "Poznan" and "Lowicz" in Poland.

[47] Blaze had a footnote. "At the beginning of the reign of Louis XIV [c. 1643] a detachment of dragoons was attacked near Pontarlier, in the Jura Mountains, by an innumerable multitude of wolves. The dragoons fought courageously, killing several hundred of the wolves, but overwhelmed by their numbers they were all devoured, as were their horses. An inscription, placed on a cross near the scene of that incident, still existed in 1789."

[48] His orderly/striker/dog robber.

[49] Referring to the chest-pounding speeches that characters of Homer's *Iliad* delivered before getting down to the business of fighting.

attacked the horses, we would have lost, but fortunately they did not. They followed us as far as the outlying houses of Kutno, which we recognized with indescribable joy. From Lowics to Kutno, is a distance of twelve leagues; we had covered it in less than three hours. You could really say that fear had given us wings.

In Spain we never travelled singly. The first tree would have been a gallows for the foolhardy who would risk himself alone on the road. It was necessary to go in an organized unit, with advanced guard and rear guard, always ready to open fire. The governor of Bayonne held the detachments and the individual officers going into Spain, until they constituted a force capable of taking care of itself, then sent them on to Irun.

When I crossed the Bidassoa River to enter into the Kingdom of Don Joseph I,[50] Sovereign of Spain and the Indies or so he said, our convoy consisted of a dozen detachments from different regiments, a large number of individual officers rejoining their commands, employees of the rations service,[51] young men going to Madrid to solicit places in Joseph's administration, and of administrators of the *Droits Reunis* who were going into Spain to organize it after the example of France, it being only proper that Spain should enjoy all the advantages that our rule could provide it.[52]

As we left Irun, the convoy commander organized the order of march of our mixed lot, a task which wasn't easy. Sixty oxcarts carrying the baggage were placed in the center of the column. Two three-horse carts could easily have carried their load, but Biscay carts are made so that four haversacks fill them completely. Their wheels are solid, without rims or spokes, and resemble the ends of a barrel connected by an axle; all that turns together with an infernal racket. When several of them are on the road together, you hear the most appalling noise, comparable to that of the ancient mill wheel at Marly.

Between Irun and Hermani, some guerrillas, whom we call bandits, fired a dozen shots at us from the crest of the mountains; our skirmishers quickly chased them away. But you should have seen the pale and ghostly faces of the young fashionables from Paris; they hid behind the baggage carts when they couldn't find cover behind the oxen. Every time there was another skirmish, everyone not in uniform separated from the soldiers, in whose midst they had been previously, and sought a shelter — that did not always protect them. Why, you ask me, were those civilians frightened? And why didn't the soldiers, who were with them, think of the danger? Here is my answer to your question.

It is said that the robe does not make the monk, but I claim that the uniform almost always makes the soldier. Among the soldiers whose ears have heard bullets whistle, there are certainly many on whom that sharp, discordant sound makes a disagreeable impression. But in that case everyone is afraid to show his weakness to his comrades; he fears the jokes and the sarcasms which would necessarily follow. A sense of duty, honor, and self-respect all unite to combat fear, and I have often seen the most cowardly be the first to shout "Forward!" If all those employees, lawyers, and auditors had a uniform on their backs, if they belonged to a regiment, if they were required to be brave,

---

[50] Napoleon's older brother Joseph, whom he had made King of Spain. ("And the Indies" was from the usual title of Spanish kings, which Joseph had assumed). He was not respected by the average French officer, being a good deal of a coward.

[51] See Elting, *Swords*, pp. 553-557.

[52] *Droits Reunis* — An expression of the French Revolution's "Rights of Man." Its application to Spain would have jerked that nation out of the late Middle Ages — something most Spaniards believed unnecessary and insulting.

(JOB)

they would not have dared to show fear and nothing would have betrayed their inner feelings. But all that did not affect them in any way; they could tremble all they wanted to without anyone noticing it. Their coats, cut according to the latest Paris fashion, left exposed a carefully pleated frill. A musket ball would mess up that elegant arrangement, and they wanted to avoid such a development. The soldiers gloated — if I may use that expression — over their uneasiness; often, to make fun of them, they would predict that in a little while the convoy would be attacked by guerillas they had seen creeping behind the mountains — that in that case the best thing that could happen to them would be to die fighting, because if they were taken prisoner they would be hanged, burnt, flayed, and so on. It is certain that, listening to these yarns, the fashionable gentlemen heartily wished that they had never left France and that they willingly renounced all their ambitious dreams.

The mountain of Salinas was famous in those days for the ambuscades that Mina, Longa, and El Pastor[53] never ceased to lay for our convoys. No locality could be more favorable — a mountain it took four hours to ascend, a road so hemmed in by cliffs and precipices that it could not be cleared by our skirmishers. The enemy hid behind the rocks; you couldn't see him, but you heard his musket shots which was some compensation.[54]

We had been climbing for three hours, preceded by our advance guard which had seen nothing of the enemy, when suddenly a pistol shot near us gave the signal for a volley from 200 to 300 muskets. A ravine separated us from the Spaniards; immediately our

---

[53] Well-known Spanish guerrilla leaders.
[54] Four lines on a proposed museum exhibition omitted.

soldiers started down into it to climb up the other side, but the guerrillas had promptly vanished. We lost fourteen men in that scuffle; a charming lady, wife of a senior official of the hospital service, who was going to Madrid to be with him, was hit in the breast by a bullet and died two days later at Vittoria. The guerrillas however did not retreat fast enough to escape a reply to their fusillade; three of them were wounded. Soon brought in by our voltigeurs who had been sent in pursuit, they were taken to Vittoria and hanged the next day. One of our dandies was slightly wounded in the leg; from then on, proud of his wound and giving himself something of the airs of a hero, he always crowded in among the grenadiers, disdaining the society of his former companions. He seemed to want to punish them because they had not had the same good luck as he had.

But when you travel in Spain, you are often obliged to stop. At every town, some fractions of your convoy find themselves at their destination, and the weakened convoy needs reinforcements to continue on its way. Half — what am I saying? — nearly all of the French army is serving as escorts to couriers. We have garrisons in all the towns and all the villages along the main roads; often even in the middle of the intervals between them, we have constructed little forts, blockhouses, or redoubts, each one occupied by a hundred or so men. All these posts, all these garrisons furnish more or fewer soldiers for escorts, according to the estimated strength of the insurgent bands in their area. That service is very difficult, and you might say that it has cost the lives of more Frenchmen than have the great pitched battles. We are masters of all the towns, of all the villages along the main roads; a hundred yards from them we no longer are. It is a war of every day, of every hour. If the escort is strong and capably commanded, it will not encounter anyone as it passes. If it is not, the enemy swarms in from all directions. In Spain you can say that they are everywhere and nowhere.

The reports we obtain on the enemy forces and their movements are almost never accurate, while they know every day and every hour what we are doing. They count us in every village, and the enemy chiefs always know our weak point. A colonel, arriving at a town, demands 2,400 rations for his regiment. "You have 1,860 men," replies the mayor, "you will get only 1,860 rations. They are ready."

The work of a spy in the army is very dangerous. To be well served by such men who, every day, risk the gibbet, a general ought to pay them generously. Our government furnished our commanding generals considerable sums for that purpose. Many of them, however, were stingy in using it. To obtain services which only greed would inspire a man to undertake, they preferred to use terror. After having imprisoned the wife and children of some poor devil, they tell him, "You will go now and return tomorrow. You will tell me what Mina, Longa, El Pastor (or whatever other guerrilla chief is particularly wanted) is doing, how many men he has, where he is. If you deceive me, or you don't return, I'll hang your entire family."

What happens? The peasant doesn't come back, and no one is hanged. Or, he talks to Mina, who gives him information to take back — and then so arranges things that the truth of today is a falsehood tomorrow. The money for "secret expenses," the cost of espionage, goes back to Paris[55] and affairs go on for the better — in the *bulletins*.[56]

Although the Spanish nation rose up *en masse* against us, although it waged a national war against us, if you pay well, you can find traitors. Love of country was not the sole

[55] Here, Blaze is uncharacteristically gentle. Frequently, it remained in the general's pocket!
[56] Official reports.

reason for the insurrection; it served as a pretext, that's all. When they found nothing to do against the French, most of the guerrillas pillaged their fellow countrymen; anything went with them.

They sought only to enrich themselves, to save their country so that they could reorganize it thereafter to suit themselves. That system isn't new; you find it everywhere, in all nations, in all epochs, during peace as well as during wars.

In many villages, the peasants regarded both the French and the guerrillas as bandits. When I had occasion to ask a mayor, "Have you seen bandits recently in your area?" he would answer, "Which? French or Spanish?" *Los brigantes de ustedes* — that's how they designated our soldiers.

And to prove what I state, I cite the famous Chacarito. This chief, after having made war on the French, attacked Spaniards in his spare time, just to keep his hand in. He became the terror of Castille, to the point where the Spanish joined the French to attempt to capture him. Betrayed by one of his band, he was seized after defending himself like a lion. Several days later he suffered the most horrible of punishments, being pulled apart by four horses in the Valladolid market place. The resulting "quarters" were placed over town streets at the four cardinal points of the compass — which did to keep any other brigands from doing as he had done. A Captain G__ one day recited Chacarito's biography to me. "That man," he said, "had no other pleasure then to pillage, steal, rape, murder, burn. In short, he conducted himself very badly."

Nevertheless, these bands would flee from a few skirmishers. They had to have greatly superior numbers before they dared attack us openly, and, in that case, they had the immense advantage of surprising us by ambuscades. The country is so cut up by mountains and precipices that it is impossible to effectively reconnoiter a road. When a guerrilla chief has completed a raid, his men split up, hide their weapons, and go home after having set a rendezvous at an agreed-on date some twenty to thirty leagues further on. The French pursue them, but find no one, and the Paris newspapers announce to Europe that such-and-such a general, with rare intrepidity, worthy of the highest praise, had driven the bandits back into their mountains, that they are cowards, unworthy to bear arms, etc, etc. But all these fine official phrases don't keep the bandits, although we call them such, from carrying out their mission perfectly. By harassing us constantly, they weary our soldiers, who fall sick. They pin down half our army to protect our couriers, and frequently a battalion doesn't suffice to escort a letter.

The grand art of partisan warfare is to always attack, and to never be forced to accept combat. The business of the guerrillas is to be undiscoverable when we look for them, to sweep on us like vultures when we are not expecting them. You can say that they have done their job very well. It sometimes arrives that they are hanged, when we capture them weapons in hand. That is the disagreeable aspect of their profession, the reverse of the medal. But they do the same to Frenchmen who fall into their power; they even have intensified their reprisals into the most revolting barbarity. Several times they have skinned alive prisoners whom the fortunes of war had put into their hands; a good many of these unfortunates were sawed between two planks. One of my friends was buried alive up to his head, which served those cannibals as the target for bowling. You could write volumes on the atrocities committed by both sides in that miserable war, but I can affirm, without fear of anyone disputing me, that we always have been less cruel than the Spaniards.

The Emperor's correspondence with King Joseph and the marshals, went every day by couriers escorted from post to post, from the Bidassoa River to Seville. As for private letters, there was no regular service; they accumulated in the post offices,[57] and every month wagons moved them to France.

The Christian religion in Spain has degenerated until it resembles Roman paganism. For the greater part of the Spanish people, the image of a saint or the Virgin, in gold or silver, is the thing they adore. The worshiper, kneeling before the image, sees nothing else, and no other higher thought rules him. If the statue is stolen, all is lost; if you make another, it will be worthless. That one produced miracles; though this one might produce a dozen, they do not find it at all fitting. The Spanish have made Christianity a routine; they think they have done everything necessary when they were young by carrying a scapular or when they have mechanically read so many pages of a book.

For them, religion could not exist without priests and processions; they require relics, miracles, bizarrely clad monks and nuns, and convents where everyone can find prayers and soup. In religion, they are materialistic without suspecting it; in love they are materialistic and say so. For the rest, they are happy after they have satisfied their material needs: that is proven from the evidence.

They respect God, but one can say that they show a greater respect for the saints. Each village has its patron; it is to him only that they pray and whom they invoke. The Virgin shares equal honors with the Saint of each locality. It is She whom a Spaniard takes for guarantor of what he affirms; it is in the name of the Virgin that a woman loves her lover, that she swears fidelity to him, that she promises a rendezvous. They don't think at all of God; Spaniards almost never mention him. A peasant said one day in my presence, "At Matapasuelos, there is a saint having as much power as God."

"And even more," responded another.

Certainly if the Spanish people could manage one day to have a government without despotism, liberty without anarchy, it should — because of it geographical position, its sun, and its character — march at the head of civilization. It will still require a long time to arrive there because you can't improvise an education for a nation. If it is to make progress, it must study, and it isn't until after many years that good books produce results.

Before our entry into Spain the importation of all sorts of publications was strictly prohibited. After our departure they made an *auto da fe* [58] of all the printed works the French had brought in. You could be denounced as readily for having a copy of Voltaire as for a plot to kill the king.

The church has always held the Spanish people in ignorance; they know that their rule will end the day the people begin to reason. By an *ordonnance* of 7 September 1558, Philip II condemned to death all those who sold, printed, bought, or resold those books prohibited by the Inquisition. To read one of those books was so great a sin that ordinary priests could not grant absolution for it; such cases were reserved for the bishops — while for theft, adultery, similar peccadillos, one is forgiven by entering a confessional for a few minutes.

Spanish clergy have always made the Catholic religion a matter of outward practices. "Think what you wish, but have the appearance of doing as we wish. With us outward appearance comes first and the heart may go where it pleases." When Angelus bell

---

[57] The French Army had a postal service. See Elting, *Swords*, pp. 106-107.

[58] Public/religious bonfire, in earlier days used for disposal of assorted heretics by the Inquisition.

rings, everyone kneels — in the streets, the promenades, everywhere. The King himself, if he is in his carriage, gets out at once to recite his prayer. The Angelus was instituted by Pope John XXII in 1316. The Hungarians were then at war with the Turks. Sometimes victorious, more often beaten, they sent a deputation to the pope to request assistance from him. His Holiness was not able to do more than to order prayers on their behalf throughout all Christendom. Since that time, the war has ended and the prayers continue; people recite them three times a day against the Turks. Also, for twenty years after peace was made, tithe-payers continued to pay their tenth for the war.[59]

These contrivances have one very odd result. During the last Russian campaign against the Turks, many religious people wanted the followers of Mohemet to win; they never thought that in reciting the Angelus three times a day they were praying to God for the success of the forces of the Emperor Nicholas. Without wishing it, without suspecting, they had lifted General Diebitsch across the Balkan mountains.[60]

You can't imagine any story so absurd, so silly, so foolish but what a Spanish monk would not attempt to make his compatriots swallow it. A certain Saint's image has wept, such a Virgin has moved her arm, feet, head — and they all believe it because a priest has said so. Soon, each of them claims to have witnessed it. How can you doubt it then when the whole village swears it is true. Voltaire said somewhere that if 20,000 men came before him to swear that they had seen a dead man resurrected, he still would not believe them. Voltaire was right, but in every village in Spain you will find men who claim to have seen that miracle.

On arriving at Burgos, I visited the magnificent cathedral. My guide told me that in the hospital they would show me a crucifix on which the Christ figure's nails grew so much that they were obliged to trim them every week. I therefore went to the hospital to see that crucifix. Its guardian was absent, so I didn't get to see it — but they showed me the nun who, every eight days, was responsible for that surgical operation.

That reminded me of the story of that poor wretch, who, to trick a few sous from Paris idlers, installed himself in a little shed on the boulevard. After having sounded a trumpet and beaten a drum to attract the loungers: "Gentlemen," said he, "Come see this rare and strange animal. It has made the tour of the four quarters of the world, to wit Europe, Asia, Africa, and Norway. Never has anyone seen the like: it was born of the incestuous love of a carp and a rabbit. The astonishing thing, gentlemen, is that the carp was the father." You paid two sous, you entered the booth, and the barker's confederate told the imbeciles, "The Count of Lacépède, Grand-Chancellor of the Legion of Honor and director of the Museum of Natural History, just now has sent for the animal, to make a report concerning it to His Majesty, the Emperor Napoleon. I therefore am unable to show it to you today, but I can let you see its father and mother." Thereafter, perfectly at his ease, the loafer could study a caged rabbit and a carp in a basket.

When we traveled we never failed to visit the churches in all the countries we crossed. They are the most curious things you can see in Spain. Nothing astonished the Spaniards more than to see us behaving respectfully in a holy place. Some of them, certain that Napoleon's soldiers were devils incarnate, could not understand why the touch of holy water did not immediately send us back to hell.

[59] I have been unable to confirm all this ecclesiastical history.
[60] Hans K.A.F. Diebitsch (1785-1831) German-born Russian general, noted for his success against Turkey, 1828-1829.

That superstition that leads Spaniards to venerate matter when it has been molded into the shape of a saint, extends also to bells. In every town, they speak of a bell that cures epidemics, of another that brings rain or protects from thunderbolts. That is a thing decided; no doubts about it are permitted.

Before the Revolution of 1789, and while the country of Venaissin belonged to the Pope, Avignon alone possessed 128 bell towers, all furnished with bells of all sizes — and God knows the clamor which you would hear on days of great religious solemnity. People with sensitive ears were obliged to take refuge out in the countryside. On the day of the Dead, for example, the town was deserted, everyone went into the country. Such is the strangeness of mankind however that many Avignonese of that period paid during their lifetime so that a certain bell would sound on the day of their death.

One of these worthy citizens was in his last agonies and much regretting leaving the world he knew to travel into another he did not know. His brother, seated at the bedside of the dying man, sought to console him. After having exhausted all the usual methods, he employed that unanswerable argument. "My brother, tomorrow at your burial, the three finest chimes of Avignon will ring: the cathedral, because I am the canon; Saint Peter, because it is your parish; and Saint Agricol, because that is where you will be buried. Now complain, if you dare."

Many ladies followed their husbands in the army, whether because their conjugal tenderness made them wish to stay together, or because a lack of sufficient money to maintain two households. However, while we were in the field they remained around the regimental depot;[61] but as soon as peace was made you saw them arrive by the carriage-load. These ladies traveled by cabriolet, calash,[62] and cart, and marched with the supply trains. Every day their chaste ears heard the strongest words; at every halt their eyes saw most hideous objects. I will not say more than that, and you will understand me if you can. In Germany, these ladies who followed the drums lived in an agreeable enough manner — no danger threatened. But in Spain, it was very different. Following the road, they were, as much as we, exposed to musket shots, and when their escort, falling into an ambuscade, left them to the mercy of Spanish bandits, they suffered the most infamous treatment.

In a skirmish near Burgos the wife of an officer of my acquaintance had her carriage wrecked, and was forced to go on sadly on foot. Soon she was overwhelmed by fatigue; the sweat ran down her face, her delicate limbs could no longer support her; it was impossible for her to go a hundred steps further. The good husband grieved to see his wife in so afflicting a state.

"That poor Laure," he said to me, "she will die on the road if I cannot find a vehicle, a mule, or a horse to carry her."

"We haven't found any of those today; but I believe I saw, back there near the tail of the column, a soldier leading a donkey, and if you could get him to sell it to you, or better to lend it to you."

"Yes, you're right. You are my friend, you are. Where is that soldier — where is that donkey? I must have a donkey for Laure. That poor Laure, she's so worn out!"

"She can't go any further."

---

[61] The regiment's home station.
[62] Both much like the American one-horse shay.

52

"I'd give a hundred louis for a donkey.[63] Money is made to use, and what good is it for me to have money, if Laure is suffering. Come on, let's see that donkey."

"I believe you won't have to pay that much."

"What difference if it is expensive, provided I find a donkey. But where will we find it?"

"With the rear guard. I think it belongs to some marauder who has made himself scarce. Let the column go by; just wait, we'll take care of your problem."

"Come on. Laure, have a little courage and keep going. I'll be back soon."

The column passed us, little by little. The rear guard appeared, and we saw a voltigeur who led a long-eared animal by its bridle. He had placed his pack on one side of it and his musket on the other as a counterweight.

"Ah, there's that donkey I'm looking for. See here voltigeur, my wife is sick, she cannot walk further. It's essential that you sell me your donkey."

"I'd be happy to, my captain."

"How much do you want?"

"Twenty francs."

"Are you making fun of me? Twenty francs! Twenty francs! And for a stolen donkey, for you have stolen it. I should report you to the commanding general."

"But, my captain, I didn't steal it. I found it while we were going through that last village."

"Yes, found, found. I'm not about to believe that."

"Even if I did steal it, you should find that agreeable enough because you need it."

"Get going. Here are two 100-sou coins. Give me your donkey."

"Oh no. I want twenty francs."

"What! Take your choice — my two 100-sou pieces or a complaint to the commanding general."

"Very well. Take my donkey."

"My friend," he said to me, "this is (censored) expensive — ten francs for a stolen donkey. But let's go. It's all the same — money was made to roll."

---

[63] 2,000 francs.

V
The Sutlers

The sutler's[1] trade is a fine one. These ladies ordinarily begin by following a soldier who has inspired them with tender sentiments. One sees them at first hiking on foot with a small keg of brandy slung over one shoulder. Eight days later they are comfortably seated on a horse they have "found." To right, to left, in front and behind, are the kegs and the saveloys;[2] the cheese and the sausages are skilfully balanced. The month never ends without a two horse wagon, full of all sorts of provisions, to prove the growing prosperity of their trade. It often happens that a party of Cossacks robs these women in the rear of the army; thereafter they begin again, and soon there is no sign of their loss.

An officer can give them no greater pleasure than to owe them money. The chance of seeing several insolvent debtors die worries them less than the Cossacks or the gangs of stragglers who often rob them of their cash. There are thieves who steal from other thieves; you see that sometimes in this world.

In camp, the sutler's tent serves as a salon, inn, and cafe; it is the central meeting place. There you gamble, drink and smoke — for what else is there to do in a camp when your whole baggage consists of a portmanteau the size of a sausage, and consequently no books? The first day of my arrival at my regiment, I was taken to the most popular sutler's, and there I found thirty officers ready to set up a game of lotto.

Though that game is not very difficult and it does not require a great mental effort to follow the necessary calculations, I was thoroughly taken that day. I had not known the method of calling the numbers; long after the prize had been won, I had no numbers marked off on my card. This is why: the habit, in the army is to say numbers only by circumlocution. A fine is inflicted on anyone who uses any other method of designation. I shall give some examples: 1 is called " the creation of the world"; 2, "the little pullet"; 3, "the Jew's ear"; 4, "the commissaire's hat"; 5, "the shoemaker's awl"; 7, "the gallows"; 9, "that which isn't old"; 22, "the ducks of the Mein"; 31, "Day Without Bread, Misery in Prussia"; 33, "the two hunchbacks"; 48, "the alarm gun"; 57, "the Terrible"; 89, "the Revolution"; 90 , the Grandfather of All.[3] I set myself to study them, and soon I was able to play my part.

---

[1] Note that Blaze uses *cantiniere* (sutler) more than *vivandiere*, which appears so frequently in other Napoleonic literature.
[2] Highly seasoned sausage, sometimes containing pig's brains.
[3] For some explanations: No. 7 was widely known as "the gallows" from its shape; reputedly 1777 had been known as "the year of the gallows." "Ducks of the Mein" was an allusion to an incident in which several companies of the 22nd Regiment, pursued by enemy cavalry, swam across the Mein River to escape: careless use of that term might end in a duel. Thirty-one's name came from the fact that the stingy Prussian government paid on the basis of a 30 day month; on the 31st you must find your own food. Napoleon had named the 57th Regiment, "The Terrible". And the French Revolution began in 1789.

Laborie, of whom I already have spoken, had little use for young officers from the military schools. My ignorance greatly amazed him.

"What in the devil did you learn at Fontainebleau?"

"Mathematics."

"And after that?"

"History."

"Afterwards?"

"Drill."

"Afterwards?"

"Fortification, drawing, geography, the—"

"But did you learn this there?" He said, putting himself on guard, as if he were about to run me through.

"That too we learned there."

"My dear fellow, that's all you need to know; all the rest is useless stupidity."

That worthy man had reason to think so, for his intelligence did not extend beyond a bottle or a pipe of tobacco. To give you an idea of it, I must tell you that one day I found him reading a book of short stories; he did not realize that 200 pages were missing from the center of it, commencing at the last part of one story and extending into the first part of

another. Laborie continued his reading without noticing this gap. Characters, plot, location — all were different; Laborie saw nothing but black print on white paper.

The sutlers were of great service to the army, even as they made their fortunes; they were really useful in certain circumstances. These females, endowed with unusual energy, were tireless; braving the cold, the heat, the rain, and the snow, like veteran grenadiers. They were always going in all directions to obtain the necessary items for their trade. Men of the world who have never lacked these things that are indispensable in life, cannot realize how important a bottle of wine, a glass of brandy, can be at certain moments.

An experienced sutler always has a small reserve for the officers; she saves that for the critical times, which doubles, triples the importance of that service. What good fortune indeed, when you found yourself in a plowed field, wet to your bones and thinking you must sleep without supper, to find beside a good fire, a slice of ham or a bowl of hot wine — or, better, both together.

That could cost a lot sometimes, but money is no use unless it can get you what you need. The moment that you can't buy bread with it, iron[4] becomes more valuable than gold. During the Russian campaign of 1812, soldiers passed by the paymasters' wagons abandoned along the road without touching a centime — because there wasn't any sort of bakery in the neighborhood. The really important things in this world are food and

---

[4] Meaning weapons.

the stomach, the periodic demands of which should always be heeded. Before Monsieur Stomach, the passions and the interests are silent; take care of him first and you can see to the rest later.

Many sutlers were as brave as veteran grenadiers. My company's Thérèse, carried brandy to our soldiers in the midst of bullets and cannon balls; she was wounded twice. Don't think she risked dangers to make money; a nobler sentiment moved her — during battles she never asked to be paid. In her quarrels with other women of the same trade, Thérèse triumphed by reproaching them for not daring to do as she did. With all these generous sentiments, Mademoiselle Thérèse Fromageot was terribly ugly, but few females, so far as I have been able to see (evil be unto him who evil thinks) had such shapely legs.

Laborie spent all the time he was free from military duties at the sutler's. He never failed to remark, while sitting there with his bottle of wine or his little glass of brandy, "Ah, we're better off here than at Eylau."

That battle of Eylau always came up in his talk. It served as a standard of comparison and was for him the superlative of misery. No one had any merit in Laborie's estimation if he had not fought on the field of Eylau. We received the *Journal of the Empire*; one day, after having read it, I told Laborie, "They advertise a book which I want to order from Paris."

"What is it?"

"The *Précis of World Geography*."

"Who wrote that?"

"Malte-Brun."

"Who is your Malte-Brun?"

"He is one of our best geographers."

"What's his regiment?"

"He's not a soldier, he's a savant, a man of very high reputation. He lives in Paris."

"He's a precious rabbit, your Malte-Brun. I would have liked to see him at Eylau, with his geography and the snow up to his knees — with his science and no bread — with his reputation and nothing to drink. Had it happened that he had been there, we would have seen if he could write those books!"

At Mademoiselle Thérèse's, you drank, ate, smoked, and gambled. You also could arrange marriages. In Posen she had a well furnished cafe which drew plenty of customers. Soldiers and civilians both frequented it, to her great contentment at seeing her profits as great while we were in garrison as they had been during the war.

Usually when a man makes an advantageous marriage as regards money, it is generally agreed that he possesses some physical advantages or that he is distinguished by his spirit, his conduct or his education, — in short, that he will have, as they say, something going for him. An officer of my acquaintance, without any of those qualities — what am I saying — possessing to an extreme degree the opposite faults, married the richest heiress in and around Posen — precisely because he had those faults.

He was the greatest drunkard in the French Army, the sort that we called a bag of wine. Seeing him drink beyond all measure, we often warned him to watch himself, that such excess was always harmful, etc., etc. "Bah," he would respond, while emptying his glass. "There is only one thing that hurts me every day, and that's the wine I wasn't able to drink." He went often to Thérèse's; there, seated alone at a table, he drank, seeking his pleasure at the bottom of a bottle. He always left his wits there, and you could say that he didn't leave very much at that. We often picked him up dead drunk in the street.

A good many inhabitants of Posen came to quench their thirst at the same place, Mademoiselle Fromageot's being the fashionable place Men having the same tastes readily become acquainted. One of these gentlemen, struck by the grace with which our officer changed full bottles to empty bottles, felt the highest admiration for him and, considering him a worthy rival, proposed a contest to see who could drink the most. The officer accepted the challenge at once with enthusiasm — it was the most agreeable proposal one could make to him. The rendezvous was set for the next day; the field of battle was a cabaret, the judges of the field were the two drunkards, and the battle began. The Frenchman kept a great superiority over the Pole; he was on his twelfth bottle; his opponent had barely begun his tenth and already his head was sagging. Two more bottles sent him under the table, while the Frenchman, pretty well gone himself, was saying triumphantly that Poles didn't know how to drink, that he had upheld the honor of France, and a thousand other foolish things. From the strain of sustaining our honor, his legs no longer could support him, and he went to join his comrade on the floor, where our two combatants snored the rest of the day.

When the wine fumes had dissipated a little, they resumed drinking, but quietly, to refresh themselves and get rid of the "counter-thirst."[5]

"Comrade," said the Frenchman, "I love the Poles, I esteem them as soldiers, but I scorn them as drinkers."

"I admit that I am defeated. You are a worthy fellow — I recognize you as my master."

"I believe it. No one is able to compete with me."

"Since you have defeated me, you will beat many others. But let's talk of something else — do you wish to marry?"

"Why not?"

"I have a young lady to offer you."

"Is she rich?"

"She has a dowry of 100,000 thalers (360,000 francs)."

"You're joking!"

"I am not joking. I am her guardian; everyone wants to marry her — I offer her to you."

"I accept, my friend."

"Come to my house tomorrow. I shall present you. It's all settled."

This would appear really incredible, but there are thousands of witnesses who can swear to it. The marriage took place; the next month the Polish girl was beaten by her amiable spouse; two years later the dowry was drunk up, and since that time I have never heard mention of either one.

We had in the army sutlers who, by the bravery and talents of their husbands, were raised quite high. Some could call themselves "madam the baroness;" others "madam the general's wife;" some even, on awakening one fine morning, find themselves "madam the duchess."[6] I have known some of them who were bored in their fine salons, regretting the lively life, full of happenings, which they had had in times past.

---

[5]   From Blaze's footnote, "A word invented by [this Frenchman] to express the thirst which he suffered when getting up after having drunk too much. Drinking to quench this counter-thirst, he called 'taking up the hair of the beast.'" (U.S. "hair of the dog that bit you.")

[6]   Considerable exaggeration here. Blaze's prime example, *Madame la Maréchale* Lefebvre, Duchess of Danzig, had been a regimental washer woman and not a *vivandiere* — and had married Lefebvre back in 1783 before the Revolution.

I have known others who, travelling in a handsome four-horse carriage, have found it quite inconvenient to see their progress delayed by new members of their former trade, perched on a stubborn horse between two kegs. They have forgotten that in the old days, an encounter with such a fine vehicle would have irked them just as much. One evening at Fontainebleau the French comedians presented "The Marriage of Figaro" before the Emperor. After the curtain had fallen, Marshal Lannes exclaimed, "When I think that I used to be willing to spend my last cent to see that comedy! Well — today I find nothing amusing in it."

"The reason is," responded Napoleon, "that back then you were in the pit, and now you are in the best box."

These ladies were never at ease. At the court, people made fun of them under their breath and often loudly. In their town mansions they never had visitors, except a few officers. One of them said to me one day, "I have always heard it said that life in Paris was very amusing; I can assure you that I am not at all amused. Look at my fine pleasures — I know nobody, I am always alone. It's really tiresome."

"If you wish to see plenty of people," I told her, "I can give you an infallible formula. Give dinners where the food is delicious, the wines are exquisite. Arrange things so that people will have a good time and your salons will be well attended. In Paris the distances are great, our period is essentially speculative. We do not care to go anywhere just for a glass of orgeat.[7] Offer turkey stuffed with truffles and pheasant à la Holy Alliance,[8] and you will have visitors."

The lady found the cure worse than the sickness, and preferred to remain by herself. Not everyone knows how to live on an income of two million francs a year. When one has dined for years on a bit of sausage, it is difficult — however rich he may be — to decide to spend 500 francs in one day. You and I know immensely wealthy men who do not spend a twentieth of their income. These men are thieves; there should be a law against them. In effect, by hoarding their money they rob the merchants, the artisans, the poor, and the tax collector. They pile up centime on centime, and finish up in a fir-wood coffin; one of oak would be too expensive

7   A liqueur made of almonds, milk, sugar, and water flavored with orange-flower water and
    brandy — suitable for invalids, old men, and ladies
8   An elaborate dish, no longer in the cookbooks. Since it was named for the Holy Alliance (a
    mutual protection society of European rulers, formed September 1815, under the disguise of
    devotion to Christian ideals) this must be considered post-Napoleonic.

VI
The Billets

In general, the place which pleased us the most was the one we left the soonest — and vice versa. Higher authority's orders very seldom coincided with our pleasures. Travelers who go by post have a new room every day and see nothing. I knew one who, traveling through Florence during a fine moonlit night, happily exclaimed, "I have seen another town." Though marching rapidly, we always lodged with the inhabitants, whom we could study. One day in a chateau, the next in a thatched cottage, we were closer to the natives of the country than someone who leaves an inn to go to another inn. You will find in this chapter some observations of customs and manners made upon the spot, day by day, with the different peoples we have visited. It is by staying with men and eating with them that you get to know them.

Soldiers traveling in France received a ticket for lodging which entitled them to a "place at the fire and a candle."[1] We Romans of the Empire therefore preferred Germany to France. With the Germans we found our dinner awaiting us; our pay remained intact and could serve for other purposes — a small dram, tobacco, and the rest. In Spain, it was often worse than in France; we got neither fire nor candle.

The soldiers have a curious method of getting special treatment. When several of them were billeted together, they agreed on their respective roles before entering the peasant's house. One of them played the tough guy; he swore, blustered, drew his saber, and threatened everyone. The women were frightened, and sometimes the men also. The master of the house would arrive; then the other soldiers would "play the saint," telling him that the brawler was really the best fellow in the world, but it was necessary to know how to handle him. Then they promptly indicated his weak side.

"He loves good cheer, good wine. What can you expect? He's crazy about it. When you treat him according to his fancy, he is as gentle as a sheep, as a newborn infant — but when anyone gives him only potatoes to eat, or sour beer to drink, he becomes terrible; none of us and even all of us together can prevent him from doing something unfortunate. Look — only yesterday, no later, just eight leagues from here, that regular demon set fire to the house of a peasant who was so rude as to put water into the wine he gave us. It does not follow that our comrade was entirely in the wrong; one should never cheat anyone. Consider — look to it — do things conscientiously, see that the food is good, the drinks first-rate, and don't worry. We'll be responsible for everything."

This oration, amplified and paraphrased by other members of the group, ordinarily made a great impression; the host took care of things cheerfully, our jolly dogs did not demand more, and everything went very well. These bits of comedy were sometimes played by the officers, but there seldom was an occasion for it since there seldom were enough assigned to the same billet to play all the necessary roles.

---

[1] "Billet" (ticket) soon came to mean the whole affair — the "lodging" (whether a nice bedroom or a bundle of straw in a stable) became your "billet." See Elting, *Swords*, pp. 465-466.

We were not loved in Germany — very far from it. The sojourn or the passage of the French regiments was an enormous expense for the country. They hated our army as a whole, but they liked individual Frenchmen. The happy, frank, and open character of the French easily won the friendship of the Germans, who are generally serious. Despite the national hatred, it was rare that a French soldier who was willing to make a little effort to be friendly was not as well thought of by his host as if they had known each other for ten years. Share their tastes, smoke, and drink their beer and the Germans will love you. And besides they had been told so often that the French were devils that when they meet well-bred men, they spare no means to express the happiness they feel.

In Spain they don't like individuals any better than armies. In a general uprising the Spaniard would cut the throat of a Frenchman sleeping beneath his roof, a German would protect him. Almost everywhere I went in Germany, I was well received; almost everywhere I have been asked to return if I had the chance.[2]

A soldier should not take such invitations literally. They were the polite formulas people utter when you leave. One day I decided to visit a worthy German again: He didn't remember me. I had to recite my name and Christian name, age and rank, also your humble servant.

In that epoch Germany was tormented by secret societies, all of which had the aim of throwing off the French yoke. A German was not a proper German unless he had written verses against Napoleon, Odes, stanzas, songs — there was a deluge of them. They spoke only of the poniards of the Sicilian Vespers,[3] but all of it passed away in verses. At Merseburg, I lodged with a lawyer, a man with plenty of wit, learned, and a sworn enemy of Napoleon. While we were not of the same political opinion, confidence was soon established between us. Certain that his indiscretion would not have unfortunate results, he showed me the verses which he had written on Napoleon.

Those verses were a masterpiece of patience. There were six, three in hexameters and three in pentameters. When you read them in the ordinary way, they were a pompous panegyric; when taken in the opposite sense — that is to say, by commencing with the last word and finishing with the first, they were a violent satire. But the most astonishing thing was that the last verse, which was a pentameter, taken in reverse, became a hexameter, by adding the last word of the preceding verse. Deprived of that word, that verse became a pentameter, and so on so that the three couplets were always regular. I made a copy of these verses, but lost them later to my great regret.

Having arrived at his billet, everyone — officer, sergeant, or soldier[4] — considered wooing the lady, or, better, the daughter of the house; often nothing came of it; sometimes you were successful. In all such cases it always was wise to keep moving on.

My captain was married, but he often forgot that. I have known a good many officers who, in certain circumstances, did not have any better memory. In all his billets he passed himself off as a bachelor; if he met a young girl, he promptly began flirting, talked of marriage — and now and then one of them listened to him. Marriage! You know that word is magical for a young lady. Whatever man she does not disdain to consider as a man, she considers with benevolence because she considers him a possible husband. A husband! That is a grand affair! Every day that melodious word invades the thoughts

---

[2]   Things became grimmer in 1813
[3]   A revolt by the Sicilian population against French rule in 1282, in which most of the French garrison and their families were massacred.
[4]   In the French Army, corporals were not considered noncommissioned officers.

of a young girl. Like a kaleidoscope, her imagination takes her through all that would mean, and on that she builds many castles in Spain — and God knows that too often they crumble.

Be that as it may, my captain could always get them to listen to that little lie. I, who always had an avowal of devotion all prepared, but who did not have the face of a marrying man, was very often disdainfully repulsed, although I was twenty years younger than my rival. The respect which I have always had for good morals, for conjugal fidelity — and perhaps a little jealousy — gave me an idea of how to supplant him. As soon as he took up the subject and began to play the suitor...

"Captain," I said to him loudly, "The wagonmaster[5] is here; I believe he has a letter from your wife."

"So hold your tongue," he replied. But I pretended not to have heard him, and continued stoutly.

"Napoleon, your oldest son (all officers' sons were named Napoleon) should be full-grown now and getting along well. He's a very intelligent young man. Is he still at the Antwerp lycee?"[6]

"What business is that of yours?"

"And little Hortense (all officers' daughters were named Hortense; later they would be Marie-Louise),[7] is she always playful?"

"All right, all right, that doesn't concern you."

"Really, it's really nice to be married, to have children, to see them grow up. This bachelor's life is often so boring; I never have felt readier to give it up than I do today."

Thereafter the young lady was colder in her responses to the captain; soon she disregarded him entirely. He was married and therefore useless. All the ground he lost I gradually gained, and sometimes I was very lucky as the result of those indiscretions.

"You devil, why did you speak to me about my wife at every opportunity? I think that you did it on purpose."

"Doubtlessly."

"But don't you know that was very wrong?"

"Do you think it was better to betray the vows you made to your wife at the foot of the altar? To attempt to seduce a young girl by getting her to believe that you would marry her? Why that is shocking, and without morals."

"Morals! Morals! Do you know what I think, Monsieur High Principles? I see very well that your talk is only a sharp trick to take my place."

"That's possible."

"And morals will be better served by you than by me?"

"Again, that's possible, for I can get married. You can't."

"You've never said anything about that."

"What do you know? For some time I've felt a certain inclination towards marriage; a notion, a whim could make up my mind for me. If I see a good example, perhaps I would follow it. You know the story about Panurge's sheep — they all ran into the water because one of them did so. For the rest, you have the advantage of being my superior officer — allow me the advantage I have over you. When there are two girls, you can court one, but when our host has only one daughter, remember that I alone have the right

---

5   The sergeant in charge of the regiment's wagons. He also handled its mail.
6   The high school.
7   Hortense Beauharnais, Napoleon's stepdaughter, then Queen of Holland.

to flirt with her. I am the younger, and gallantry is in inverse ratio to length of military service."

Several days later, on arriving at Magdeburg, I went to see my captain and found him with a face a yard long. He was sad, breathing long sighs, intermixed with very energetic interjections.

"What's happened to you?" I said to him. "You don't seem happy today."

"That which I have, my dear fellow, that which I have — you'll find out. It's an end to laughter — wedlock arrives."

"What do you mean?"

"My wife is coming to rejoin me. I received word this morning."

"Oh well, my captain, receive my sincere felicitations on the pleasure — the happiness — that — which —"

"Thanks, thanks. You're trying to be funny, but I wish the same to you."

Germans did not like to have married officers billeted on them. These ladies were usually very demanding. Since they wish to appear to be "well born," they made a show of never being pleased, either with their accommodations or their meals, to make you think that things were much better under their paternal roof. During the Restoration[8] the officers on duty at the Tuileries dined at the chateau; it was the height of style in the Royal Guard to find that mess unpleasant; they gave themselves a certain air of the *grand seigneur*,[9] trying to persuade you that things were much better done in their own homes. I don't know how those gentlemen's kitchens were organized; as for myself, when I compare my father's food with that of the Tuileries, the latter is the one I prefer.

Everywhere I've been billeted, my host has told me that he would rather have ten soldiers than one officer's wife. In Germany, they would rather receive four Frenchmen than one German from the Confederation of the Rhine. The Bavarians, the Westphalians, the Württembergers, were unmanageable; they began by blows with the flat of their sabers, and sometimes went further, while the French almost always went no farther than threatening.

When we traveled alone in Germany, a police officer never failed to come greet us at our inn to ask us to write our full names in his notebook. One day we were eating when the policeman arrived and everyone went through the usual formality. When my turn came, I read with surprise the odd Christian name which the man next to me had written — he called himself Monsieur Topinambour Duval (or Dubreuil or Dufour — it makes no difference).

"That is undoubtedly a joke you; you've played on the police officer," I said to him.

"No, monsieur."

"But didn't you call yourself Topinambour?"

"Why not?"

"I have never known a saint of that name."

"Well, it's not the name of a saint; it's the name of a plant[10] that is more useful than all the saints in the calendar."

"Ah, I understand. You were doubtlessly baptized in the year of grace 1793."[11]

"Monsieur, I have never been baptized."

"My sincerest compliments."

An employee of the rations service joined in our conversation. He claimed that the republican calendar was much more sensible, that it was better to call oneself cabbage, carrot, and turnip than Georges, Pierre, or Polycarpe. That the peasant very well understood those first names with which he had frequent business every day, while the second set was unintelligible to him All the stories about saints were only falsehood,

---

8 After Waterloo.
9 High nobility.
10 The Jerusalem artichoke.
11 The French Revolutionary (or Republican) calendar was adopted in November, 1793. The names of the months were changed and saint's days abolished.

vague tales, and silly things, while by contrast, using the names of vegetables was a clear and practical idea. "For my part," he said, "in 1793 I discarded my name of Bernard, and I have taken that of Betterave."[12]

"Why rave," an old Hussar officer responded.[13]

The King of Württemberg has established an unusual tax in his state: any young lady who takes the great liberty of giving birth without being married, must pay a fine; and that brings in 300,000 francs a year to his Württemberg majesty. One should not neglect such small profits. That money goes to the king's kitchens; the grand master of that essential part of a proper government exercises control over all those infants who are born without the permission of monsieurs the parish priests. A word to the commission preparing our next budget, to those studying ways and means; finally to all commissions present and future: in France, every year approximately 70,000 natural infants are born. Tax all of these young fellows. That way will be not at all vexatious, for it is understood that you can live without making babies. It will be essentially moral because it will push those men who have a decided inclination for the procreation of their species, into marriage. I invite monsieurs, the ministers, to consider my proposition; in all events, I count on the credit for introducing it.

After having been billeted on a cobbler, the next day we reached the area of Ulm and found ourselves in a palace. Prince Henry of Württemberg had been exiled by his father, the King;[14] while waiting until he was forgiven he led a merry life at the chateau of Wippling. His highness had the kindness to invite us to dinner. We accepted — officers always accepted.

The prince drank nothing but champagne, from the beginning of the dinner until the dessert. It was poured lavishly; we initially found such doings strange, but we quickly got accustomed to it. Our national spirit became involved; for the benefit of the champagne wine growers, we pushed its consumption. Many other wines were served, but the prince did not touch them. They were only for us, and his royal highness did the honors most gracefully.

"Monsieur captain," said he to one of our comrades who chanced to be seated across the table from him, "may I offer you Bordeaux, Chambertin, Malaga, Xeres, Johannesberg?"

"Yes, your highness," — successively.

One of the guests was a Bavarian officer. I noticed at once that this brave man wore on his left thumb an extraordinarily large gold ring; it was at least four times the diameter of his thumb. A black ribbon, tied around his wrist, held it in place. I asked myself if it really was a ring — and, if not a ring, what was it? I had never seen one so large and worn in a similar fashion. During the whole dinner, my attention was continuously taken by that ring; even the champagne barely diverted me occasionally. If I had gone to bed without learning the why and the wherefore I would not have been able to sleep.

I wanted to get to the bottom of it. After we had left the table, I approached the officer to strike up a conversation. We had made the same campaigns, we had been in the same

---

[12] Sugar beet.

[13] "Bette" is "beet" and "Rave" can be either "turnip" or "radish." To have a vegetative name, "bette" would have sufficed.

[14] King Friedrich I, the very fat, very ruthless, and very able first King of Württemberg (by grace of Napoleon).

battles on the same side, and we quickly became friends. We commenced by talking about our profession, but my eyes were always fixed on that ring.

"Sir," I finally said, "Could I, without being impolite, ask you what that is that you wear on your left thumb?"

"As you see, it is a ring."

"It's certainly a big one."

"Yes, that's why I have it attached to my wrist."

"Excuse me — but how do you come to wear so large a ring?"

"Because in my family all the oldest sons have worn it since times immemorial. It was made expressly for one of my ancestors, Othon de Ringesbaum. Think of what a man he must have been. We are sadly degenerated."

He took off the ring and showed it to me. Resembling one of those big brass rings we use to hang our curtains, it was solid gold and weighed at least a pound.

"Sir," said I, as I handed it back to him, "You have more patience than I have, for that must be really uncomfortable."

"Yes, it's very uncomfortable, it's very heavy — but you must realize that all of my forefathers have worn it; it is only proper that I do the same. It is even a privilege my family enjoys. I can not, I will not renounce it."

"And you are absolutely right."

Among the rulers whom chance and my billeting assignment[15] have given me the honor to see intimately, I should give first rank to the Duke of Anhalt-Dessau. That excellent prince combined the patriarchal morals of the German middle class with the qualities of a learned courtier. No French officer left Dessau without pleasant memories of the welcome he had received. It is only in Germany anymore that you see that old-fashioned simplicity, that unaffected civility right from the heart, that sincerity in the talk and features of the host.

The moment that we had mentioned the word "Worlitz," the duke ordered his officers to take us there. We knew of that famous garden from several verses of Delille,[16] and I quoted them. That seemed to please the duke; promptly everything was placed at our disposition, horses, carriages and all.

That excursion was certainly the most agreeable I have made in my life. Nothing is as pleasing or as beautiful as the garden of Worlitz. Nature and the fine arts have completed to embellish it; everything the imagination could conceive is there, in an area several leagues square. First a prairie of immense extent, divided by a river, offers a delightful view with its bridges, sometimes elegant, sometimes bizarre. Here were flower beds, there cascades, here rocky crags; further on were obelisks, statues, and museums.

You lost yourself in a grove, to emerge in front of a temple with Corinthian columns, which was the library. Then came a farm with all its animals, tools, and workers. A white marble dairy farm was staffed with appropriately costumed young girls. You could believe yourself at the Opera! Further on, a more nobly designed building housed a collection of medals; still further was an art gallery. In short, Worlitz was, for the Duke

---

[15] "billet de logement."

[16] Abbe Jacques Delille (1738-1813). Besides poetry and songs, he was noted for studies of light, including naming the colors of the rainbow — a work he botched by including indigo, which is not a 'pure' color.

of Anhalt-Dessau, all our museums, our libraries, our natural history collections combined in a magnificent English garden.

In traveling through the Duchy of Anhalt-Dessau, we felt a vague desire to always live there. After seeing the duke who then governed, we willingly obeyed all his laws without asking any pledges from his officials. He was a good father amid his children; they never asked the reasons for his actions, knowing that they would be for the best.

That happy country is not as large as some French *departements*[17] but it is one vast garden. All the roads are bordered on each side by three rows of cherry trees, which present a wonderful sight in June. Also they make an enormous quantity of *Kirschwasser*[18] from all those cherries.

This fondness for gardens is general in Germany. From the rulers to the least important citizen, each has his own which he continually embellishes. Cities which were fortified in times gone by have changed their old bastions into hills of lilacs, their walls into avenues of flowers. The marshy moats have become pretty sheets of water, interspersed with little islands. Leipzig and Bremen could be cited as models of that style. One could walk completely around those towns under beautiful trees and along rows of flowers.

These fortifications provide an irregular terrain which, converted into English gardens by men of good taste, present a delightful aspect. The view changes with each step and there is always something more to see. It is not like our symmetrical French promenades where you see everything as soon as you arrive.

A country where we lived either very well or very badly — that was Poland. Poverty and luxury confronted you at each step. Villages there were unbelievably dirty; in each peasant's house you found one room — or, more exactly, a stables — where the cows, the horses, the poultry, and so forth slept. A quarter of the space is occupied by an enormous canopy which serves as a bed for all the family. The father, the mother, the daughter, the son-in-law sleep together on straw placed above it, and everything goes on very much as with a drove of hogs. Leave that shack where you have left humanity in its primitive state, and go to the chateau and you will find all the refinements of civilization — select libraries, the politeness of well-bred men, agreeable conversation — and you will be as comfortable as it is possible to be in Poland. Travel in that country is a perpetual series of antitheses.

In general, the Polish nobles pass eleven months of the year in their chateaus. They live very economically, but they make up for that during the periods of the carnival and of Saint John; they then go to Warsaw, Posen, and Cracow. There, everyone makes a show of ruinous luxury; dinners and entertainments follow day after day; the streets are jammed with splendid carriages; they gamble for high stakes. At the end, the travelers go home and try to restore their finances by the work of their peasants.

That chateau life is not very agreeable in Poland; each family is isolated in each village. The roads are horribly bad; you can not go visiting except when they freeze hard or during the summer. I do not advise the professional gastronomes to go to Poland for a practical course of the sublime meditations of Brillat-Savarin. Nowhere, except in the cities, is there a butcher or a baker. The noble must provide everything that would sustain life from own resources. A cow that he has had slaughtered will provide his family with fresh meat for three days, or with salt beef for three months — that is all.

---

[17] French equivalent of U.S. states.
[18] Potent, colorless cherry brandy, made from wild cherries.

Bread very seldom is a part of the Polish diet; their meats are dressed up as pates and pastries. Their usual drink is a foul tasting beer; in many chateaus where I have dined, I have seen only one glass in the middle of the table, and each person emptied it in turn. I have seen very pretty young ladies, charming, well brought up, drink from it after an ugly sloven of a steward with a long beard without the least repugnance. As soon as I learned of such habits, I got myself a goblet for my personal use alone.

In Poland I have seen young ladies with the odd habit of sticking kernels of black pepper to their faces, like the patches with which our ladies used to tattoo themselves in times gone by to emphasize the whiteness of their complexion.

"I am surprised," I said one day to one of them, "that you have managed to put your patch in exactly the same place that it was yesterday."

"But I never remove it."

"You mean that you don't wash your face?"

"Why should I? My face is always clean."

In Warsaw, half the inhabitants are foreigners, especially Germans. Polish Jews handle all, or nearly all, the businesses; they are the innkeepers, the merchants, the tailors and shoemakers. The Germans are doctors, surgeons, pharmacists, and lawyers. The Poles, properly speaking, are either nobles or peasants, slaves or great lords; in that country there is no intermediate class.

Warsaw society much resembles that of Paris. The ladies are most amiable and are fully equal in every way to our charming compatriots. They follow French fashions, and affect the Parisian ways. These Poles speak only French, even among themselves; it is in the worst possible taste in Warsaw to speak Polish, except when you speak to servants. The Polish language is banished from society, just as the Provencal[19] patois is in Marseilles. The study of foreign languages is the basis of the education of Poles of both sexes. They really have a reason for learning the languages of other nations, for no one, I think, would want to learn theirs. I have wished to try to, but how can you manage to pronounce a word that has four or five consonants in a row?

A public cab horse in Paris[20] is a little bit less unfortunate than a Polish peasant, who works all year for a lord who gets all the profits. The country produces an abundance of grain, and the peasant never eats bread.[21] Potatoes, milk, and millet are his nourishment. These people are always clad in sheepskins, with the fleece inside during the winter and outside in summer. Their extreme dirtiness produces, besides the fleas and lice which devour them, a disease which, I think, is known only in Poland and Russia. The hairs of a man attacked by this plague are matted and twisted like the serpents of the Furies; when you cut them, blood flows. It is a disease without a remedy, and the sick man dies in appalling convulsions.[22]

Nothing can give you an idea of the filth of a Polish village. No Polish peasant ever sweeps his doorstep. In those cantonments occupied by the French army, we made the inhabitants clean their streets — it was the greatest vexation we could have inflicted on them. However, these dirty, indolent peasants could become proper soldiers and

[19] The common version of French in its Mediterranean coastal area.
[20] Traditionally, an overworked, underfed, and much abused lot a crowbaits.
[21] To a Frenchman, for whom bread was literally the stuff of life, this was the epitome of hardship.
[22] This sickness was plica/plique polonaise. The Furies, of course, are from Greek mythology — avenging female spirits with serpents for hair.

especially very brave ones. Under their peasant's clothing, they seemed foolish, stupid, and brutish. But once they are put into a uniform and assigned to a regiment, you wouldn't recognize them. These blockheads become men, proud, clean, intelligent, and fully equal to the soldiers of the most civilized nations.

Polish horses are small, and are harnessed four abreast. These *"Konia"* are excellent; they go very fast and can live very well on whatever food they get, even the old straw from thatched roofs. They can stand up under all the hardships one has to in war, while our fine Norman horses look like skeletons when they've had to go without oats for fifteen days. The luxurious coaches of the nobility are drawn by four to six horses, harnessed two abreast. Their traces are unusually long. In Warsaw a four horse carriage takes up more road space than the king's eight horse carriage does in Paris. That way of doing things is quite pompous — which is why the Poles have adopted it. They love everything brilliant, everything with an air of magnificence. Their servants' livery is covered with galloons of imitation gold lace, which may be false, but looks like the real thing from a distance. Especially in winter, the Poles display a great luxury in their vehicles. You see sleighs in every shape, horses loaded with bells, servants covered with furs, presenting a peculiar appearance. In the summer, northern Europe is very much like France, but during the winter it has a peculiar look all its own.

I had established my second lieutenant's headquarters at the chateau of Kladziensko, five leagues from Warsaw. The owner had abandoned it, so I was landlord and master. The story of a little adventure I had there will demonstrate, better than anything I can say, the extreme misery of the Polish peasants. I was alone in my bedroom, the soldier who lodged with me being in an adjoining room. One night I was awakened by the sound of my door being cautiously opened, and I saw by the light of my dying fire, the bearded face of the peasant caretaker who ordinarily cut the wood with which I warmed myself. He looked in and, since I pretended to be asleep, he entered. Not knowing why that man came into my bedroom at that hour, I carefully reached out for my saber which lay close to my bed and made ready to run him through if he made a hostile move. However, the poor devil was far from wishing to shorten my life — a packet of candles was the target of his nocturnal excursion. I had hung them beside the chimney; the thief went there, took them, departed, and closed the door behind him. If by misfortune the candles had been placed near my bed, I would have thought he had come to murder me and probably would have killed him.

Astonished that anyone would have risked his life for so little, I wanted to know what he would do with my candles — for in Poland, and even in many German villages, the peasants use only pine splinters, which they light one after the other, to light their evening hours, and I did not believe that my man wanted anything more luxurious to illuminate his smoky cabin. I immediately got dressed and, knowing where he lived, went there. Through a cracked window pane I saw him frying potatoes with my candles. All the poor devil's family waited impatiently to taste such a delicate dish; they joyfully watched all the details of that culinary operation, and soon they appeared very happy while devouring that unusual stew. I went away with my head full of philosophical reflections, and that peasant never learned that I knew who had stolen the candles.

As regards pleasures, excepting the finest of all,[23] to which none of the others can compare, nothing is positive in this world. Every enjoyment is relative to its surrounding

---

[23] Since Blaze was a Frenchmen, the reader probably can hazard an educated guess as to the identity of that pleasure.

circumstances. Pleasure is sometimes greater when privations have been the harsher. Thus for the shipwrecked passengers of the *Medusa*[24] a sip of mouth wash, containing alcohol, was an invaluable favor, sought by each of them. My candle-eater, who never had swallowed anything better than potatoes cooked in water, made — by eating them browned in tallow — a delicious meal, as good as, and possibly better than, those fancy combinations the best Paris restaurants offer blasé dilettantes with their wild fowl puree covered with larded partridge wings, ortolans[25] *à la provençale*, and other delights of high gastronomy. The cossacks, accustomed to plum brandy and the stinking fermented sap of the birch tree,[26] prefer brandy spiced with pepper to our best wines of Burgundy, which give them only a dull taste while passing down their horn-lined throats. Their supreme pleasure is to drink "thirty-six."[27]

Some time later, chance and my lucky star had me billeted at Kozerky, with Count Lesseur, ex-chamberlain to the former king of Poland. It is with the greatest pleasure that I mention a name that I shall always remember; I received the most friendly hospitality from M. Lesseur, and my heart shall retain an eternal gratitude.

Monsieur Lesseur was born in France. He rose to high positions at the court of Stanislas,[28] and since the partition of Poland, he lived the life of philosopher with his wife and Mademoiselle Annette, his very witty, very virtuous and very pleasant daughter. This respectable family combined the education, talents, and kindness of civilized people with patriarchal manners. I shall describe the chateau of Kozerky, so that my readers will have an idea of what the Poles consider a chateau. Without doubt the great noblemen have finer ones, but the number of those who have less desirable ones is much greater; I therefore take Kozerky as an average.

At the end of a long avenue of sheds, cabins, hovels, and whatnot, serving as stables and living quarters for the peasants and their horses, you see a nice enough cottage. It appears superb because of its surroundings, but it has only one floor, two steps up from ground level, and an attic above. The front door opens on a hall that runs the length of the house; four doors open from it — to the right is the dining room, to the left the drawing room; in the back are two bedrooms, and that is all. The rooms have birchwood floors and are neatly furnished; in each is a big stove which is lighted from the outside.[29] The windows are double, to keep out the cold. The Poles put flowers and sometimes birds between the two window panes. The roof was thatched; the house itself did not differ from the average noblemen's country home except as to the number of its rooms; the others having more or fewer according to the size of the family living there. The kitchen, the servants, and the horses were in a nearby building where the steward also lived, though he ate with his master and, as I have said already, drank from the same glass. This steward-bailiff is almost always an educated man. I have seen many who spoke Latin perfectly, though the professors of our French universities would not have comprehended the Polish manner of pronouncing it. In Paris we have the craze to

---

[24] A French frigate. Its crew and passengers suffered terrible hardships in a shipwreck before their survivors finally were picked up.

[25] Buntings.

[26] Birch beer.

[27] "Alcohol" (gin, vodka, etc.) heated to 36 degrees centigrade.

[28] Stanislas II Poniatowski (1732-1798), incompetent last King of Poland.

[29] Like our pot-bellied stoves, not through an opening from a servant's corridor in the wall behind it.

"Frenchify" Latin; we say "u" in place of "ou" and "ain" instead of "in", and so on. In the south of France we speak it a little less badly, but I had to work to learn how to speak it like the Poles — who, I think have the best style since they imitate the Italians. Everyone knows that you can use Latin to talk familiarly with all the world, but in Poland the habit of using servile expressions gives it a twist never found in Virgil or Cicero. Instead of saying "thou,"[30] the Poles say *"dominatio tua"* (your lordship) and that expression is used constantly in their talk, varying according to their sex and number, until you are bored half to death. A peasant always bows low when he speaks to his lord — or anyone who is dressed in anything better than sheepskins. Every time he opens his mouth, he extends his right hand and bows his head until he touches that person's feet. This got our soldiers in the habit of saying, whenever a peasant wanted to speak to us, "My lieutenant, here is a man who wants to measure your gaiters."

After seeing a Polish gentleman travelling and then in his chateau, you wouldn't believe that he was the same man. At home he eats only salt pork, cabbage, and dumplings; he drinks only bad beer and an even more detestable brandy. On his travels he has his four or six horse carriage; he is escorted by a squad of tall, moustached lackeys, gleaming with lace; and he drinks only champagne. He does not count the cost; for he must make a show. If he does not have money, he borrows it — the Jews are always ready, and God knows what interest they charge! Nothing in the world would keep a Polish noble from making his yearly trip to Warsaw, especially to the festival they hold there every year. Because his ancestors have done so, he must do the same. If he fails to do so, he will feel that he has dishonored the remotest of his posterity. There is a great similarity between the French and Polish characters. Like them, we like to make a show; like us, they are brave — they have given thousands and thousands of proofs.

When a Polish noble travels in winter, he always has a sleigh on top of his coach. If it snows, the sleigh carries the coach; if it thaws, the coach carries the sleigh. In that way his trip is never interrupted. He must take along his bed, if he wishes to sleep on something better than straw, and all sorts of provisions if he wishes to be certain of eating every day. Accordingly you see one or more carts, packed with baggage and servants, following the coach; it's a real caravan.

In every village you find "the Jew's house." It's the inn — Good Lord, what an inn! Enter and ask for anything more than beer, nasty brandy, or the half baked paste they call bread, and the answer will always be *niema* (we don't have it). In Poland that is the universal response, except when you ask for water — in that case they say *zara* (right away). You should see the filthy condition of these dwellings of the children of Israel. I was staying in one of these inns one time and saw that they had had given me soiled sheets. I called my host and asked him to change them.

"But why?"

"Because they aren't clean."

"But you're mistaken — only three or four French officers have used them."

I could not get that son of Jacob to comprehend that sheets might be dirty before they were black.

The Jews of Poland are a people to themselves They very much resemble the Jews of other countries in that they are always trying to get rich, but they are different in that

---

[30] The familiar form (tu) of the French "you" (vous), used between friends or condescendingly to an inferior.

they never spend anything. They pile up penny upon penny and are content, though often beaten. In France and Germany a rich Jew lives like a rich Christian, but in Poland he goes dressed like a pauper and if — fooled by his appearance — you give him two sous, he will keep them.[31]

It is an unusual thing that the Jewish race has spread throughout the entire world, always having the same customs and keeping the same type of features. Before the Revolution of 1789, the Jews of the County of Venaissin[32] led a sad existence. The Christians of that area did not believe that a child of Israel was a human being like themselves. The Jews were restricted to a certain section of the town and could leave it only during designated hours. If by mischance they found themselves on the street while a religious procession was passing (which happened frequently) they had to flee at once to escape the stones which were thrown at them from all sides.

They were required to always wear a yellow hat; Jewesses wore a scarf of the same color across their breast. Woe to those who left their district without those distinctive badges. All Jews were required to bow to any Christian vagabond, who would tell them, "Make an offering." The Jew had to obey and give him five sous. God alone knows how many twenty-five centime coins a rich Jew might have to pay out every time he left his house.

One of those gentlemen, a zealous follower of the law of Moses, who detested Christians as much as they hated him, possessed several million francs, and increased that sum every day by his industry. But "Miser father, prodigal son" says the world's wisdom, and his son proved the truth of that proverb every day. His expenditures balanced his father's profits. This young man signed notes for (borrowed) enormous sums, which Christians with Jewish tendencies loaned him at fifty-percent interest. When these were presented to Father Abraham for payment, he always refused, but the son would intervene. "Don't pay it if that makes you happy," he would say. "The vice-legat[33] won't ask for more — he'll pay it for me any time I ask him. For that I'll only have to say one thing; I WANT TO BE BAPTIZED."

The old Jew would rage inwardly while digging into his strongbox. What torments he had to suffer all his life, his religion on one hand, his money on the other! Well, the laws of Moses always came first with him. How many Christians are incapable of making a comparable sacrifice!

Polish roads are neither graveled nor paved. You may have trouble tracing them through the forests. During the winter and while the French army furrowed the country in every sense of that word, we encountered oceans of marshland which were impossible to cross. The bogs of Pultusk are sadly famous; cavalrymen have drowned there with their horses; others, finding themselves unable to escape, have blown out their brains.

Concerning those Pultusk swamps, I have heard a sad story about an engineer officer. He was engulfed up to his chin and could not save himself. A grenadier came by.

"Comrade," cried the officer. "Help me! I am doomed, I drown! This bog will soon swallow me."

"What are you?"

[31] Blaze missed the fact that an obviously well-off Polish Jew would probably be "persuaded" to make forced loans on very poor security.

[32] The enclave of Papal territory around Avignon. This account may very well come from Blaze's boyhood memories.

[33] The Pope's deputy, who ruled the Avignon area for him.

"I'm an officer of engineers."

"Ah, you are one of those who creates problems. Plan your own way out of it."

And the grenadier continued on his way. Soldiers did not like engineer officers because they never saw them in the hand-to-hand fighting. It was difficult for them to understand how anyone could be useful to the army with nothing but a pencil and a compass. In this they resembled Laborie who didn't believe that Malte-Brun could be a good geographer because that savant hadn't fought at Eylau.

When the roads have become so bad that it is impossible to travel, then — and only then — are they repaired. The Poles place logs, cut to the same length, across the road and fasten them together.[34] If you like to bump about you have only to ride at the trot along such a road. The pieces of this unusual road are of varying thickness; no effort is made to overlap them, and God alone knows how you are jolted about. Roads thus "repaired" are very dangerous for horses, for often two logs pull apart or break in two, and the animal gets a foot twisted. But that's of no importance — horses are cheap in Poland. Between Warsaw and Posen, the road is frightful in winter, the villages are the dirtiest one can imagine. Lowics, a pretty little town, is the only passable station — Kutno, Sempolno, Klodawa, and Slupcee are regular sewers!

Posen, like many Polish and Prussian towns, is built of wood and bricks; stone is very rare in that country. However its streets are paved, and here is how that was done. Every peasant who comes into town with a cart is obliged to bring a stone of specified size and deposit it at the gate; only if their owners have paid this unusual toll can vehicles enter the town. You see a heap of stones at every gate; these are used when repairs must be made. At first glance it would seem easy to pay such a tax, but the men who come every day, and must bring in 365 stones a year, are obliged to go great distances to find them, the neighborhood of the towns having been stripped of them long ago.

I have said that the Poles practically never eat bread. Serve them a morsel the size of a small coin,[35] and they'll leave half of it on their plate. The first time I dined at a Polish chateau, the servant offered me a plate containing fifteen small bits of bread, and I took all of them. Then I noticed smiles on everyone's face; the person seated next to me told me that I had just devoured bread enough for fifteen people. However it was far from enough to satisfy my appetite, so — to the great astonishment of the company — I had to demand more.[36]

After a dinner, it is the general Polish custom for all the men to kiss the hands of all the ladies. When the guests are numerous it can be a long ceremony, and it is curious to watch the movement which takes place accordingly in a large drawing room while the men cross back and forth in all directions, for it is necessary that every one of them kiss all the hands. The ladies quietly keep count, and it's an unfortunate man who fails to give them the required kiss.

The balls commence with a "promenade," in which everyone joins. The oldest man chooses a lady and, to the sound of music, walks solemnly with her arm in arm. As soon as they are on their way, all the gentlemen take their ladies and fall in behind, down to the little three-year-olds who are there. This column of promenaders meanders around the room to lengthen its route, rather like the soldiers in a melodrama who go all around the theater in order to sortie from the wing opposite to that in which they had been

---

[34] The "corduroy road" of the American frontier.

[35] Very loose approximation.

[36] As noted earlier, bread was a Frenchman's primary food.

stationed. To be in the promenade, there must be two people, man and woman. When a gentleman can not find a lady, he presents himself to the head of the column while it is moving. There he bows and claps one hand against the other while clashing his spurs by bringing his heels together.[37] There upon the gentlemen at the head of the column gives him the hand of his lady, turn about, strikes his hands and heels together, and receives the hand of the next lady. This process continues all down the column until the last gentleman finds himself left alone, and may start the whole maneuver over again by dispossessing the man who is then heading the column. However going on this way hides the real reason for finishing the promenade. Ordinarily you continue until the original leader, having given his hand to all the ladies, finds himself at the end of the line. As he is always the oldest, he naturally sits down, and everyone follows his example.

Lovers find the promenade very pleasant because, without being noticed, they always reach the lady of their choice, and everyone knows how, by taking the hand of the one you love, you can tell her all sorts of pretty things without speaking. The music played for the promenade is known to everyone, being also a national air; at its first bars, every man takes his lady and goes to their place. King Alphonse of Castile, surnamed "the Magnanimous," said, "The only difference between a madman and man dancing is that the latter's lunacy is of shorter duration." I have always agreed with that worthy monarch. I have never known the art of the *entrechats* or the *jetés battus*. Neither have I learned how to deploy my graces in making "the tail of the cat." However I excel at doing the promenade; I can clap my two hands in a decisive fashion, and I know how to reinforce that by the jingle of my spurs — whenever I'm wearing them.

The promenade also serves to go to the dinner table and to return to it for they have the excellent custom in Poland of serving supper during a ball. They do not send the dancers home at five o'clock in the morning with a glass of orgeat and a cup of tea, as they do at many great houses in Paris. When the Poles extend an invitation, you can be certain that nothing will be left undone to make the guests comfortable.

I have introduced you to the Germans and the Poles. Since we now have the time, you and I, we shall travel in Spain. Usually when one crosses a frontier you have been prepared well in advance for gradual changes in the customs and the language. Here one speaks French entirely and understands German; further on they speak German and murder the French language. It is only after traveling ten leagues beyond the Rhine that you find yourself in Germany. It is the same on the frontiers of Italy and Poland, but when you have crossed the Bidassoa River, you are in Spain. Two minutes before you were in Prusse,[38] but when you pass that river you have gone a thousand leagues — manners, language, costumes, all are different. The change is as great from Saint-Jean-de-Luz to Irun as from Calais to Dover, and yet the Bidassoa is only a brook.

Everything was new to me in this unusual country, and I spent my days exploring the streets, cafes, and shops to make my observations. The Spanish language is easy enough for a south-of-France man, like myself, who knows Latin, and I soon was able to speak it as well as anyone. But the Spaniards are not talkative; in place of the gaiety, the open-hearted, frank, and straight-forward manners that characterize our nation, I never met anything but anxious, gloomy faces with the sly features which the actors playing the

[37] Footnote by Blaze: "In Poland everybody wears spurs; you never take them off, even while dancing, and I am not certain that they remove them before going to bed."

[38] A small frontier village.

part of the tyrant in our melodramas have so ably copied. See those groups at the street corners in public places — to smoke a cigar while doing nothing seems to be their idea of supreme happiness. In France, when ten people come together, nobody listens, everyone wants to talk, everyone tries to dominate the conversation. In Spain, all is silence. Wrapped in dirty cloaks over their still dirtier coats, showing nothing more than half their face and the two fingers that hold their cigar, Spaniards remain gathered together for entire hours, exchanging clouds of cigar smoke without speaking. Occasionally one of them decides to speak, which he always does as briefly as possible. Then the most loquacious members of his audience reply *"pues."* This *"pues"* is a preposition, a conjunction, an interjection which fits all occasions. According to the way it is pronounced, according to the movement of the head — affirmative, dubious, or negative — that accompanies it, it means "yes," "no," "but," "however," "you're right," "I don't believe it," and so forth and so on.[39]

One also finds in the Spanish language another word that is as frequently used — *"carajo."* If you took these two words out of Spanish conversations, nothing would be left but cigar smoke. Instead of saying *"carajo,"* prudish women employ a diminutive form; *"cara"* is to *"carajo"* just as *"je m'en fiche"* is to a certain expression which the French Academy has not yet consecrated.[40]

How different from our billets in Germany, and especially from the kind faces of our hosts. The most careful cleanliness and the friendliness of over-the-Rhine were replaced by the dirt and scowling looks of the Spanish. What is more, though hardened to Poland's climate, we were cold in Spain. In Biscay, in Castile, it is impossible to keep warm in winter; it is doubtful that even one door or one window is made so that it can be closed. They don't know what wooden floors or carpets are; the chimney-sweep's trade is unknown because there are no chimneys. In the kitchens you see a hole through which the smoke escapes, when it feels like escaping.

In the big towns like Burgos and Valladolid, you might count one or two chimneys on the great nobles' houses, yet most of these have been built by French generals who wanted comfortable lodgings. General Dorsenne[41] had a chimney built in all his quarters everywhere he was stationed.

Everyone everywhere warmed themselves at a brazier, an iron pot filled with charcoal which is set alight out in the street in the morning. It then is placed in the main room of the house where all the inhabitants gather. Then they form a circle around it and grill their knees while — to establish a proper balance — their backs are always frozen. Men and women pass a cigarette around the circle, each taking a puff in turn, and the conversation has the same animation that it does on the street corners. The prettiest woman shows no repugnance in accepting a cigar that has just left the mouth of a monk. As for myself, I smoked alone, just as in Poland I drank from my own glass.

A young and pretty comedienne wrote one day to the Duke of Alba that she was freezing in her bedroom for lack of money to buy charcoal. That great lord sent her a

---

[39] A modern Spanish/English dictionary gives "since," "because," "for," "inasmuch," "well then," or just "well."

[40] *"Fiche"* was the polite version of "foutre", used by soldiers and other crude types to express the original sense of having something "thrust in." It is another form of that basic word, the constant use of which by Tommy Atkins led even Rudyard Kipling to conclude that soldiers really needed another adjective. *Carajo* is the equivalent of *merde*.

[41] General Lepaige Dorsenne, a handsome, hard-case veteran of the Imperial Guard.

brazier filled with *piastres*.[42] You couldn't think of a more handsome remedy for such a malady.

In France, the owner of a house rents you an apartment or a room; you provide your bed and eat what you can purchase — all of which does not concern him. It is the same in Spanish inns; they rent you a room which you will occupy for the length of your stay; it's up to you to search for food if you are hungry, and to procure a bundle of straw if you do not intend to sleep on the floor. The next day you pay the landlord for the rent of the room, plus extra for the noise you have made the evening before. That custom is natural for a people who never speak, for whom the least noise is annoyance, and who answer all your questions with *pues*.

When we were billeted in inns under military jurisdiction, we did not have to pay for noise — the bill would have been too high for our slender purses, for we sometimes avenged ourselves, by singing loudly, for the privations which Castilian frugality imposed upon us. That vengeance hit its target, always striking fairly. Of all the peoples of the world, the Spaniard certainly is the one who eats and drinks the least. You could feed 1,000 Spaniards with what 100 citizens of Paris consume. That sobriety is not a virtue with them; it is the daughter of avarice and indolence. These gentlemen are epicures and gluttons when it doesn't cost them anything. If given a chance, they will spend the day eating tartlets and preserves and drinking ratafia and rosoglio.[43] The women of the Peninsula are very pleased when you speak sweetly to them, but they are happier when you feed them. Invite a Spaniard to dinner, feed him plenty of tasty food, and your man will not leave the table until he has gobbled up the makings of a first-class case of indigestion.

The first man who drank wine from a goatskin bag must have had a copper-lined throat. The first time I tried it, I thought I'd been poisoned; I quickly spewed out that treacherous liquid, and started drinking water. However after someone reminded me that this would have the inconvenient result of actually going without wine, I forced myself to try it again. A man can adapt himself to anything; little by little I managed to drink without making too many grimaces. This *pelieco* or *botta* is a goat skin which has been tanned and sewn together with the hair on the inside; they fit a plug and mouthpiece to one of the hoofs of the animal, through which they fill and empty its contents. Unlike any other possession, the older the wineskin, the more expensive it is. The tavern keepers use them first; some time thereafter they sell them to middle class citizens, who later resell them to the nobility. Consequently, in the taverns and inns you always get freshly tanned wine. When these wineskins have passed through all the hierarchies and reached the height of their glory the wine they hold has a very agreeable taste. They do not use wine casks in Spain because of the lack of roads. With the exception of several very good highways which traverse the kingdom from border to border, all the roads are very bad. Goods can be transported only by mule trains; casks are very difficult to pack; also they weigh almost as much as the contents.

From the skins of small kids, they make leather bottles holding one, two, three, or even four liters. We found them very useful, and each of us had his *botta*, which fitted very well across the front of our saddle, between the two pistols.[44]

---

[42] An older name for the Spanish peseta.
[43] Ratafia are cordials, usually home-made; rosoglio/rossoglia, is a liqueur, colored with cochineal and flavored with oil of roses.
[44] Carried in holsters on either side of the pommel.

The *olla*, or pot-au-feu, by itself makes up the three courses of a Spanish meal — no, I am wrong, the cigarette always serves as a light dessert. Put chick peas, cabbage, strong red pimiento, and a small bit of lard or meat into a kettle full of water, cook it all thoroughly, and you will dine as all Spaniards dine — when they dine well.

Nineteen Spaniards out of twenty live with the *olla*. The lords of high degree, by contrast, make a great show of luxury, but it is only in the largest towns that one finds these privileged beings. They have kitchen utensils with casseroles and cauldrons, while the average middle-class or noble family has nothing but a kettle and some minor utensils, which all together might be worth the modest sum of two and half francs. But great or humble, rich or poor, no Spaniard knows of that useful clockwork instrument which we call a roasting-jack. In the rich Spaniards' kitchens, a kitchen boy takes its place; seated before a blistering-hot fire he must keep the spit turning until the meat on it — and he himself — are completely roasted. Day after day the menu never changes. It is the same menu, without any variation. Men living by themselves eat bread and raw onions; they don't take the trouble to prepare an *olla* because they would have to light a fire to do so. The basic necessities of life are so cheap in that country that a household that has an annual income of six hundred francs can live in relative opulence, envied by all the neighborhood.

While in Spain, I often thought of a sort of comedy which I had read in my childhood. It must be, I told myself, that the Spanish know it by heart. That *Morality*,[45] for such was its title, was written by Nicole de la Chesnaye; it had a cast of twenty-eight characters and was *"The Condemnation of Banquets to the Praise of Diet and Sobriety, For the Profit of the Human Body."* That curious work was printed at the end of a Gothic quarto volume entitled, *"The Ship of Health with the Rudder of the Human Body."*

The author wanted to prove that overeating is dangerous. His *Morality* ends with the trial of Banquet and Supper. Experience is the judge. Banquet and Supper are accused of killing four people by excessive wining and dining. Experience condemns Banquet to be hanged. Diet is the executioner. Banquet confesses, acknowledges his faults, and receives absolution. Diet slips the noose around his neck, and pushes him from the top of a ladder; thus that poor devil Banquet dies. Supper is condemned only to wear lead cuffs, so that he will not be able to put too many plates on the table; in addition, he is warned — on pain of being hanged — to remain always six hours away from Lunch. I recommend this *Morality* to all our hack writers; with a few minor changes, they could make a very nice modern drama out of it.

While I am talking to you concerning ancient books, I'll tell you about an old book where, among some nonsense, you can find plenty of good things. "Tell me," said a man, "What are the different degrees of happiness?" Response: "If you live only from day to day, get a shave. If from week to week, go on a spree. If by the month, buy a good horse. If by the half-year, buy a fine house. If from year to year, marry a pretty woman. If for two years, become a priest. If for all your life, stay sober."

The Spaniard, who never reads, however puts into practice all these precepts concerning sobriety. The peoples of the Mediterranean area are generally recognized as needing less than those of the North. Consider the Arabs, who live on a few dry figs or dates a day, with occasionally a little corn meal. The Spaniard does not know the pleasures of the luxury and the superfluity which are necessities to us. Their arts, agriculture, and

[45] Morality play.

mechanics have not progressed since the times of Charles V[46] — in fact they have retrogressed. The inns have not changed, retaining the character of the times when Cervantes' heroes lived. With the finest olive trees, the Spaniards eat a detestable olive oil; with fine vineyards, they drink foul wine — without feeling the least desire to improve their lot. When I have commented on that subject, their answer always has been: "Our fathers did it this way, why should we do differently?"

In Spain comfort is unknown — perhaps disdained. The inhabitants of the Peninsula are not interested in those childish things we think so important. The fact that he can always find the necessities of life at the monastery gate has long ago infected him with carelessness and sloth. But if he is lazy when faced by sustained, regular work, he is active when it comes to smuggling. No nation has men more physically fit for long marches, more audacious in attempting dangerous enterprises, or more persevering and headstrong in carrying through once they have commenced.

The religious wars which the Spaniards waged against the Moors forced most of them to live in walled towns. Rarely do you see hamlets scattered across the countryside; summer houses such as you see around our towns are unknown, and this is the origin of that proverb "Build castles in Spain." That concentration of the inhabitants in certain places leaves the countryside unusually empty and the roads unsafe. Spain always has been the country for adventures; it is only natural that it was the native land of Don Quixote. The many customs barriers which split up the country[47] gave rise to smuggling. An unsuccessful smuggler sometimes turned highwayman. The Spaniards, always ready to praise the exploits of the former, came gradually to exalt the second. Thus, bandits and smugglers, alike considered heroes, found themselves all prepared to become guerrilla leaders. Their band was already formed, and grew bigger, like a snowball around the original nucleus.

All those men who have acquired a name of renown in a guerrilla band probably would have remained unknown in a regular army. Everyone wanted to be noted for something; fighting under the eyes of his neighbors, he was certain to be seen, praised, and made the hero of improvised ballads. Every day, his courage was rewarded by the praises of his countrymen; in a regiment he would be lost in the crowd, and, if he did win distinction, his native village would not know it. That love of celebrity is always an outstanding feature of the Spanish character; that is why the bullfighter risks his life for the uproar of applause — which he feels he deserves as much as if he had saved his country. And it also is why that a Spaniard, lacking lawful occasions to distinguish himself, will become a bandit or a smuggler.

No country on earth is more favorable for guerrilla operations; you find excellent military positions everywhere, and if you add the sobriety of the natives, who need next to nothing to exist, to those topographical advantages, you have the secret of all the insurrections past, present and to come.

You will realize also why Spanish civil wars are endless. The leaders of all those bands have a certain importance, which they will lose the day peace is signed. Each commander is a sort of viceroy who has uncontrolled rule over the area he occupies. He requisitions foodstuffs and levies taxes; in peace he would be reduced to a minor, ill-

---

[46] Holy Roman Emperor and King Charles I of Spain, 1500-58.

[47] Before the 1808 French occupation, goods moving from one Spanish province to another had to pay customs fees.

paid position. That is why the war now desolating Spain has lasted so long and why no one can see an end to it.[48]

Marshal de Villars[49] was in Catalonia; one day his nephew, who served as his aide-de-camp, arrived all out of breath.

"Marshal, I bring you great news; I have positive information that a force of 6,000 Spaniards will pass through that defile in two hours. By sending off a regiment, we can occupy the hills that command it and capture all those Spaniards at one crack of the whip."

"That's good. Have my breakfast served."

"Yes, but shall I take your orders to the colonel later?"

"I told you that I want my breakfast!"

"But, Marshal, if you let this opportunity slip, you won't have another like it."

"Let's eat."

The marshal made a lavish breakfast without saying a word. The aide-de-camp was unhappy and could not understand what was going on. Pulling out his watch, he exclaimed, "It's too late — the Spanish have passed."

"Imbecile, why shouldn't they pass? Certainly I *could* have bagged the lot of them and ended the war today. But what would be the result? I would return to Versailles, to be lost in the crowd, or perhaps to Villers to bore myself. I prefer to remain here as general-in-chief of Louis XIV's armies."

An insurrection like that in Spain against Napoleon would be impossible in France whatever the possible cause. With us, the most minor bourgeois owns personal property, a stock of food, a certain ease; he values them as he does his life; he would not leave his house for fear of finding it looted when he returned. In Spain, everything is reduced to its simplest form; the Spaniard — for it is the man who has that responsibility, buys daily everything necessary for life. He purchases the wood, charcoal, the wine, the bread, the oil, and the salt for that day at the market. That evening all is eaten, burned, or drunk; nothing remains. If he has to go away, he would leave nothing behind but a few old furnishings of no real value. Compared to the Spanish middle class, the craftsmen of our towns have all of life's material luxuries and are Sybarites and real Sardanapaluses.

Spaniards have little linen: the peasant wears a brown cloak, the townsman a blue one — which permits them to wear a dirty shirt or even none at all. Thus they save a little money. In Madrid and the big cities you see dandies dressed in the French fashion, but those are the exceptions.

All the arts owe their origin and their perfection to the need to eat which reoccurs every day with mankind. If there existed in nature a universal and plentiful food which everyone could procure without labor, just as there is a drink with which we may refresh ourselves as we wish — if that food were available to all, like water is, we would still be in the woods, clad in the skins of wild animals and not troubling ourselves to build towns or construct railroads. It is the need to eat which produced all the arts, crafts, and civilization Rabelais named the stomach "Master Gaster, First Master of the World's Arts," and Rabelais was right. After getting the necessities, we want the extras. From

---

[48] The first Carlist War, 1833-1839 — a civil war between branches of the royal family.

[49] Claude Louis Hector de Villars, Marshal of France, 1653-1734.

a cake baked in the ashes to a loge at the opera, there exists a long series of things, an unbroken chain of necessities which have their origin in our stomach.

The Spaniard is stuck halfway there; when he has twenty sous, he is sure of eating for a week, and he will do nothing during that time The love of gain can not overcome his hereditary laziness. This carelessness about tomorrow forms a barrier higher than the Pyrenees between France and Spain. For the Spaniard *farnada*[50] is the supreme happiness; like the *far niente* for the Italian.

The Spaniard lacks the fortitude for work — but that is of no importance for he has the fortitude to endure privations The happiest man is the one with the fewest needs; that also can be applied to nations.

In France and elsewhere, just to eat does not suffice us; we must have the proper coats, linen and household furnishings which we renew from time to time. The Spaniard renews nothing; his furnishings, his utensils, reduced to those absolutely necessary, served his grandfather and will suffice for his great-grandson. Fashion does not influence him in the least; a reigning deity with us, it has no altars in Spain. They dress today as they did in the days of Philip V,[51] like they will a hundred years from now. Men and women everywhere dress the same; in Madrid, Seville, Valencia and Vittoria it is always the black gown and the black veil for the women, the brown or blue cloak for the men.

I have never understood why, in our theaters where we generally take pains to get the costumes correct, the directors allow Rosine and the Countess Almavira to wear white and pink.[52] Rosine never was so clothed; she never owned anything but a black gown, decorated with jet and a black mantilla — always black — which was excellent for emphasizing the whiteness of her complexion. Dress a Spanish woman in pink — you might as well represent Manlius[53] as wearing a costume from the Middle Ages with moustaches and dagger. It is odd that, under the scorching climate of Spain, that black should be the only color used for female costumes. It gives their appearance a certain austerity — and makes a most effective contrast to their brilliant and wanton eyes and emphasizes their voluptuous figures. The young women look like nuns who had fled from their convent to seek their fortunes; the old ones have the air of ancient sibyls who need only a tripod to fall into convulsions.[54]

I have said that when you pass Bidassoa, you are in Spain. That's true, but you don't yet hear Spanish spoken. The people there have a language which is said to be derived from the Phoenicians. I don't know if anyone is capable of deciding that; but it is most extraordinary that in a little border of the Pyrenees, which has always been in close contact with France and Spain, they have kept a language unintelligible to both Frenchman and Spaniard. In the Biscay area they speak Basque; educated men learn Spanish as a foreign language. The common people don't understand it any better than they could Chinese, except for those living in towns along the main highway — who, out of both need and practice, can speak a garbled Castilian.

---

50 Doing nothing.
51 King of Spain, 1700-1746.
52 Characters from Beaumarchais' *Barber of Seville* and *Marriage of Figaro.*
53 Probably Marcus Manlius, tragic Roman hero, 4th Century B.C. He must be the hero of some play Blaze had seen.
54 A reference to the priestess of the once-famous Oracle of Delphi — come to think, I haven't seen it mentioned in years.

A gourmet among my friends disliked pot-luck dinners. When he arrived at a house just as they were setting the table and was invited to share their meal without ceremony, he would quickly reply "Today it's impossible. I'd prefer to come back tomorrow." He hoped, of course, that the next day, with one more guest to feed, the cook would be instructed to produce a more elaborate meal. A Spaniard wouldn't take the trouble. If you invite him, he is certain to accept; and you need not worry — whatever you can put on the table will be perfectly acceptable to him.

Since the beginning of the war in 1808 a swarm of French restauranteurs descended across Spain. They were set up at every halting place, from Irun to Seville, inclusive. They offered the best products of the French soil; well-heeled gourmets found them a healthy change from the Spanish *ollas*.

These merchants of beef steaks and cutlets charged very high prices for the products of their kitchens. Only those of us who managed to triple their pay by illegal means could afford their masterpieces.

Generals, *commissaires des querres,* and store-keepers[55] could meet their prices. After having watched a skirmish through a telescope from a safe distance, a clerk of the rations service could seat himself in one of these fancy restaurants and relax by dining à la carte just as if he were in the Palais Royal in Paris. At first I wanted to imitate these rich notables, but I soon had to stop. Not having an inexhaustible source to keep me in funds, I had to live on my rations, for it is mathematically proven that it is impossible for a captain with 2,000 francs pay to spend twenty francs for his dinner every day.

The day after my arrival in Vittoria, I went to a cobbler to have a shoe repaired. No one was in the shop; the cobbler was seated across the street, smoking his cigarette. With his shoulders covered with a cloak full of holes, he looked like a beggar, but a Spanish beggar — carrying himself in his distress so that he appeared proud of it, rather than ashamed. He approached me, I explained what I wanted.

"Wait," he told me, then called to his wife, "How much money do we have?"

"Twelve pesetas."[56]

"Well then, I'm not going to work."

"But," I said, "twelve pesetas won't last forever."

"Who has seen tomorrow," he replied and turned his back on me.

I went to one of his fellow cobblers who, apparently not having command of such riches, was eager to work for me.

Spanish pride has become proverbial; in that country the most miserable beggar believes himself as well-born as his King. Clad in tatters he drapes them as gravely as a Roman senator did his toga; you need tact to refuse him alms — and that is a ceremony which you must repeat continuously because of the innumerable beggars who cover Spain. It is the country of Guzman d'Alfarache;[57] that hero of beggars could not have been anywhere else.

The proverb "Proud as a Spaniard" is true for all classes of their society. There is probably no country where there is less sense of equality than in Spain, but no place where the people are less servile. The beggar retains a certain dignity; if he meets a great

---

[55] *Commisssaires des guerres* were civilian administrative officers. Store-keepers *(gardes-magasins)* and clerks were their assistants. All were accused — too often correctly — of theft, and all related offenses.

[56] Standard Spanish coin worth fractionally more than a franc.

[57] The "hero" of a picaresque novel by Mateo Aleman.

noble, he treats him as a equal. He may ask him for a light for his cigar: "Lend me your light, marquis." And the marquis finds that very normal. These two men who blow out clouds of smoke together, nevertheless remain what they are. The one will always be a beggar, the other always a marquis. For in Spain, unlike everywhere else, the world is changeless. "My father did this; I shall do as he did."

Begging is a profession. Every church door, every street corner decorated with a statue of the Virgin or of some saint has its attached beggar. It is a property which he exploits and which he sells. A ruined man, who does know what to do, buys a second-hand image of a saint, baptizes it with the name of Saint Jacques or Saint Pancrace, sits it up near a milestone, and becomes a *santero*.[58] The peasants give him alms; for a small fee, he prays for the dead. He will recite the seven psalms of the Penitence in your presence, applying them to whatever person you designate; that costs devotees two sous. But if you wish to purchase some of the psalms he has already said in his spare time, those will cost less — he will sell you as many as you wish at fifty percent discount. In such a sale, since the vendor does not deliver anything material, you might worry that he has sold to others that which you are going to buy — but there's no way of determining that!

When a servant deserves punishment, his master gives him a certain number of blows with the flat of a sword, a chastisement fit for a noble. When a Spaniard wishes to impose silence on his child, boy or girl, he says, "Be silent, man!" Other people have children, the Spaniard thinks of his as adult men. "The oldest sons of Kings are princes," said Napoleon, "Mine shall be a King."[59] The Spaniards are not only personally proud, but proud of their sun, their towns, and their villages. Read one of their proclamations — it praises the heroic city of Madrid, the invincible Valencia, the glorious Seville. In the *Gradus ad Parnassum*[60] all the nations are treated as brave and mighty in arms. The Spaniards have a similar attitude toward everything pertaining to their country; they never describe themselves except in superlative terms.

The Moors left the Spaniards these ideas of grandeur, along with the bull fight. A King of Spain can not believe that any man on this earth could be his equal. His widow must remain always a widow; no King is thought worthy to succeed him as her husband. That extends even to his horses — a horse once mounted by the King of Spain may not be ridden by anyone else. The queen's person is so sacred that no man may touch her, even if it would be necessary to save her life.

Among the Spaniards, the Castilians are especially conspicuous for their pride; if the Spaniard scorns all other races, the Castilian despises all other Spaniards.

Galicia is the least honorable province in Spain to have for a birthplace. When the Spaniard wishes to really insult someone, he calls him a Galician. That corresponds to the use of Savoyard with us. Whenever they give an example of silliness or grossness, a Galician always is the hero. The word always serves as an example in comparisons, and they say "stupid as a Galician" — "uncouth as a Galician."

All Spanish towns have a market place surrounded by arcades. These are a necessity for their inhabitants; indeed, without them where would those men go who spend half the day seated together without thinking, without speaking — for there is no point in

---

[58] Keeper of a shrine.
[59] Napoleon gave his infant son the title "King of Rome."
[60] *A Step to Parnassus* was a dictionary of prosody widely used in schools during the 18th and 19th centuries. Another indication of Blaze's extensive education.

speaking except to direct here or there a few words enveloped in a cloud of smoke. They need a place sheltered from the sun and rain, so what would they do without the arcades in bad weather or when the sum has sent the thermometer above 100 degrees.[61] He would have, to remain indoors, and no one can take a siesta all day long.

In Spain, everything is the same; the towns, the villages, the costumes of the men and women all appear to have been cast from the same mold. And, if all the ladies are not pretty, you must admit that they have a grace and a figure such as you wouldn't imagine.

Nowhere will you find women gifted with that "I-don't-know what," that ravishing grace that the Spaniards call *salero*, a word for which no other language has an equivalent,[62] because you can't really find out exactly what it means in Spanish. What eyes! What magic in their glance! One is almost tempted to say to them, "Please do me the favor of not looking at me." Add to those means of seduction an enchanting voice which combines marvelously with the world's most beautiful language, harmonious and nobly expressive. If you want to remain free-hearted, don't go to Spain. These ladies appreciate the effect of their black costumes, which show off their charming figures; they carefully do not imitate the French women's constant fashion changes. No hat ever perches on their head or hides the ardor of their regards. An artfully disordered *mantilla* covers their hair; while it may conceal certain charms for an instant, you can be sure that a lucky chance will soon reveal them to you.

Rich men ordinarily hear mass in their own homes; their womenfolk, who are very indolent and slow to arise, often hear it from their beds. Those who go to church sometimes attend ten or twelve masses, and you can say that during that whole time the thing that occupies them the least is religion. Rendezvous are ordinarily arranged at the church; Spanish women are expert at expressing themselves with their eyes and fan, by which two means they know how to make themselves perfectly understood. As long as the mass lasts, they fan themselves, even during the winter. Since neither chairs nor stools are allowed in the churches, they are continuously on their knees or seated on their heels — a position little becoming for a female.

When a Spaniard dies he is careful to leave the necessary money for a great many masses for the repose of his soul. If he has creditors, so much the worse for them. They may be paid afterwards if any money remains. In Spain they call that "making your soul your heir." Philip IV ordered in his testament that 100,000 masses be said for the good of his soul. If he proved not to need that many, the rest were to be devoted to the souls of his father and mother — and if they did not need them all, the surplus was to be said for those who were killed in Spain's wars. I am curious as to the king could judge here below the number of masses that would be required or how anyone would know when to stop saying them.

Spaniards, and especially Spanish women, were very much afraid of ghosts; everyone has seen at least a half-dozen of them during his life. Therefore they are very careful, before going to bed, to make many signs of the cross to keep ghosts from coming to trouble their sleep — a method, as everyone said, that had always proved infallible.

Generally speaking, in Spain all customs are marked by a certain glaze of piety and mysticism which you find nowhere else, not even in Italy. If you enter a social gathering,

---

[61]   Blaze wrote "at 34 degrees." He probably was using the Reaumur scale.
[62]   My prosaic dictionary gives "grace" and "charm."

a drawing room, or any place when a number of people have gathered, you greet them by saying: *"Ave Maria purissima."* Then they chorus: *"Sin pecado concebida santissima."* Among the women every exclamation of pleasure or pain in preceded by *"Ave Maria."* The men use it less often, usually substituting *carajo*, doubtlessly because it is more emphatic.

If the men of Spain are taciturn and short-spoken, their women are lively, babbling, fond of gossiping and very good at it. Generally, they have very little education, but their natural spirits and the grace with which they can say little nothings keeps you from realizing that right away. They know the whole vocabulary of flirtation; all of the expressions of love and fine feelings are familiar to them — they have an immense repertory. Occasionally all that floods out as if from a spring; you might say that they knew every word of it by heart. As soon as I understood their ways, I composed several very high sounding speeches I could deliver by letter or word of mouth — and everything went splendidly.

When Spanish women uttered the word "devil" they made the sign of the cross in front of their mouth with the thumb of their right hand; "Napoleon" received the same treatment. In Pampeluna I was billeted in the home of a charming young lady. I wanted to flirt with her, but I was always rebuffed. Every time that I encountered my pretty hostess and attempted to play the gallant with her, that poor lady shrank back as far as possible in a corner and there, trembling with fright, her right thumb moved with incredible speed making thousands of signs of the cross to prevent the devil — who undoubtedly was me — from speaking or introducing myself to her. While that was most unfriendly, I replied that I would not trouble her then, hoping for a better opportunity. But she kept too careful a watch. Always there was that sign of the cross, and however much a devil you might be, you could not fight against such a means of defense.

And all that because I was a soldier of Napoleon! Certainly the hangman, returning from an execution, would not have inspired such horror as I did. At first, out of self-respect, I tried to change her sentiments, but she was always ready to swoon whenever I attempted to detain her for a moment to get her to listen to me, so I had to give up. Soon I simply avoided her — and certainly I could have done nothing that would have pleased her more. For a long time the memory of Senora Juana de Artieda troubled my thoughts. You can learn to forget a woman whom you loved, or one who left you for another man, but the thought that I had inspired a woman with horror is one I never could accept.

VII

Masters of Arms and Duellists

In every regiment there was a man whom the soldiers respected as much as their colonel, and that man was the regimental "master at arms."[1] He had several assistants who, under the title of "provost," exercised whatever part of that moral authority he delegated to them. On my arrival at my regiment, I asked Monsieur Malta to give me lessons in his art, of which I knew very little, and he taught me by demonstration just how he went about killing his man without ever being killed himself. For, as Monsieur Jourdain's[2] fencing master wisely said, "The whole secret of fighting consists of two things: to give and not to receive. To avoid receiving, turn the sword of your opponent away from your body. This needs only a slight movement of your wrist , either to the left or the right."

M. Malta, who, I believe, had never read *Le Bourgeois Gentilhomme*, told me exactly the same thing, which should prove that Moliere really understood human nature. Malta was a real original: the deeds he bragged about the most and which he regarded as claims to glory were those that an honorable man would blush to admit. He had picked quarrels with the most famous fencing masters of his time and had killed dozens of them. (I think he exaggerated the number of his victims somewhat; however I can assure you that whenever anyone mentioned some famous swordsman, Malta's greatest ambition was to measure himself against him.) The title he wanted most of all was that of "Executioner of the Brave."[3] I was attentive to his lessons, and he seemed well content with my progress. "My lieutenant," he told me one day, "If you continue this way, in two months you will have mastered the politeness." He meant that he would have trained me in the salute and all of the other fuss that ordinarily preceded a duel.

When we had reached the point where I could learn this "politeness," M. Malta urged me to stare wide-eyed when I saluted by opponent. "My lieutenant, open your eyes — more — still more. When you salute, you must have your eyes open like the glass in your watch; it makes him realize you are there." When we wished to get him angry, we would praise the fencing masters of other regiments in his presence. Then, Malta would shrug his shoulders disdainfully and finally finish by declaring, "I wouldn't let any of those characters sweep out my school room."

Among his provosts, "Mister Dupre,"[4] a drummer, held a distinguished rank; he was Malta's assistant, his successor; the heir presumptive of his so-great renown. In the bars

---

[1] This chapter contains the major difference between the daily life of the *Grande Armée* and contemporary American soldiers — who generally settled their differences informally with their fists. "Master at arms" meant fencing master. American officers might duel, but they would not have allowed such nonsense in their units.

[2] The leading character in Moliere's play *"Le Bourgeois Gentilhomme."*

[3] Blaze's original is *"Bourreau des cranes,"* which could have several slightly different translations.

[4] This mâitre-d'armes/provost system was "in addition to" other duties and formed no part of the regiment's official organization. Apparently that is why Blaze gives them civilian titles.

Dupre made the first-comers pay for his drinks; if anyone objected, he invited the recalcitrant outside to "refresh himself with saber cuts" — that was his favorite expression. No more insolent person ever cocked his shako over one ear or went armed with a clanking *briquet*.[5]

"You see that cuirassier drinking by himself?" Dupre said one day to his comrade, L'Etoile.[6] "Watch. I'm going to demolish him."

"Careful. If he falls on top of you, you'll be squashed."

"My saber will make him fall on his back."

And Dupre went up to the cuirassier, seized his drink, and downed it in one gulp. I should tell you that an infantry duellist always prefers to pick a fight with a cavalryman — the cavalryman is his natural enemy. Among cavalrymen, he especially chooses a cuirassier, since they are so tall and heavy — if he kills one, it brings him more praise.

"Comrade," the cuirassier said, "you are mistaken."

"It is you rather, who does not understand"

"Have you mistaken me for someone else?"

"Not at all, my dear fellow. That was done on purpose."

"You came over here to pick a fight with me?"

"Certainly! Why, it is beginning to comprehend."

"If I put you into my boot, it would serve as a guardhouse for you."

"Yes, but you'll have to put me there, and you'll be dead before that happens!"

"Thousand thunders!"[7]

"Don't yell, my friend — gently. Between Frenchmen, things should be arranged properly. Come over here to put me into your boot — and my saber also."

Five minutes later the cuirassier drew his last breath.

However, one day Dupre met his master — the saber of a young conscript ran him clear through. Someone brought us the news, and everyone was delighted. Everyone said that the evil rascal had gotten what he deserved. However the surgeon went to the scene of the duel. He tried to draw the blade out of the wound so that he could apply a bandage, but at first that seemed impossible because the weight of Dupre's body, in falling, had bent the point of the saber. The armorer had to be summoned to straighten it. The operation was long; Dupre must have suffered horribly,

**A MASTER OF ARMS
(KNÖTEL)**

---

[5] The short infantry saber, then worn by grenadiers, drummers, and noncommissioned officers.

[6] "The Star" — A good many soldiers used such nicknames.

[7] Probably an euphemism.

but his face showed no sign of that — on the contrary, he joked with the bystanders while urging the surgeon to do his best. The saber was withdrawn, the wound dressed. Dupre spent two months in the hospital, and then — he came back, more of a worthless scoundrel that ever. A hundred thousand honest men would have died. Dupre did not.[8]

It is remarkable that these bravos are generally poor soldiers. The man who, relying on his strength, forces a fight on a weaker individual is necessarily a coward. On days of battle these brawlers always have a new excuse for remaining behind; you don't see them until the next day. A conscript in their place would receive the *savate*,[9] but the "excuse" which they always presented at the point of their sword or saber shut the mouths of all their company.

A drummer is usually a duelist, a fencing master, or at least a provost. He is taunting, hard to live with, a grumbler, always ready to draw his sword. A Paris gamin in uniform, he does not carry a musket. His saber is his only weapon, and he handles it better than other soldiers. He caresses it, polishes it, and handles it all day long, and when the time comes to draw it, its blade will not stick in its scabbard. Not only does he know how to cut, but also how to use its point.[10] When he is marching, look at the top of his pack — two capped foils, wrapped in his overcoat,[11] showing lovers of that art their keen points, covered by two corks to keep them from rusting.

While he is on garrison duty, the drummer/provost carries the regulation *briquet*. He has to, because if he loses it, he will be compelled to buy a new one from the regimental supply room. But when he goes into the field, he rejects that vulgar blade and replaces it with a *carrelet's* blade,[11] which he very carefully attaches to his *briquet* hilt. That is the mark by which you can recognize all the regiment's goons: all of them have a sword an ell[12] long banging against their right heel at every step. It is not convenient while marching, but they are willing to suffer a bit in order to look ferocious. It makes them feared, and that gives these scamps great pleasure.

I have seen fencing masters fight in earnest, without motive, without hate, without any of the reasons that usually cause duels. They fight to test their skills; if one of them is killed, the other vaunts himself on having added one more triumph to his past exploits. I have seen those, who, during a fencing contest, have quarreled over a questionable hit and have by mutual consent taken up swords in place of their foils, and fought to the death in front of fifty spectators — who did not interfere. "You won't deny that," said the victor as he ran his opponent through. It would indeed be difficult not to acknowledge a sword thrust that pierced your chest. Another fencing master had placed this singular signboard on his door: "Here we fight from 10:00 A.M. to 4:00 P.M." That was very handy for fencing enthusiasts. They were sure of always finding a champion ready to oppose them. Like those ancient knights who rode out ready to break a lance with anyone they met, my man awaited customers and gloried in their absence.

M. Malta's son was taken into the regiment's band as a triangle player — a great favor for which that bullying brat showed himself thoroughly unworthy. He picked quarrels

---

[8] This *was* remarkable: surgeons of the time could do very little for wounds of the body cavity.
[9] Blaze's note: When a soldier played the coward, or committed a serious offense against his comrades, they would condemn him to receive fifty *coups de savate* [whacks with a hobnailed army shoe] more or less on his rump. The judges then executed their sentence.
[10] The saber was basically a cutting weapon.
[11] A sword with a long, thin triangular blade.
[12] Obsolete unit of measure, approximately 44 inches long.

AN HUSSAR DUELS WITH A GRENADIER

with the bandsmen, played tricks on them, spoiled their music — and, when rebuked, offered to fight them with either sword or saber, according to their choice, by way of apology. One day I complained to his father, urging him to discipline his son. "My lieutenant," responded Malta, "He's a worthless bum, I know. Do you know what gives him so much energy? It's because he carries my name. I haven't dared train him thoroughly in swordsmanship — he has too much natural talent for that. If I taught him several of my old secret passes,[13] he soon would beat me, who is his father. He only respects me now because he knows that I know the old *coups de Jarnac*,[14] which I keep for myself. It is not my fault that he has not turned out better; I have not neglected his education. Only yesterday I gave him a real thrashing — the devil wouldn't have wanted to be in his skin."

---

[13] Systems of attack.
[14] "Jarnac's thrust" — a semi-mythical thrust, possibly designed to hamstring one's opponent — generally, any treacherous or unfair attack.

One day while crossing the Stettin bridge, on my way to the Lastadie suburb, I met a provost, a *sapeur*,[15] a drunkard, and an eight-ball — all in the same soldier. Today, we'd call him an "accumulator." Drunk as usual, talking to himself, staggering crookedly, our man — to use soldier talk — had confused his equilibrium and was hanging festoons.

"Why," he was saying, while tugging at the hairs of his long beard, "can't I find in all the garrison a good lad who will duel with me? Nobody wants me to make a buttonhole in the middle of his belly! Other times, I'd find a hundred ready to draw their sabers — today, not one! You all are soldiers of the Pope.[16] If I were the Emperor, I'd stuff you all into the muzzle of a cannon and fire you off to teach you how to live."

"Eh! What's bothering you now, my friend?" answered one of his comrades who was fishing with a line from the top of the bridge.

"What's bothering me — you ask what's bothering me? Very well, I'll tell you what's bothering me. For two hours I've been looking for a good lad who wants to refresh himself with saber cuts, and I've found no one I've insulted everyone, and no one took offense."

"If you wish, I'm ready to do you that service."

"Good! That's the way to talk! I've always said you could be relied upon. Come, so I can hug you. You are a Frenchman; you are a friend. Tell me of a comrade who equals that."

"Wait — let me coil up my line and I'll be with you right away."

"Ah! The fine boy! That's a true grenadier! We'll go down to that little wood along the road to Dam. We'll be alone; nobody will interfere; we'll fight completely at our convenience. Your saber has a good edge, doesn't it?"

"It does — don't worry."

"Good. Mine cuts better than the razors of our company barber."

"That's as it should be. Let's go."

I thought that it was a joke, and that the fisherman, having all his wits about him, had not agreed with the drunkard for any other purpose than to get him to sleep it off. Not at all: that evening I learned that there had been a serious fight and that my two gaillards, both well cut up, had come back to the barracks arm-in-arm, each proclaiming the other his best friend.

I know that civilians will not believe me — if they had had a chance to study the customs of the barracks and guard rooms, they would learn a lot more. But let us go higher up in the military hierarchy — I'll tell you of a scene I witnessed in Paris. An officer of my regiment quarreled one evening with a captain who lived in the suburb of Courbevoie. The dispute became heated, and they agreed to meet and settle the affair [by a duel] the next day in the woods of Boulogne.[17] It being almost midnight, the captain had turned to leave us when we called his attention to the storm that was threatening to break out momentarily. He responded that since the hotels would be full at that hour, he would take a cab; besides, he did not fear the storm.

Then his adversary approached him and said, "Stay here. You can stay with me. I offer you half my bed. We can leave together for the woods of Boulogne in the morning. That will be much more convenient, since neither of us will have to wait for the other."

[15] In this case, one of a small detachment of picked infantrymen trained as combat engineers, attached to regimental headquarters. They customarily wore beards.
[16] The Papal Army was a joke in uniform.
[17] A wooded area just outside of Paris.

"I accept. But we are going to fight."

"Except for that, I wouldn't have offered you half my bed."

Our gentlemen slept in the same bed talked of politics, war, and their "gallant adventures" — and the next day, after having eaten a cold chicken and drunk a bottle of champagne, they went gaily off to try to cut each others' throats. One of them was seriously wounded, but did not die.

I have known many officers laboring under a "duel-o-mania." They feel obliged to take part in an affair of honor [duel] every month. If they aren't the duelists, they want to be witnesses [seconds]. When there is to be a duel they feel offended if no one asks them to be judges. Passing their lives competing in fencing schools, they feel the need to really fight every so often, just to keep their hands in. Often these bravos with their secret passes are killed or wounded by inexperienced opponents who never have learned the sublime rules of swordsmanship.

We also have generals of that same type; killing a man in a duel is a pastime for them. It doesn't trouble their digestions or their sleep — any more than killing a few partridges does ours. One general whom I don't wish to name[18] fought a young lawyer with pistols. "You were the offended party, monsieur, fire first. It is your right, but aim carefully. If you miss me, you're dead."

The young man fired.

"Imbecile! Your ball went into the tree tops. Mine will strike the third button of your coat; it will pierce your heart; you won't suffer." Like a cat that prolongs the agony of a mouse which it holds between its claws, the general looked at his adversary for a long time. "Yes," he said, "It is a pity to die when one is only thirty, with fine hopes, a fine career at the bar, a sweetheart — I understand your regrets — it just so happened that you got in my way. Come, say your farewells." At once he fired; the young man was dead.

At Ragusa[19] thirty officers were gathered with a general. While dining they talked of duels and pistol marksmanship. Everyone told of splendid shots. One had killed sparrows in flight; another could hit the edge of a knife blade. The general saw a grenadier passing on the street outside and had him bought in. While entering, the grenadier took the little pipe he was smoking from his mouth and thrust it into his pocket. "Keep your cutty-pipe," said the general, "Continue to smoke. Take the position of attention without arms, immobile, head up. Attention to orders: By the right flank — Right![20] Don't move." And at that moment the general drew a pocket pistol, fired, and broke the pipe.

"Good. Here's twenty francs to buy a few drinks. Gentlemen, that's what I call a pistol shot."

"Thank you, my general," said the dazed grenadier. "The next time I'm brought before you, I won't be smoking."

Hémére, the man of the windmill, who had consulted Laborie's map with such results, was a skilled fencer. Being very short and having a contentious disposition, he was always thinking that someone was making fun of him. The slightest smile, the least gesture could be misunderstood; he would demand satisfaction,[21] which sometimes he

[18] Probably Réséda Fournier, "Demon of the *Grande Armée.*" He had behaved indecently toward the lawyer's wife.
[19] Now Dubrovnik, in what was Yugoslavia.
[20] Our "Right face!"
[21] A duel.

got, but most of these groundless quarrels — thanks to the intervention of witnesses — were explained away then and there without recourse to sword play.

One day he picked on the biggest officer in the army, a gallant of six feet two inches,[22] well-built in proportion, a living colossus. He could have put Hémére in his pocket and his handkerchief on top of him. They agreed on a rendezvous where they would fight with pistols. When he arrived, the big officer flattened his enormous person against a wall, and his witness drew a careful outline of him with a stick of chalk. That completed, he came up to Hémére.

"You want to fight me," he said. It seems to me that you aren't difficult to please. Many others in your place would like to do the same if I would agree. You can plainly see, my dear fellow, that the match isn't fair. I am much taller, much bigger than you. I offer over four times as big a target for your bullets as you do for mine. I know that you might answer me like someone responded to Desessarts the comedian under similar circumstances — that hits in certain areas won't count — but jokes are not reasons. I am most willing to exchange several pistol shots with you, because of my great desire to please you. However, I set one condition, without which I must tell you that I simply will leave you here. There is my exact outline. You will place yourself in front of it facing me and we will fire. But first you will give me your word of honor that, if my bullet misses you but hits within that outline on the wall, you will go to your billet and lie down on a stretcher. You will be considered seriously wounded and will remain in bed for three months."

That proposal was so droll that we all whooped with laughter. Hémére himself quit scowling and imitated us. He might have quoted Baliveau,[23] "I laughed, behold me disarmed," but Hémére didn't read much poetry.

To finish with Hémére, I shall say that because of his tendency to taunt and to get angry over trifles, he finally found someone who didn't joke. The poor devil was killed in a duel, the evening of the battle of Wagram.

During the forty days before that great day, all the army worked at fortifying the Island of Lobau.[24] Our soldiers got fifty centimes extra pay a day for this. A young engineer officer, whose duty it was to inspect their work, found some grenadiers loafing on the job and rebuked them. The grenadiers promptly complained to their captain concerning the way in which *"Monsieur Problem"* (as soldiers called all engineer officers, for whom they generally had little respect) had treated them.

The captain, furious that anyone else had presumed to reprimand his grenadiers, twisted his moustaches and hunted up the engineer officer to demand his reasons for such remarks. He was one of those fighting men who talked only of breaking backs and killing, who — to use an expression of Moliere's — are "all sword thrusts," and whom our soldiers call "dealers in sudden death."

"Monsieur, you have allowed yourself to say that my grenadiers —"

"Were not working. Yes, Monsieur, and that's the truth."

"I warn you, little greenhorn, to watch your talk."

"Greenhorn! Greenhorn!"

[22] French measurement, equalling 6 feet 6 ½ inches U.S.
[23] French poet, apparently long forgotten.
[24] A large island in the Danube River, to which much of the French army had withdrawn after being repulsed at Aspern-Essling, on 22 May, 1809. Napoleon converted Lobau into a fortified base for his subsequent crossing to defeat the Austrians at Wagram, 5-6 July.

"Yes! Greenhorn, conscript, and I'm going to prove it right now!"

"Oh that. Captain, do you by any chance think you can scare me with your big moustaches? Do you really think yourself terrible because you haven't shaved for the last fifteen days But consider, monsieur, that if I wished, I also could go without shaving."[25]

"Ah, you dare to mock me! We'll see if you're still jesting while I run my saber through you."

"Gently, monsieur. If we come to that, I hope that I'll do any running through."

"Enough talk! On guard!"

"On guard is all right by me. But I would remind you of one thing: I am calm, you are excited — the match would not be fair. Wait until tomorrow."

"Tomorrow? Tomorrow you will have been dead for twenty-four hours. I will have run you through your liver, and gotten you off my conscience. On guard? I want my grenadiers to bury you under these fortifications — thereafter they'll work happily."

"As you wish, monsieur. I'm ready." The young graduate of the Ecole Polytechnique[26] and the moustached captain drew their swords and had at each other in the midst of all the workers, who were happy to drop their shovels and wheelbarrows for a moment to see their troublesome supervisor punished.

The engineer officer parried the captain's first blow; his saber glanced down on his opponent's hand, hitting its little finger which was nearly severed. "You are wounded, monsieur," said the engineer. "We can stop now, if that satisfies you."[27]

"Scoundrel! Don't you know that the *coups de manchette* are not allowed?"[28]

"Monsieur, I'm perfectly ignorant. This is the first time I have fought. I strike when I can. You do the same."

"Ah, you bastard of a conscript! I'm going to give you a lesson you'll remember."

"Monsieur, you're wounded; I have too much of an advantage over you. Let's postpone this match."

"On guard, rascal! On guard!"

"Here I am."

After several blows delivered and parried, the captain received a gash extending from the top of his thigh to his knee. He was forced to quit fighting, but nothing could compare with the fury that he felt over having been twice wounded by a youngster without moustaches — a greenhorn — a conscript! "I shall have my revenge," he told the engineer, "Get out! I'll settle with you later — I'll hunt you down even if you hide with the devil, and we'll see, you damn conscript, if *coups de manchette* will save you then."

They carried the captain away. He was laid up for a long time, but eventually recovered. But during the fever that followed his wound, he was always heard repeating, " A conscript! A greenhorn! *A coup de manchette!*"

[25] In other words, "I'm no beardless youth."

[26] France's major technical school, producing artillery officers and military and civilian engineers.

[27] Duels frequently ended once blood had been drawn.

[28] Blaze's note: A *coup de manchette* is a saber blow which touches the wrist. The dueling code especially forbids its use, and such a hit never counts in fencing matches.

All countries have passed laws against dueling without ever being able to stop it. The medieval tournaments were often forbidden by the popes because of the bloodshed they caused; kings prohibited them for another reason — because their nobility spent too much money on them. In 1240, sixty knights were killed during a tournament at Nuys near Cologne. "It was unusual to see a tournament end without some lord having been killed, but that no wise affected the joy and pleasures of these fetes. And that was in a time when those taking part in tournaments, were excommunicated and threatened with being denied church burial after their deaths."[29]

After the tournaments came the duels, admittedly less showy, but just as deadly. All men entitled to wear a sword wanted to prove their skill and courage to all comers. A gesture, a word, a look was enough to bring the swords out of their sheaths. Cardinal Richelieu, despite his absolute authority and the death penalty, could not eradicate that unhappy mania. Men wanted to be talked about; certainly they would achieve that, the more so that in dueling they risked the gallows and a sword thrust to boot. A post chaise would carry the victor over the frontier; the Versailles salons would resound with talk of his exploits; his family would smooth over the affair. Soon he returned, to be noticed everywhere; the women talked of him — that was everything he wanted.

The older civilizations did not practice dueling. If we find some examples in the Bible and in the history of Greece and Rome, those single combats do not resemble our modern duels. David and Goliath, Achilles and Hector, Aeneas and Turnas, the Horatii and the Curiatii all fought for their country and not for their personal interest. The only duel on could cite — that of Elcocles and Polynices[30] — appears to be legend rather than history. The heroes of the Iliad (those on the same side) insult each other frequently, but never fight. This custom of dueling was introduced into Europe by the northern races; it gradually infiltrated our customs to that point where kings and even popes approved of it.

If I were really important, I would propose two methods of ending dueling, and certainly that evil which is corroding our society demands someone's attention. Every year it deprives France of men of whom we are proud. I shall spare you all the words I could write concerning that horrible practice; you can read the best ones in Rousseau's works; both of us can profit from that.

I wish that the witnesses to a duel would be punished by a very heavy fine of ten, twenty, or thirty thousand francs, and that those of them not able to pay that would be sent to prison for a number of years. But, you say, the duelists would fight without witnesses. Some of them perhaps, but that would be very rare, for they would risk being charged with murder. More than that, they would fear being assassinated by a treacherous opponent — just recently the Seine assize court has ruled on such a case. If that measure did not abolish duels entirely, it would greatly diminish the number of duelists, and that would always be advantageous. Who would want to pay 20,000 francs, or go to prison for ten years, for a quarrel that was none of his business?

If that measure wasn't enough, I would borrow one of Russia's laws. In that country, when two men quarrel, the witnesses are obliged, under pain of severe penalties, to at once report them to the governor of the town or the colonel of their regiment. A council is promptly assembled; the disputants are summoned and witnesses examined; each

---

[29] Blaze's note: *"Memoirs sur l'ancienne chevaliere"* by Lacune Sainte-Palaye.
[30] Brothers in Aeschylus's *"Seven Against Thebes."*

man states his case. If the case is without importance, if reconciliation is possible, the council decides that they must make up. Each gives his word of honor that the affair is over and everything forgotten. But if serious insults have been given, if it is established that blows have been exchanged, the council will order a duel. "Gentlemen," says the presiding officer, "tomorrow, on the parade ground, you will duel." All the troops of the garrison are assembled there and form a hollow square. The two champions are brought in, and the heralds tell them, "Gentlemen, you have a clear field — fight! One of you must leave here dead." If one of the combatants is wounded the affair is only suspended. As soon as he is healed the presiding officer tells him again: "You fight tomorrow." The herald repeats, "One of you must leave here dead." And so it goes until one of the quarrelers has given up the ghost.

That law, decreed by Catherine II, stopped the rage for dueling in Russia. One may very well want to look like a swordsman, because he hopes to get out of any duel with nothing more than a scratch — but the prospect of kill or be killed is not reassuring. The grim face of the herald causes serious second thoughts, and the sacramental words, "One of you must leave here dead," have stopped more duels than the gallows, which everyone could hope to escape.

During the Middle Ages, people believed that God would not allow the guilty to triumph; thus, in single combat, the winner was always right. This "Judgment of God" thus became a hunting license for the bravos of that period, permitting them to do anything. Today we no longer think so; our skepticism or our humility leads us to think that God does not bother to occupy Himself with all the human miseries which swarm down here like gnats.

How many times have we seen the guilty triumph because he has frequented the fencing schools and the pistol ranges. The honest man who does not expect to ever need the art of killing someone to show off, neglects the science of the tierce, the quarte, the half-circle, and the thrust in second.[31] He does not waste his time breaking dolls, while the duelist makes that his sole occupation.[32]

---

[31] All fencing terms.
[32] "Breaking dolls" is the only translation I can find for *casser des poupées*. In Blaze's time, it may have had a slang meaning.

VIII
A Day of Battle

In days of old when the Romans gave battle, the two sides often met on a plain. Both generals drew up their troops, and then, the signal given, with clouds of dust obscuring the sun, each man did his best to kill his opponent without being killed by him. On the fields of Fontenoy, the French and the English began like this.[1]

"Very well — since you are kind enough to allow it — Ready! Fire!"

All that took place as if it were in a fencing school. It was characteristic of the period of Louis XV — of the Marquises with red-heeled shoes who, having left the Versailles salons the day before, could not fight like obscure plebeians. They did it with elegance — which did not mean that they lacked courage.

Today we no longer give a signal when we begin fighting — commence who wishes to, kill who can. Our generals don't harangue us now as generals did in Homer's day when those gentlemen were terribly loquacious. Ajax, son of Oileus and one of Agamemnon's generals, could never begin a battle without making a speech three pages long. If that is amusing for the haranguer, it's very boring for the harangued. Witness Pope Urbain IV: the deputies of Carpenters made him a long speech during which His Holiness yawned constantly.

"Are you finished?" asked the Pope.

"Yes. But if you do not grant what we have asked of you, we have precise instructions to repeat our harangue without omitting a single word."

As you can guess, the Holy Father agreed to all their demands.

During a day of battle at present, one says little, but it is effective. From the commanding general down to the corporal, when it's a question of marching against the enemy, everyone uses the same formula. "Blessed name of God, forward!! Forward, sacred name of God!" That is understood from one end of our line to the other:. At Marengo, at Austerlitz, at Wagram, we did not make any greater expenditure of language. Truly that method of expressing yourself produces more effect in certain circumstances than fine academic phrases. If you speak too precisely, everyone may not comprehend you, while even the most affected fop always understands interjections.

After having read some history, civilians generally think that a battle resembles a review on the *Champ de Mars*[2] and that 100,000 men placed facing another 100,000 amuse themselves by firing as they please with the accompaniment of cannon to produce the effect of contrabasses in an orchestra. I shall enlighten them as to how a battle is fought.

An apothecary of Avignon was the lucky husband of a pretty woman. Extremely jealous, our Monsieur Fleurant did not like to lose sight of her He had read Voltaire and knew what might happen two or three times a day if he were careless enough to leave his wife. The wife wanted to go to the theater; the husband, unable to accompany her

---

[1] War of the Austrian Succession, 1745. Here, Blaze repeats an old fable. The French, being determinedly monolingual, never realized that what they took for an invitation to fire first was actually a dare by a (possibly intoxicated) English officer to stand and fight.

[2] Field of Mars — the drill and parade ground of the Paris garrison.

because of his work, would never permit it. On Sunday, he could have taken her, but he feared the unexpected meetings, the oglings, the love letters — those distressing harbingers of even more disastrous events. On those days our apothecary was overwhelmed with caresses and demands, but — firm as a rock — he would not listen and always refused. "Listen, sweetheart," he would say, "We'll stay home, we will be more comfortable, it will be cooler. We'll spend a pleasant evening, and I'll read you the play that they staged today."

The lady pouted, but had to give in. The husband took his book and the play began. At the end of each act, after having drunk his customary glass of sugar and water, he never failed to comment on what he had just read. "You see, my dear, when the actors say that they are going to fight, or promenade, or leave for America, you must not think that they're really going to do so — they remain offstage in the wings."

When you have finished reading my chapter on the battles, you will know as much as the apothecary's wife.

Our army is on the march, preceded by our advance guard, composed of light troops. Our hussars go like devils; they trot, they gallop, the enemy flee before them. But suddenly the enemy halts — as do our hussars. A village held by a few hundred men confronts us; our skirmishers attack it. At the moment that our men break in, an enemy battalion drives them out. We send in a regiment to support them; our opponents commit two. We move up ten regiments; the enemy throws in twenty. Both sides bring up their artillery; the cannon rumble; soon everyone is taking part in the party. You fight, you are exhausted. One man cries for his leg, another for his nose; others yell about nothing, and behold the food for the ravens and for the authors of bulletins.[3]

The science of a commander in chief is simply this — to mass as many men as possible at a given place on a certain day. Napoleon said that, and Napoleon would know. The general must decide, from a study of his map, what points the enemy will attempt to hold. It is there that he will have to fight, and consequently he will direct his troops there by twenty different routes. An order poorly phrased or poorly understood often upsets the best strategic plans — witness how Grouchy's corps never arrived at Waterloo. The First Consul, before leaving Paris, had marked the plain of Marengo with a pin, as the scene of a new triumph; the result justified his forecast.[4]

The science of a general also includes knowing the enemy's strength at one place and his weakness at another. To learn this, a spy service is indispensable. You must have good ones and above all pay them well. Napoleon gave them gold by the handful; it was a well-justified expense. We have seen generals defeated because they were stingy with their secret funds.[5]

The spy's trade is a terrible one; every day he risks his life in a game of "heads or tails." Ordinarily these men serve both sides; they have two passports which they use according to circumstances The general who pays the best is always the best served. But when a fortress is blockaded or a corps is cut off from the rest of the army and no one is allowed to leave them, passports become useless. Then a spy must be able to slip through like a smuggler.

---

[3] After-action reports. Napoleon's were propaganda sheets — as he himself said "Not history."

[4] This is another legend, taken from the unreliable "memoirs" of Napoleon's false friend, Bourrienne.

[5] Funds given them for spies, guides, bribes, etc. Some generals confused them with their personal savings.

While the emperor was in Madrid, an aide-de-camp managed such a difficult mission with successful daring. Marshal ____ (I don't know which one) was cut off from the rest of the army by a greatly superior Spanish army. Its position and the nature of the country left no hope of defeating it. There was urgent need that the Emperor learn all the circumstances so that he could deliver an effective diversionary attack elsewhere. But one could not reach him except by fighting his way through, and the Spaniards — holding all the high ground and the passes — would have too many advantages.

"Well," said the marshal's youngest aide-de-camp, "I'll take the responsibility for getting through to Madrid. I'll be there tomorrow and inform the Emperor of the situation."

"And how are you going to escape being hanged?"

"Leave that to me — just give me your dispatches."

This officer promptly went to a monastery, where he accosted the prior, an estimable man who was deeply respected and considered a saint for twenty leagues around.

"My father," he said to him, "you will give me a habit of you order immediately. Have the best mule in your stables saddled at the same time The two of us will mount him and leave for Madrid."

"But, my son, that's impossible for me."

"No arguments."

"However-"

"Not one more word. Here are two loaded pocket pistols — one is for you if I am detected, the other for me. We'll pass through the Spanish army together — your habit, your reputation will easily open all the roads for you. I shall pass as one of your brethren; if they question you, tell them what you wish; if they question me, you will answer for me. I am sick, my tongue is paralyzed; I'm going to Madrid to consult doctors. Also, my father is a Grandee of Spain; my illustrious family is anxious that I be cured; you have taken the responsibility, and so forth. Find good excuses — that's your business. If we are captured, you will die as certainly as I will; I shall have only one thing to do — to kill you. If we succeed, as I do not doubt we will, the marshal promises you his potent protection. If we don't return, your monastery will be burned."

"But, my son, what are you thinking? At my age?"

"At your age, my father, one can travel on a good mule. At your age, everyone respects you — that's why I have chosen you. Think of the important matters confided to you — you will be responsible to God for your death and my suicide."

Everything went well. The Spaniards knelt before the prior who gave them his holy blessing. They even received that of the French officer into the bargain. The travelers arrived at Madrid safe and sound. As they entered the town the aide-de-camp was recognized by some of his comrades who carried him in triumph to the Emperor's palace. It's unnecessary to say that such devotion received its reward.

Sometimes, to avoid attacking a fortified and well-defended position, we turned[6] it, but the enemy, having foreseen the danger, has placed troops at other points, and the battle breaks out instantly along a front of several leagues. To reach Ratisbon, for example, we fought at Eckmühl, Tann, and Landshut, over a distance of fifteen leagues.

When you move up into combat, nothing is more discouraging to young soldiers than the remarks of wounded men straggling to the rear.

[6] Maneuvered widely around it to cut the communications of the troops holding it.

"Don't go so fast! Don't be in such a hurry!" they say, "You don't have to be in such a rush just to get killed!"

"The enemy outnumbers us ten to one."

"They cut off my foot — they'll cut you somewhere else."

"You look like the living dead."

"Hey — look at that one. Doesn't he look like a dead man?"

"He sure does. They forgot to bury him yesterday, so he's still following along today."

You can try to silence them, but an arm in a sling, a gashed face assure them impunity and give them the privilege of insolence and their jeremiads continue as long as they can find anyone to listen to them.

One of those poor devils passed before us with his head split and his arm broken. Everyone pitied him.

"What misfortune!" said one: "Two wounds! What a distance to go without being given first aid!"

"You are a lot of imbeciles," retorted the wounded man. "You'll soon know a lot more about it. I know what's happened to me, but you don't know what will happen to you."

You should see the faces of the conscripts when they hear such talk and especially when they see the first dead men. They will detour twenty feet around them, for fear of touching them. Soon they can come nearer to them; later they walk over them without a thought.

A man can get accustomed to anything, whether pleasant or painful. How many times have you yourself not discovered that, after fifteen days, any deep grief or great joy

INFANTRY GOING INTO ACTION (SERGENT)

becomes dulled and something quite ordinary. Remember that when you first feel grief and tell yourself, "This will pass as all my other unhappinesses have passed." The true philosopher should take his misfortunes in stride, considering them unavoidable evils — for example, like the rain. You should try to protect yourself from it, but if that isn't possible and you get soaked, a sunny day will come to dry your clothing. That fine day always will come, sooner or later. Be patient, and you'll see that I'm right. But if pleasures come your way, be careful not to let them escape — you must, as they say, grab them by the collar — clutch them to you — get the last drop out of them, and review them as often as possible.

I have always followed that principle: imitate me — you'll be delighted with the results. Finally, if you do suffer an irreparable loss, what good will despair do you? Worry yourself sick, beat your head against a wall — what will that remedy? Nothing! On the other hand, if you go out and have a good time, it will cure you — and doctors are expensive.

To prove to you the truth of my reasoning, I'll tell you a little story. You know that after the siege of Toulon [1793], the Republic shot all those who opposed it at that time. After the cannon had mowed down entire ranks, a voice cried out, "All those who are not dead, stand up! The Republic pardons them." Some wounded unfortunates, some others whom the canister had missed, seduced by that promise, raised their heads. Instantly a squadron of executioners (history says a squadron of dragoons, but that history is wrong) fell upon them, saber in hand, finishing what the cannon had begun. Soon the sun set on that enormous butchery.

Under a bright moon, one of these victims recovered consciousness amid that ocean of corpses. He had ten wounds — in the head, arms, legs, chest, everywhere. He rolled and crawled.

"Who comes there," shouted a sentry.

"Kill me."

"Who are you?"

"One of the miserable ones they shot — put me out of my misery."

"I'm a soldier, not a hangman."

"Kill me. You'll do me a service — an act of humanity."

"I'm not an executioner, I tell you."

"Kill me, I beg you. All my limbs are broken, my head split. It's impossible that I recover. You will spare the horrible sufferings. Finish me off."

The sentry came up to him and verified the extent of his wounds. Believing that they were mortal, he took pity on him. Knowing that if he fired, the guard would turn out,[7] he preferred to use his bayonet, which he ran through the body of the canister-shattered unfortunate. But, believe it or not, that man did not die; the next morning while burying the dead, a grave-digger realized that he still lived. He took him home, and nursed him back to life. All his wounds healed. That man was Monsieur de Launoy, naval officer under Louis XVI; he really could have spared himself that last bayonet thrust.

The regimental surgeon establishes his first aid station some distance behind the battle line. All the wounded are sent there; after being given first aid, they are sent to the hospitals behind the army, until they can return to duty. The first aid station is a curious sight, all the surgeons cutting and carving; the cries of the wounded, the amputated

---

[7] Causing explanations and possibly getting him in trouble with the merciless agents of the Republic.

98

limbs which litter the courtyard, the wagons carrying off those who have been bandaged, the stretcher-bearers bringing in new customers. It is a sad gathering of human sufferings. At Wagram, a grenadier of my regiment was wounded by a musket ball; his buddy hoisted him on his back and carried him to the surgeon — but, on the way, another ball killed the poor wounded man without his comrade knowing it. The latter continued on his way, reached the first aid station, and laid the grenadier on the table where our medical genius was working.

"Why do you bring me that? He's dead. What do you expect me to do for him?"

"Major, he is wounded."

"Blazes — look, imbecile! You can plainly see he's dead."

"Well, so he is. See now how one is deceived in this world, and by his best friends too. That sneak told me he was only wounded."

Do not believe that everyone in the army is brave. I have seen men who never could become accustomed to the roar of the artillery. At Wagram, a soldier in my company was felled by a violent epileptic attack, set off by the whistle of the first bullet. When a soldier does not unhesitatingly do his duty or when he remains behind for reasons not clearly stated, he receives the *savate* at the hands of his comrades when he returns. Often that punishment was unjust; a soldier unexpectedly taken sick the evening before a battle got little belief that his illness was genuine — about the only way he could persuade them that it was true, was to die in the hospital. Then all his comrades, who had been waiting for a long time to give him his "correction," would chorus, "He was sick after all!"

An officer of my regiment had never been under fire during his thirty years of service, like the son of Mary Stuart,[8] the sight of a bare sword made him turn pale and he frankly admitted. "I wish I could go into action, but that isn't possible. I'd pull foot at the first shot, and that would be a very bad example." During hostilities, he remained at the regimental depot where nevertheless he was very useful in drilling conscripts.

When we went into the field, he went back to France and did not rejoin us until peace was declared. That was customary and expected; no human power could have detained him. He often brought replacements forward to us during the war, but the next day he went back alone. One day, however, he was obliged to stay over; detachments of enemy cavalry were prowling through our rear area, and the danger of going back was as great as that of going forward. The poor fellow had a fever; he found himself in a state of nervous stress that defies description — and yet the whole day passed in marches and counter marches without a shot fired. One fine morning in the gorges of the Tyrol, one of our outposts was attacked. There was a short fusillade, to which we paid no attention since it was over a thousand yards away from us. But behold our man, who left and without stopping fled twenty leagues to the rear. Malicious jokers claimed that he leaped two 15 foot ditches though he was big and obese. We had no news of him for a long time, and thought him either dead or a prisoner of war, but later we learned that he had arrived at our depot in Antwerp.

We teased him constantly, but he endured it with good grace; he even joined in the chorus of laughter, and every time someone spoke of a coward, he would always say, "Exactly like me." Later he told us of his trip from the Tyrol to Antwerp, the fear he had

[8]   Mary, Queen of Scots. Her son (1566-1625) was James VI of Scotland and James I of England and Ireland.

felt, the two ditches he had leapt, and all the rest of it. He claimed with much simplicity that fear was an incurable malady with him, but he was none the less well-liked by everyone. How many others were no braver, but spoke constantly of running through and cleaving asunder? And those who purposely got themselves captured during the first skirmish, to escape at once from the dangers of the campaign? And finally those who wounded themselves, lightly it's true, to have a pretext to go to the rear until peace was declared? Later, you would see them return; to hear them talk, they were entitled to all rewards[9] — and yet you'd need a microscope to see the honorable scars of their pretended wounds. Such examples were rare, but you could name several in every regiment.

If everyone in the army was not brave, you could see those whose courage was beyond all comparison — and that in all the ranks, all of the grades, from King Murat to the simple buck private, from General Dorsenne to a drummer. I could fill ten volumes with stories of the truly incredible valor of our warriors. I will tell only one, which the III Corps witnessed in Spain.

General Suchet attacked Mount Olive,[10] despite the Spaniard's predictions, "The ditches of Mount Olive will be the burial ground for all of Suchet's army, and the ditches of Tarragona for all of Bonaparte's armies." He met a wounded soldier whom comrades were carrying to the first aid station.

"Victory! Victory! The Olive is taken!"

"Are you seriously wounded?"

"No, my general, but unfortunately enough to have to leave my unit."

"Well answered, my friend. What reward would you like for your services?"

"To lead the assault, when you storm Tarragona."

"Better and better."

"You promise me?"

"Yes."

On 30 June 1811, that is to say a month later, Suchet was ready to launch his final assault. The troops were forming their columns of attack when a voltigeur in full dress, all correct, gleaming as for a parade, came up to Suchet.

"I have come to remind you of your promise. I wish to be the first in the assault."

"Ah, it's you, my brave. That's very well, but soldiers of your sort are too rare for me to waste their blood. Stay with your company; by giving everyone the example of your noble courage you will render more service than by getting yourself killed all alone."

"I want to lead the assault."

"You will certainly be killed, which I can't allow."

"General, I have your promise and I want to lead the attack."

"So much the worse! My brave, so much the worse for us! Do as you wish."

The columns moved out, with my voltigeur twenty yards ahead. He threw himself through the blasts of canister, was the first man into the breach, and there he fell, riddled with bullets. Retrieved by Suchet's orders, this brave soldier was taken to the hospital; during the remaining hours of his life all the army's officers, led by Suchet himself, came to visit him. And Suchet took off his own cross of the Legion of Honor to decorate the chest of the voltigeur, who died admired by all the army.

---

[9]   Decorations, promotions, sometimes cash donations.
[10]   Commanding hill mass outside Tarragona.

This brave man was named "Bianchelli."[11] Chateaubriand[12] has written, "Glory must be something of genuine worth, for it quickens the heart of those who only think of it."

I shall tell of another sort of courage.

During the civil wars in the Vendee, a Republican soldier was captured and condemned to death with all his comrades. They had been taken out to be shot, when one of the Vendean chiefs, admiring the fine bearing of this grenadier, demanded his pardon from the Vendean general.

"No mercy," replied the general. "The republican army never shows us any."

"What does that matter? If you are generous, you save a brave man. He is a Frenchman; he will be another supporter for our cause and a devoted friend to you because you have saved his life."

"I'll consent," replied the general, "on condition that he marches with us and shouts, 'Long live the King.'"

"I'll take the responsibility. Grenadier, come here. I have asked the general to pardon you; he will do so if you shout, 'Long live the king!'"

"Long live the Republic!" responded the soldier.

"Shoot him."

The grenadier returned proudly to his comrades, many of whom already had been killed. He stood with arms crossed, head up, facing the muskets, when the Vendean chief threw himself on his knees before the general.

"You know that I have always served honorably; as a return for the blood I have shed so many times, I demand mercy for this grenadier, without conditions. Will you refuse me?"

"So be it. I grant it to you."

"Come here, grenadier. The general spares your life, and I hope that you will not employ it against us."

"Is that without conditions?"

"Without conditions."

"Oh well — 'Long live the king!'"

I do not know the name of that hero. I once read it — and, I am ashamed to say, I have forgotten it. If he had lived in ancient Greece or Rome, the writer and sculptors would have certainly immortalized him.

Frederick the Great often repeated to those who would listen, "Do not say that a man is brave, but that he was brave on such and such a day." Indeed, our actions are so intermixed, our feelings sometimes produce such unexpected results that it is impossible for us to say whether we shall be able to do tomorrow that which we have done today.

"I challenge anyone to frighten me," said a bravo with a long sword and bristling moustaches like those of the King of Clubs. "We'll see about that," responded several of his friends. A wager was made; a large sum deposited, to go to the winners. They agreed as to a date after which — if the bravo had not said, "I am afraid," he would win the stakes.

The bettors took all possible precautions. By secret dealings, they got into their man's bedchamber. There, they drew the balls from his pistols and sawed the blade of his

[11] J. T. Headley, *Napoleon and His Marshals* (New York: baker and Scribner), 1850, Vol. II, p. 236 identifies him as "an Italian soldier named Bianchini."
[12] Viscount Francois R. Chateaubriand (1768-1848), French author and statesman of a sort.

sword three-quarters through. Several days before the ceremony they were preparing, they were careful to get him to swallow several good-sized doses of rhubarb to clean him out.[13]

One fine night they came into his chamber. He awoke with a start and saw twelve walking cadavers covered with shrouds. They carried a coffin and chanted unintelligible words. Putting down the coffin, they surrounded it with candles and gestured to the bravo to lie down in it. He gave a shout of laughter, and the chanting continued.

After a half hour had passed without any sort of change, the bettor — mesmerized by the monotonous chant, the lighted candles, the open bier — began to feel uneasy.

"Gentlemen," he said, "enough is enough, I think. I want to sleep; get out."

The chanting still continued.

"This finally has bored me, and if you don't get out of here at once, I'll use other means."

The chanting went on.

Our man drew his sword and struck at one of the phantoms. It broke.

The chanting still continued.

Furious, he seized his pistols and threatened to fire. No one answered. They chanted. He fired, and two chanting phantoms handed him his pistol balls.

"Gentlemen," he said, "it's finished. I am frightened. I have lost my wager. Speak to me and go. It's time you did."

The chanting still went on.

The bravo fell over backwards — he was dead.

I shall not boast here like a matamore captain, claiming that I never have been afraid — something I have often heard others say repeatedly. I declare, to the contrary, that when the first bullet whistles overhead, I salute it by an involuntary movement.[14] With the second, I am less polite; I ignore the third — but each time that I went into the fire I must admit that I followed those same forms of politeness exactly.

Yes, certainly one must have a breast lined with triple steel to remain perfectly cool amid shot and shell. I have often analyzed the sensations I have felt during that ceremony, and I admit that I have been afraid. Very often the infantry plays a purely passive role during the battle; it supports the artillery and catches the shorts and overs from the fire the enemy places on it. It must remain steady, receiving without giving. If a sense of honor, of self-respect were not there, it could be a debacle. But each soldier has his comrades who are watching him, everyone wants to be respected by all of his regiment, and nobody budges. The officers especially have to set an example; they stand unshaken, give the order to close up the ranks in a strong voice — but you can be very certain that the devil loses nothing thereby.[15]

I have no secrets to keep from you, and it would be wrong of me to pose as a hero and give myself a dashing air. I tell you frankly the most enjoyable battle I ever saw was that of Bautzen. Why so, you ask me — how was it more diverting than the others? Did the cannon balls, the shells, and the bullets rain less heavily? No, but what made me always find that battle very enjoyable was the fact I wasn't there. I really was, but on the top of a clock tower. A long telescope in my hand, I saw everything, I judged the course of

13 To avoid possible messes if their man panicked?
14 He ducks.
15 They're still afraid.

102

INFANTRY IN ACTION AT ESSLING. (SERGENT)

events from a safe place. While the battle raged on the plain, we were in reserve in a village and — since we had nothing to do while waiting for orders, we climbed to the top of the church and from there watched all the exploits of our warriors. That method of taking part in a battle is the most agreeable I know. When you are actively engaged, you see nothing — and less — and less — and less.

When you maneuver, when you fire, when you are fully engaged, your feelings disappear — the smoke, the uproar of the cannon, the shouts of the combatants intoxicates everyone. You don't have time to think of yourself. But to have to stand steady in ranks without firing, while receiving a storm of bullets, is not at all comfortable.

There are men, however, who, gifted with an extraordinary strength of spirit, can cold-bloodily face the greatest dangers. Murat, bravest of the brave, always charged at the head of his cavalry, and never returned without blood on his saber. That can be easily understood, but what I have seen General Dorsenne do — and never have seen done by anyone else — was to stand motionless, his back to the enemy, facing his bullet-riddled regiment, and say "Close up your ranks," without once looking behind him. On other occasions I have tried to imitate him. I have tried to turn my back to the enemy, but I

---

[16] Approximately 20 miles northeast of Avignon.

could never remain in that position — curiosity always made me look to see where all those bullets were coming from.

At the beginning of the Revolution, the inhabitants of Avignon and those of Carpentras[16] were in full civil war. The first wanted the Pope for their ruler, the other, the king; still others were for the Republic, and there were even some who wanted none of them. Everyone, to support their cause, armed themselves to the teeth and fought — or should I say, made the motions of fighting. It was tacitly agreed that everyone would flash their powder without using lead.[17] This was a very sensible saving; further, it gave both sides a certain appearance of being heroes without running the least danger. One day, whether by carelessness or malice, a bullet left the Carpentras army and whistled over the Avignoneses' heads. A general cry, followed by one of "Save yourselves," promptly followed. "We are betrayed! Someone's shooting balls." From that day, the civil war was over.

At the battle of Ratisbon one of my comrades was horribly wounded by a cannonball which struck him exactly on that fleshy part on which one is accustomed to sit. The surgeon cut and trimmed away two kilograms of flesh; finally the whole part — the entire "moon" to use an old expression. Now before his wound, that officer was five feet tall, at most. After his recovery he became six. He became unrecognizable and had to give his name to old friends when he met them. Not only was his height greatly increased, but he grew big in proportion; few men were as tall and large as he. I deliver this recipe to all those who would like to grow larger, and I guarantee its efficacy. What's more, it's not difficult; with one cannon shot accurately applied you are sure to succeed.

A whole army can not march by a single road with its artillery and trains — the advance guard would have reached Strasbourg while its rear guard was still in the Place de Carrousel in Paris. Also, you have to feed that army; concentrated, it never can find enough to eat, especially since the gentry who compose it ordinarily have astonishing appetites. When you see separate divisions come together, when detached generals rejoin the main body, it is easy to predict a battle. Of all the battles fought in our times, Wagram was anticipated for the longest time. The field was known; both sides had studied it. On both sides, for forty days, all the preparations for attack and defense had been made at leisure.

The storm of 4 July 1809 was one of the most violent that has ever inundated our poor planet. It has been said that it aided Napoleon's operations by concealing our movements from the enemy. I know nothing about that, but what I can conscientiously affirm is that evening found about fifteen of us officers gathered at the sutler's and that we were trying to neutralize the effect of the rain by numerous libations of hot wine.

Fleuret came in; he was our eagle-bearer, a brave soldier of Valmy, Fleurus, and Hohenlinden. He had always followed the path of honor, but he strayed frequently from that laid out by grammar; we called him the "box of T's and S's." That worthy man perpetually transposed those two letters. For example, he would say *"il faus aller à l'exercise"* for *"faut aller"* and *"il n'est pat encore"* for *"Il n'est pas."*[18] I hoped there would come a day when those letters would be properly pronounced, but chance never permitted it.

---

[17] Would shoot blanks.
[18] "Time to go to drill." "It's not yet the time—"

[Four sentences detailing more of Fleuret's scrambled French omitted.]

A good many men made fun of Fleuret's dangerous liaisons of words[19] who did not know any more than he. I gambled one day with one of the eagle bearer's sharpest critics. When I complained of always having bad cards while my adversary constantly got the high ones, our purist replied.

"What can you expect my dear fellow — you have paid me today, I'll pay you tomorrow. When one gambles that's the way it went."

"Ah, my captain, I have caught you — you've used the wrong word."

"What did I say?"

"'That's the way it went' — when you should have said 'That's the way it goes.'"[20]

"Oh, I know that, but I used the wrong verb purposely to see if you'd notice."

"Very good."

That good captain sometimes posed as an intellectual. We were talking one day in his presence about the cornets of the Voltigeurs, and someone said that that name was ignoble and that *clairons*[21] would be much better. "Certainly I prefer *clairon*," he said, "The Romans had clarions, you can see that in history. First-rate rabbits[22] all those Romans then! They were the troubadours who did not often jest. They bore a cuirass, a bow, arrows, a javelin, a shield, rations, camp equipment, cartridges — but no, I'm mistaken. They did not yet know about gunpowder. That was not until much later that it was used, when Alexander went to conquer the Incas."

But I was telling you that Fleuret joined us to take his share of the bowl of hot wine.

"It looks," he said, "as if there'll be plenty of empty shakos tomorrow.[23] So much the better, for my own is in poor shape and I'll be able to chose another. Here's one that will do me perfectly."

While saying that he tried on the shako of one of my friends, Monsieur Gaillemot, a distinguished officer who commanded our regimental artillery company.[24]

"Be careful, Fleuret," responded Gaillemot. "After tomorrow your shako could very well serve someone whose shako perhaps is in worse shape than yours."

"Impossible, it's too old."

"Well then, it will be picked up to some peasant, or put into the same ditch as you."

"What are you trying to say?"

"I am saying that you, who wish to inherit from others, have all the look of a man who will not see the sun go down tomorrow."

"Bah! The bullets and cannon balls know me. I have fought for twenty years and never yet been touched. The Kayserlichs are too awkward."[25]

---

[19] A play on the title of a popular novel *Les Liaisons Dangereuses* by Pierre Laclos, a French artillery officer.

[20] Words substituted here. The original dealt with the proper liaison of two words.

[21] At this time, both terms meant generally "horn," the "cornet" being specifically a hunting horn, "Clairon" later meant "bugle."

[22] Believe it or not — Strong, brave soldiers!

[23] Casualties will be heavy.

[24] Blaze's note: "On our arrival at Vienna, each regiment organized a 2-gun battery of artillery." Blaze's memory failed him however, when he added that, "These artillery companies remained until the beginning of the Russian campaign." They were abolished in 1810, revived in 1811.

[25] Austrian soldiers.

"The pitcher that goes to the well too often finally gets broken."

"To the health of those who survive!"

That meant me, and I emptied my glass.

The conversation finished there. Everyone returned to his company and laid down. The cannon fired constantly to protect the men working on the bridges, but that didn't concern us — we slept. At two o'clock in the morning, Gaillemot was smoking his pipe and supervising the repair of a gun carriage that had been damaged the day before, when he saw Fleuret walking alone. He called to him. "Already up and around!" He said, "You certainly have gotten up early! We won't cross the last branch of the Danube for a long time yet."

"What you said to me last night has kept me from closing my eyes. I am sure to be killed today."

"Bah! An old soldier and afraid — for shame!"

"Fleuret never has been afraid; he has never even thought of danger. But today I sense that I am a dead man."

"Come, you shouldn't be anxious. This battle will pass like so many others, and...".

"Adieu."

At four in the morning we passed over the last bridge. At ten o'clock our division was placed in the first line. And the first shot from the Austrians caught Fleuret in the head.

That gallant fellow had carried his savings in his cravat.[26] It was stuffed with gold 20 franc pieces. The bullet sent flying all those prisoners, which hadn't seen daylight for a long time.

The battle of Wagram did not have great results in the material sense, which is to say that it wasn't one of those great hauls like Ulm, Jena, or Ratisbon. We made very few prisoners, and we took nine guns from the Austrians and lost fourteen. When this was reported to the Emperor, he replied with great composure, "Nine from fourteen leaves five."[27]

Ordinarily after a battle, an order of the day would tell us what we had achieved, for — like M. Jourdain — we spoke prose without knowing it. In these proclamations to the army, which Napoleon prepared himself in faultless style, we learned that he was content with us, that we had surpassed his expectations, that we had rushed forward with the speed of an eagle. Following that he gave us the details of our deeds and conduct and the number of soldiers, cannon, and supply wagons we had captured. That was exaggerated, but it was sonorous and had a very good effect. After Wagram, we didn't get the least little proclamation, not the shortest order of the day. For three weeks we didn't know the name that famous day would have in history; among ourselves we called it, "The battle of 5 and 6 July." We learned the name of Wagram only from the Paris Newspapers.

That battle led to the victory of Znaim, the armistice and peace. The Austrian army retreated in good order; it was defeated but neither cut to pieces or demoralized as it had been in other campaigns. Also, for example, the battle of Ratisbon had brought us to the walls of Vienna, and that of Wagram brought us only to Znaim, that is to say four days of marching. There, we would have to begin again, and we were ready to recommence.

---

[26] At that time usually two good-sized handkerchiefs, the inner black, the outer white, folded about the neck.

[27] There is no agreement as to guns captured and lost. Actually, the French seem to have bagged over 5,000 prisoners.

That evening the whole Austrian army was trapped; we could see its bivouac fires inside a great circle of ours. We were expecting that the next day would bring some great and decisive battle when a rumor spread that an armistice had been declared.[28] Our astonishment was great on hearing that news — why didn't the Emperor crush his enemy when he had such a fine opportunity? Why did he consent to stop fighting in a place which inevitably would have become a new Caudine forks[29] for the Austrian army, or perhaps a vast tomb? Everyone lost himself in reflections on that subject.

When much later the question of Napoleon's [second] marriage became public, all recalled their memories of Znaim, and all the army believed that the hand of the Archduchess Marie-Louise had been the express, secret, and sine qua non[30] price for that suspension of hostilities. But, you say, his divorce from Josephine had not only not been completed, but had not even been mentioned. Doubtlessly true, but did Napoleon have the habit of making all his plans public? There was no talk of marriage until the French army had evacuated Austria — it would not do to have it appear that the new empress had been won by force of arms. The demand [for her hand] was made later according to the rules; they granted it; we took all that for a comedy in which everyone played a part agreed upon in advance. But, you still insist, you can not find anything to support that assertion in all the related diplomatic correspondence. I reply that it is quite possible that nothing on that subject was put in writing, since the self-respect of the two emperors would have been compromised. One would not like to have it known that he had captured the woman he was going to marry by force, or that he had been forced to give his daughter to a son-in-law whom he did not like. Perhaps all was arranged by a word of honor given in the bivouac. However it was, the army generally believed that the hand of the Archduchess Marie-Louise was bestowed on 11 July 1809.

In reporting the talk which went on at that time, I don't pretend to present established facts. In the minor position where I have always served, you don't see very much. That which I do certify as the truth is that most officers and soldiers believed what, which I venture to repeat today. My reader can take it for history or for barracks gossip[31] as he pleases. He is perfectly free to do either, and it won't bother me.

Concerning barracks gossip, I have read in many books written during the Restoration[32] that there were secret societies in our army working to overthrow Napoleon and reestablish the Republic. It was said that the "Society of Philadelphians" counted many officers of all grades among its members, that its leader was Colonel Dudet of the 9th Line Infantry Regiment, that he and twenty two of his officers were ambushed and murdered during the evening after Wagram. How could anyone make up such yarns and, when he tries to spread them, how can he expect to be believed? I have carefully searched my memory, which still is accurate enough, and have found nothing which

---

[28] Here, Blaze's memory seems to have played him false. The Austrians were under heavy pressure, but not surrounded. The armistice had been proclaimed during the afternoon — though news of it may have been late reaching Blaze's regiment.

[29] A double mountain pass in southern Italy where a Roman army was trapped in 321 B.C. and forced to "pass under the yoke."

[30] "Without that, no" — Latin for "indispensable."

[31] Which it was.

[32] The last period of Bourbon rule (1815-1830) in France. Naturally it produced many books denouncing Napoleon.

would agree in the least with that story. I have questioned many officers who were at Wagram: none of them had heard anything about that bit of melodrama. Certainly such an event would have produced an uproar in the army — you just can't shoot a colonel and twenty two officers of a regiment and remain incognito. *La Contemporaine* [33] speaks much of Dudet in her *Memoirs*: she does not tell of him being killed in that fashion, but she does mix in some extraordinary items. She also writes about "The Philadelphians," a name that none of us had heard until that book on the secret societies had appeared. The real Dudet was a brave officer who died at Wagram from enemy fire, as every soldier should desire to die, doing his duty on the field of battle, and not in a squalid trap. He was colonel of the 17th Regiment of the line, and not of the 9th. He was hit by a bullet that pierced his chest and came out through his left shoulder — and that ball certainly wasn't French. The officers of his regiment put up a monument to him in Vienna. Would they have dared to do that if he had been shot by order of the Emperor?

It is not enough for a general to have talent; he must also be lucky. In war, events combine in so many ways that you are always having to improvise. [34] When anyone proposed to Cardinal Mazarin that he employ a new man, that wily old fox [35] always asked if the applicant were lucky; if the answer were "Yes", he was accepted. Napoleon believed in his star although he had an astonishing genius; that was expressing it modestly. How many times during his life did chance or the stupidity of his opponents save him? At Essling, for example, the Austrians cut our bridges by sending boats loaded with stones downstream against them; one blamed all that on a sudden flooding of the Danube; the poor Danube got the blame. With our bridges broken, our army was cut in two. If the enemy, profiting from our situation, had attacked us all-out, I believe that our situation would have been extremely critical. We had little ammunition and only fired from time to time to keep up a front. There still were our bayonets, but there are limits to human effort. Fortunately, the Austrians did not know that the bridges were broken, even though they had done everything possible to break them — in such a case, why not inform yourself if you've accomplished your mission. [36] Certainly if we had been in their place, and they in ours, all the enemy army would have laid down their arms.

Many Frenchmen were lost in Russia [in 1812], but put us in the Russians' place and not a man would have seen his native land.

It is certain that great men never want to be in the wrong. "The sudden flooding" of the Danube, the "premature winter" in Russia have been the pretexts to excuse the want of foresight. In Russia, a winter that begins in November is not premature. One does not expect it to wait until the first of December to make itself felt, which is to say never before. Couldn't anyone determine that from an almanac? Besides, it often freezes in Paris at about the same time. For the rest, it was not the cold that killed off the army — it was the lack of food. If the soldier had had bread and a bit of beef in his belly and a

---

[33] *The Contemporary,* an anonymous post-Waterloo authoress. Though Blaze seems to present her as influential, she is not listed in the latest Napoleonic bibliography.

[34] Napoleon said that war was nothing but a series of accidents, and that a "lucky" general was one calm and quick-witted enough to take advantage of them.

[35] Jules Mazarin (1602-1661), Italian-born French cardinal and statesman.

[36] The Austrians *did* know the bridges were broken and *did* attempt an all-out attack, but fumbled it and finally were so battered that they quit trying.

shot of brandy, he would have survived. Since rulers never fail to credit their vast genius for results that often were simply the result of chance, it would be proper for them to acknowledge their mistakes, when they make them, and say their mea culpa.

Certainly in the army you must expect chance in everything. It is like a lucky stroke at billiards, like killing several partridges with a snap shot while hunting. Moreover chance may even upset the deepest diplomatic calculations. When Frederick I,[37] King of Prussia, was still only the Elector of Brandenburg, he instructed his ambassador in Vienna, M. Bartholdi, to negotiate with the Holy Roman Emperor to secure permission for him to assume the title of "King." Bartholdi was to, above all, to keep the matter secret from Father Wolf, the Emperor Leopold's confessor.[38] These instructions were in cipher; the copyist mistakenly used the code for "employ" in place of "avoid." The ambassador accordingly approached Father Wolf who was thoroughly astonished.

"I was always strongly opposed to this, but I can not resist this proof of the confidence the Elector has shown me. He will have no reason to regret making this proposal through me."

The Elector's request was granted — which it probably would not have been except for the copyist's mistake.

How many generals have become famous because of the stupidity of the adversaries!

An aide-de-camp is sent with an order, but his horse breaks down, he is hurt, and does not arrive in time; the general is defeated — and because of that accident alone, the victor is considered a genius. The tiniest causes may have the greatest results. Sometimes, by an odd stroke of chance an army does everything it possibly can to be defeated — like a swordsman who runs himself through.

We were encamped near Patzeburg in Holstein; the enemy was two leagues from us. We were not fighting — or at least we seldom fought, only to check from time to time on what the enemy was doing. Each general knew that they would not win the war; all that depended on the Grande Armée, which was then near Leipzig.

One day Marchal Davout decided to push out a large-scale combat reconnaissance to determine the strength of the enemy facing us. A formidable column moved out early in the morning, and two hours later we were facing the Russian-Prussian-Swedish camp (their army was composed of all those nationalities). The camp looked occupied to us; fearing an ambuscade, we advanced cautiously. Scouts were sent out; they checked all the huts and saw no one. What had become of the enemy? While we waited for someone to find the answer to that question, the order was given to set the camp on fire. The camp burned; in an instant all those straw huts became piles of cinders.

While we watched that immense midsummer fire, and while everyone made conjectures concerning the disappearance of the enemy, cannon thundered behind us. The uproar grew louder, and everything convinced us that our own camp was being attacked. "We're cut off," the soldiers said, "the Russians knew of our movement, they let us pass, they're taking our camp, and then they'll easily get the better of us."

The French soldier easily lets himself become demoralized; four hussars behind him worry him more than a thousand in front of him. "We are cut off," they always say in

---

[37] 1657-1713, Grandfather of Frederick the Great.

[38] Brandenburg was Protestant and the Catholic Church tended to oppose its aggrandizement. Actually, Frederick had to promise military support for Leopold before his request was granted.

such a case. You have to expend plenty of strong language to prove to them that, if anyone is cut off, it's those four hussars.

"My captain, I have taken a prisoner," cried a conscript during a scuffle.

"Good! Bring him here."

"He won't come."

"Use your saber."

"He's taken it away from me."

However, in our present position, the soldiers seemed to have the right idea, and their fears to be well-founded. Learning of our movement, the Russians had let us go ahead while they seized the opportunity to destroy the garrison left in our camp. Any hesitation was out of the question — we must rush to rescue our comrades — and we must at once seize certain hills from which 300 men could block our return.

We moved out, almost running and soon arrived at the Gros-Mulsahn defile, which we found unoccupied. Then we began to understand; the enemy would not have left such a fine position unguarded if he had known of our expedition. He knew no more of our movements than we had known about his an hour earlier. These conjectures became certainties when, getting near our camp, we saw it under attack from all sides.

Chance had caused the two opposing generals to have the same idea the same day at the same hour. They both had decided to attack, and each had taken a different route.

General Walmoden, commanding the allies, was most astonished to see our column coming up behind him — it took him some time to comprehend who we were. Then, concluding that Davout had cleverly outmaneuvered him, he hurriedly retreated. All his skirmishers[39] were trapped and forced to surrender. It was time we arrived, for the weak garrison left behind to guard our camp had barely been able to hold out. If Walmoden had known how small it was, he surely would have made an all-out attack, and the consequences would have been unfortunate for us. But we arrived in the nick of time and everything was saved.

Something like that happened at Wittenberg. The same night, at the same time, the besiegers and the besieged got under arms — the first to deliver an assault, the second to make a sortie. The two forces met nose to nose; there were a few shots, but everyone thought they had been ambushed, and both sides ran for it, fleeing in opposite directions. It was difficult to rally them.

Voltaire said somewhere: "God is on the side with the big battalions." Voltaire talked nonsense. Big battalions poorly commanded, poorly organized, maneuvering awkwardly are cannon fodder. The history of our wars during the Republic prove that great truth on every page. How many times has a battalion or a squadron charging all-out, forced units three or four times their strength to surrender?

Skirmishes and minor clashes are as dangerous as the great battles for those involved in them. But they are less profitable for they seldom have decisive results.

Captain G. always talked of his combat at Rueda, which — he held — should immortalize him. Well, here are some details on that brilliant expedition. He was marching at the head of 200 men when he met several hundred guerillas who seemed determined to block his advance. The captain halted, quickly reached a decision, and

---

[39] Blaze's meaning here is unclear. Possibly these were the troops Walmoden detached to cover his retreat.

summoned his lieutenants, "Gentlemen," said he, "this is not the time to throw away my twenty-five years of good service — we must retire."

The lieutenants, however, did not approve of that pacific oration. They called for volunteers; fifty responded; they swept the road and ran the Spaniards into the hills. The captain was the butt of many jokes for his proposal to retreat and because he had taken no part in the fighting, leaving all the work to his lieutenants. "Gentlemen," he would respond. "I command here. The Emperor does not engage in personal combat, and I follow his example: I give my orders; I am the intellect which controls the limbs."

However jokes and gibes rained down on the poor captain. His lieutenant told him every day[40] that he should silence the mockers by some well-directed sword thrusts, and that after he had killed three or four of them — the others would quickly change their tune. "We are on campaign," he replied. "France and the Emperor have need of us. It would be a crime to deprive him of the assistance of our arms. We'll take care of this later. I shall wait." From that moment we gave Captain G. the nickname of "the modern Fabius."[41]

The Emperor loved to award decorations and promotions. After a battle, he held reviews, distributed ribbons and epaulettes. Everyone hoped for something. But for a minor affair in which 200 to 300 men took part, what happened? The commoners — junior officers and soldiers — could not even hope. The commanding officer would carefully prepare a superb report, sprinkled with glory, intrepidity, clever maneuvers — and if there was any recompense later, it was always for him alone.

I'll give you an idea of how they wrote history then. In the 1813 campaign we had an advance guard squabble at Sprottau, a small town in Saxony. The Russian rear guard defended it briefly; no more than three or four companies of skirmishers were engaged on either side. In brief, the enemy retired, leaving some prisoners and several baggage wagons in our possession. An hour later we were strolling around the Sprottau marketplace and talking of our prowess that morning.

"There's food for the bulletin writers," said one officer. "You'll see later how we have done superb things! Magnificent!"

"I don't know," said another, "if we have done so very much, but I agree that it should be mentioned."

"They say that the general claims to have gathered laurels by the bundle;[42] but that our regiment won't be mentioned."

"Go on — we'll get a line and he'll get a page."

"We'll get nothing at all."

"We can't speak to him personally — that wouldn't be worth the trouble."

"You'll see, when the Paris newspapers arrive. But to judge the matter better, let's not forget to write down what the brilliant results of our fight were. Here are the prisoners, count them. Good! They come to sixty-four, plus three baggage wagons drawn by twelve horses, plus one cannon and its caisson."

Fifteen days later the newspapers arrived. Good Lord — what splendid things had we done! (When I say "we," I mean one General S___. With incredible daring, by skillful

---

[40] With, I fear, ulterior motives, including a desire for promotion.

[41] From Quintus Fabius Maximus (BC 275-203), Roman general nicknamed "the delayer" from the evasive tactics he used against Hannibal.

[42] Writing a report glorifying himself.

tactics, he had surrounded, attacked, defeated, captured, and killed everything and everybody. Three hundred dead, a thousand wounded, two thousand prisoners, ten cannon, sixty baggage wagons were the glorious results of his scientific strategy and his noble courage. He had done all that by himself, our regiment not even being mentioned.

Actually, had the general said that he did all those fine things at the head of such-and-such regiment, everyone would have thought that quite natural, and the honor could have been shared. But in writing that "gripped by his natural impetuousness, with a small detachment of his advance guard, he routed the enemy who got away only thanks to the speed of their legs," he kept the glory all to himself. That small detachment of the advance guard is an imaginary being, fantastic, impossible to see as individual soldiers. It is possibly four men, and since the general did everything with so few, he must be a rough customer indeed. Ah, if I dared, how many heroes of the same breed could I recall!

Virgil's *sic vos non vobis*[43] is applicable every day in the army. In everything you need to know your way around to get ahead. After the battle of Eylau, a conscript brought his captain a Russian flag which he had found in the snow, amid twenty corpses. "Imbecile, do you think that's a flag? It's a company guidon of no importance whatever. Every day I find others like it, and I wouldn't bend over to pick them up."

Fifteen minutes later, the captain is addressing a marshal: "Here," he declares, "is a flag I took from the Russians. Four men defended it — they all are dead." The next day the captain was a battalion commander.[44]

The word 'promotion' lodges in the military mind at the moment you enter the service; it doesn't leave until the day your retirement is finalized. It is almost the same as the word "husband" with a young lady. Every day she thinks, "we're going to a ball this evening; perhaps I'll find a husband." The soldier thinks, "We're off to the wars; there's going to be promotions." That idea preoccupies everyone in the army, from drummer to marshal. While we imposed our laws on Europe, our generals dreamed each night that representatives of a neighboring kingdom were offering them a golden crown on a velvet cushion.

The example of Bernadotte[45] turned everyone's head. "This marshal wants to be a king; that grenadier wants to make corporal." These were very natural ways of expressing ourselves; all of us thought we might have a royal scepter in the scabbard of our sword. A soldier had become a king; every soldier thought he also might become one. Certainly if since the creation of the world there exists a single example of a man who has never died, all of us would think that we might be the second exception to that general rule. In his innermost heart, every individual considers himself immortal.

The speed of promotion depends on the number of officers who are killed — the more killed, the more promotions. When a captain, who was one of my friends, heard of the death of a field-grade officer[46] or general, he always exclaimed, "So much the better! It's about time. Every dog has his day, and his has lasted too long." But when it was a question of a lieutenant or a second lieutenant, he'd say, "So much the worse! The poor devil! It's shocking; I pity him with all my heart." In effect, the deaths of those below him in rank did not serve him in any way, while those of his superiors moved him up a notch. What this captain had the frankness to say, all the rest of us thought.

[43] "You; not us."
[44] *Chef de bataillon* — U.S. Major.
[45] Marshal Bernadotte, was invited to become heir to the Swedish throne in 1810.
[46] *Chef de battalion*, major or colonel.

There is much talk today of military advancement during the empire, and especially of the gratitude of the soldiers to the Emperor. Gratitude is a very nice word, but is it not strangely abused here? In all honesty, should we be so thankful to Imperial and Royal Majesty because he was willing to give dead men's positions to those who survived? All those years we drew the short straw[47] to see who would replace a dead comrade. And often the winner could not keep the stakes. After every battle a swarm of officers sent from Paris pounced upon our regiments to take over the better vacancies. The new nobility was like the ancient nobility;[48] all possible nobilities are like that. If the empire had lasted ten more years, one would have thought it remarkable if a commoner had made colonel. The term "officer of fortune"[49] was coming back into use, and we were getting to the point of seeing the most ambitious plebeian grow gray in the obscure honors of the grade of major.[50] The sons of the marshals, generals, counts and barons, councillors of state and prefects got a promotion every fifteen days. It was by rewarding them in the army, where they had done nothing, that Napoleon encouraged their fathers.[51]

Not that the marshals and generals lacked courage — they had proved the contrary a thousand times, but their profession was beginning to weary them. When one has a fine mansion in Paris, a handsome chateau on its outskirts, it isn't agreeable to fritter away one's life in the smoke of a bivouac. Ten years, twenty years, and more — but always!!

It was necessary to dazzle the prefects,[52] to make them deaf to the lamentations of mothers and the cries of their conscience so that they would send everyone capable of carrying a musket to the army. A general said to his soldiers who were fleeing before the enemy: "Idiots, you've sure made a mess of this! You're all going to get killed — if not today, then tomorrow." Napoleon appeared to have the same attitude toward us; but with him, you say, one became rich. Who became rich? Here and there some senior officers, but what could the immense majority show? Old coats and glory. As for glory, what is it? It is an after-action report, where one is mentioned by name. How many were nominated after each battle? — Maybe ten persons out of 300,000. Yet everyone did their duty, but you cannot mention everyone.

I constantly heard it said that you joined the army to serve your country, to serve the Emperor. You went, you go, you will go as long as there are armies — some because you had to, some in hope of advancement. Promotion — that's the country, the Emperor, the King. I except the times of great political crises, where passions and social status may overcome your personal interests. You join the army because you know that so and so,

47 Drew lots. This would be possible only among officers of equal seniority.
48 The "New nobility" was that created by Napoleon after he became emperor (a good deal of it had decidedly plebeian origins); the "ancient nobility" was that existing before the Revolution.
49 In the Royal Army, an officer, usually promoted out of the ranks, without family influence or wealth.
50 Equivalent to U.S. lieutenant colonel.
51 Blaze may have missed some promotions he thought due him and so was suffering from a case of sour grapes. There is some truth – but a lot more exaggeration – in this paragraph. For one thing, Napoleon always was short of officers after c.1807 and had no "swarms" to send out from Paris! Also imperial correspondence constantly stresses standard promotion procedures.
52 Heads of the *departements*, equivalent to our state governors, but appointed by the central government, not elected.

simple soldiers, have become generals, marshals, princes, kings. "Why can't I do likewise?" says every soldiers as he slings on his pack. We all had a commission as marshal of France in our cartridge box; it was only a question of how to get it out.

"My buddy has won the top prize in the lottery. Why can't I too win it?" So reason all the kitchen boys! How many 10-sou pieces have been lost in the hope of reaching that prize, without ever attaining it!

When we are promoted, we are very satisfied. The next day we aren't — our thoughts are directed toward that day when we will receive the next one. It's like that old song:

We want that which we do not have,
And what we have has ceased to please."

Man is made thusly and does not change; he chases after a shadow which flits always just beyond him. His life is short, and he always desires to grow older, in the hope of possessing those riches which he soon will have to leave behind. "Congratulations," I said one day to a captain who had just been promoted to battalion commander. "At present I still need the officer's cross,"[53] he replied promptly. "That will perfect my status." To thus get ahead, everyone tries to keep on the good side of his commanding officer, because it is that commanding officer who determines his future; you had better be in his good graces, or you are in danger of remaining in a shameful status quo. From a corporal to a marshal of the Empire, everyone bowed before whoever held the roster of awards. All of this necessary bowing and scraping had, little by little, changed the character of our army. The thirst for baronies and donations had given our old officers, once republicans, all the habits of Versailles courtiers, and often the most humble huts witnessed scenes worthy of the *œil-de-boeuf*.[54]

After a battle, the Emperor granted a certain number of the crosses of the Legion of Honor to each regiment [that had distinguished itself] — eight, ten, or twelve for the officers and an equal number for the non-commissioned officers and privates. After Friedland, eight were given to one regiment, but only seven newly decorated offices were visible. Everyone wondered who the eighth might be. Three months later we knew: a relative of the colonel, arriving from France, had received the cross en route — putting on his uniform for the first time, he had found it decorated with the [Legion's] red ribbon. We complained, but so quietly, so quietly that the colonel could not hear us. Those gentlemen were high-and-mightys whom it would not do to have as enemies. Only imbeciles expressed their opinions loudly, and I was always one of those imbeciles.

Captain "G.", the hero of Rueda, talked about nothing but battle; all the promotions others received should have by rights been his; no one should have had as many titles. His mother and sisters believed him to be a giant-killer, a gallant who on various occasions had fought off two or three enemy battalions. I went to see him one day and found him with a weeping lady. It was his mother.

"You must go? You've hardly arrived, and you're leaving me already?"

"Yes, mother. Sacred name of God, I'm going. Dry your tears. This is not a farewell worthy of you. You'll see me return a colonel." At the same time he called a waiter.

"Bring Bordeaux wine, pastry, and three glasses!"

"Ah, my darling, I am neither hungry or thirsty."

---

[53] This meant a promotion to the next higher grade in the Legion of Honor, the grades in which were cavalier, officer, commanders, and grand-officers, headed by "grand-crosses."

[54] At Versailles a drawing room next to the king's bedroom, where nobility seeking favors gathered to greet him.

"Mother, drink. Your son shall always be worthy of you! To your health. I shall return a general of brigade."

"And to yours, my dear. At least don't get yourself killed."

"Killed! What is my life worth? Is it not devoted to my country, to my Emperor? I idolize them both! To your health! You will see me return a general of division."

"If only I could go with you!"

"Go with me — impossible! We don't want women with us — at least not mamas," he added, giving me a roguish glance. "Instead of crying, tell me like the women of Sparta, 'Come back with your shield — sacred name of God — or on it'. Waiter, a bottle of Bordeaux and pastries for my mother. It is that, you see, mother, in Sparta or really in Lacedaemon, for they are the same, the women — to your health — if I am one day marshal of France — eh! — what would you say then! — The women bring up their children for their nation, and when they leave for the wars — pass me that plate of pastries — it is a holiday for them; the mothers don't weep, you see. This Bordeaux is delicious — your tears are capable — this ought to be the true Laffitte [vintage] — would be capable, I say, of diminishing my natural energy, if anything in the world could influence — the habitual manner — which — I mean — that — "

But the captain's tongue was thoroughly thickened by the fumes of the Bordeaux; he wasn't able to finish his sentence and could find no other way of getting out of his muddle than to summon the waiter. He thus cut his Gordian knot by demanding a third bottle and more pastries — again for his mother. The poor woman listened to her son as if he were an oracle; she wept while he got himself drunk. In the end he left her with the calm dignity of a hero who goes to single-handedly throw himself upon the enemy's battalions. You believe perhaps that our man left the next day for Russia, or at least for Spain? Neither: he went to Chalon-sur-Saône to pick up a detachment of conscripts.

We had another real original [in our regiment], to whom we gave the nickname of Mr. "Humbug Town;"[55] I will not further identify him. He was one of those men who had seen everything, done everything, said everything. He appropriated to himself the deeds and exploits of everyone he had ever known or had heard mentioned. In Germany, he had had seventeen horses killed under him and twenty-two in Spain. "It's too bad you never served in the navy," someone told him one day. "You could tell us how many frigates you had shot out from under you!" Speak of a battle; not only had he been there, but it was to him that we owed the victory — either by charging at the decisive moment or, better, by giving the Emperor wise advice. He knew Egypt, Italy, Germany, and Spain like his own bedroom. He had even done deeds of high valor in battles fought 200 leagues apart on the same day.

Never was there such a liar as this jovial blade — but he had no memory. If someone mentioned Paris, he had lived there twenty years and knew all the lively ladies and all the celebrities of that period; if the talk was of Italy, he had resided there fifteen years, had visited all the monuments, and brought home sketches of them; if of Germany, he had crossed the Rhine with Moreau[56] in 1796, and hadn't returned until six months previously. One day we added up all the years he had spent fighting the enemies of France and visiting Rome and Naples, Greece and Palestine, Europe and Asia; they totaled 115 — and our braggart was around forty years old!

[55] "Monsieur de Blaguenville."

[56] General Jean-Victor Moreau, French revolutionary general, killed 1813 at Dresden, fighting against Napoleon.

He was a poet, a musician, a painter, an astronomer, a chemist; he knew everything, and was a universal man. In his room you saw superbly framed drawings of the monuments of Greece and Italy. At their bottoms you read, in Latin, "Made by Humbug Town in Rome, Athens, etc." On a piano, spread out in calculated disorder, were the ballads, for which he had written music and words, dedicated to his friends Kleber, Kosciusko, LaHarpe, and so on.[57] Such "friends" were always illustrious men, recently deceased; as soon as a famous person left this world, Humbug Town dedicated a 50-page ballad to him, and claimed him as a friend. Humbug Town showed us a poniard given him by Selim III of Turkey; a Bible, a touching souvenir from the Bishop of Mesopotamia; a pair of pistols which were a pledge of friendship from George Washington.

Concerning that poniard that Selim III had given him, I must tell you that while examining its blade — ornamented with turbans, crescents, and Arabic lettering — I asked our traveler to read me two or three words which I could make out among the engravings. Humbug, who knew everything, and consequently could read Arabic, told me with the greatest seriousness, "That signifies 'God is great; death to the unbeliever.'" Being one of those people who always believed what was told them, I thought his translation correct. One day however, finding myself with a real Arab, I asked him to interpret the phrase. "Nothing could be simpler," he told me. "It's a merchant's stamp — Mustapha, Armorer of Damascus."

He talked all the time of his travels in Greece, Egypt, and Jerusalem, without ever telling us anything that we hadn't read twenty times in various books. In his tales of his stay in Athens, I recognized the descriptions of Chateaubriand. Never having been to the Orient, none of us could catch him in his lies by asking embarrassing questions. One day I had the luck to meet a very agreeable gentleman who had lived in Athens for three years. I persuaded him to help with a certain joke I had long considered. He was happy to dine at our officers' mess; I seated him opposite Humbug Town, turned the conversation to traveling, and got my gentlemen into Greece, where I wanted to see them.

"You know that country, monsieur?"

"Very well," replied our comrade

"What a fine climate!"

"Superb, admirable, and the monuments! For it's the monuments that especially interest you in Greece. Sunshine you find everywhere, but it is only there that you find that purity of style, that — that — well, it is the classic land of the fine arts."

"How sad it is, monsieur, that that country is ruled by the barbarous Turk, by ignorance and stupidity! You know the Aeropolis?"

"Like an Athenian — possibly better than many Athenians."

"The Parthenon?"

"I could hardly leave it."

"Those are very beautiful monuments, without a doubt, but there are a good many others, less well known, which merit the attention of artists. For example, that little temple to Jupiter — you know — very close to the Acropolis, as you turn to the left."

"Very fine! Very fine! I have sketched it, and now have the drawing in my portfolio. These gentlemen have admired it."

---

[57] Kleber and LaHarpe were Revolutionary generals; Kosciusko the famous Polish patriot.

"Thirty-two columns on each face."

"That's right, a total of 128 columns with capitals —"

"Corinthian."

"That's it. The whole building is in very good condition. The Greek climate is quite preserving."

"Yes, but the Turks don't share that same quality. Would you believe it? They recently destroyed that magnificent triumphal arch which, while we were there, stood on the road to the Piraeus."

"What? That triumphal arch is destroyed?"

"Yes, monsieur, completely."

"What a shame!"

"Destroyed to put into the oven."

"To make plaster! The barbarians!"

In short, our traveler talked for an hour about twenty temples and thirty triumphal arches, none of which ever had existed in Greece. He described each of them as having a hundred or so columns in black and white, or red and yellow marble, not sparing any details. Humbug Town kept saying that he knew of them, had copied their plans and sketched them. He lost himself in exclamations over the genius of the ancient Greeks and the perfection of their masterpieces. At last, after our man had gotten himself thoroughly entangled, we all burst out in a storm of laughter, certifying that none of those monuments had ever existed, and that if Humbug Town has ever seen them, it must have been in a dream.

Humbug Town wanted above all to be thought rich: it was his greatest craze, his cock-horse, his hobby. I would never finish this book if I tried to describe all the ruses he employed to make us believe that he owned wide lands and chateaus; he invented new ones every day. Thus, for example, he dined in his bedroom on bread and cheese, and you would thereafter see him strolling with calculated nonchalance in the neighborhood of Very or Beauvilliers, a toothpick in his mouth, saying to whomever he met that he had just dined at that famous restaurant, and that while in Paris a man such as he really could not eat elsewhere. He shut himself up for eight days and when he reappeared he told us with all possible details about a pleasure trip he had taken by post coach. He had been all over Europe in that manner. After a picnic at the home of one of our friends, each of us gave the servant five francs; Humbug Town let go of a double Louis.[58]

One day I met him at the Palais-Royal; his face was radiant, and he had the bearing of a victor in the Olympic Games.

"You look really happy," I told him.

"Yes, I have just left my banker, I received a quarterly payment of my allowance, and that is always pleasing."

"I agree — is that a large allowance?"

"Not too big — however one can get along."

As he said that Humbug Town showed me an enormous purse, crammed with golden louis; there must have been four or five hundred.

"The devil," I said, "but that's immense; you have at least seven or eight thousands francs there."

"More than that," he replied indifferently.

"And you consider that sum insufficient for three months?"

---

[58] Forty francs.

"What do you expect, my dear fellow — when one leads a certain type of life in Paris, you need money — lots of money. Besides, if I had only this little income, I couldn't do very much, but beside this allowance from my father I personally own several farms; all of these together enable me to keep up my place in society."

We separated, and I continued my walk. I had not gone a hundred yards when chance brought me to an officer I knew. He was as sad as Humbug Town had been happy. I asked why. "I have lost all my money gambling," he told me. "I've just left one of those miserable gambling halls of the Palace Royal where I was robbed of my last sou by that gang of organized bandits who had set up their infamous headquarter there. Fortune never was so contrary to anyone: I lost every throw. While I was playing on the red, Humbug Town — whom you know — played on the black, and won every time. He ought to have carried off at least 6,000 francs."[59]

"So that's how," I told myself, "our boaster was able to draw a quarter of his allowance, and his banker is none other than one of cards and dice."

Since chance happened to bring this officer who had lost all his money on to the scene, I shall profit from it by introducing him to you. It is proper that I exploit him in his turn. Why not him like the others?

All of his intellectual facilities were constantly occupied in looking for new ways to gamble. Every day he found one which should "blow up the bank," and it was only after he had blown himself up that he realized the inefficiency of his calculations. Superstitious as an old 12th century gossip — because one day he had won while wearing a disreputable green coat — he would go two leagues to put it on before gambling.

To a passion for cards he joined one for the lottery. He asked everyone he knew for numbers they had dreamed; often he burst in upon me as I was getting out bed and begged me to tell him of my dreams. Tired of these visits which dragged on and on, I ended by giving him four numbers, every time he visited me. He would leave promptly to place his bets, and I was free of him. Later, he would tell anyone who would listen that I had misled him, that I had abused his confidence. "He gave me numbers and made me believe that he had dreamed them, but I am certain that was not true, for they never were winners."

He pretended that you could find only one reliable lottery office in Paris — the one which used to be on the Place Bastille, opposite the Garden Beaumarchais. Winning a small sum there led him to have as much confidence in it as he did in his green coat, and you could say that one was quite as reliable as the other.

He had creditors who pursued him. "Come back the 5th of next month and I shall pay you," he'd tell them. "If I can't then, it will be on the 15th, or at most the 25th. It is impossible that my money will not have arrived by then." These days that he assigned for the payment of his debts were those when they drew the numbers at the lottery; always he counted on winning.

[Pages 234-240 are omitted, being merely a drawn-out story of the fool this officer made of himself when he thought he had won 1,000,000 francs — but hadn't.]

---

[59]   He was playing *rouge et noir* (red and black), a popular card game.

IX

The Camp

In the times of Louis XIV and Louis XV, a camp was often nothing more than a sort of opera given for court ladies weary of the pleasures of Versailles. Most of the officers under canvas occupied themselves with gossip and love notes; they left the daily routine to the majors and "officers of fortune." The business of the colonels and generals was to arrive in camp with handsome vehicles, numerous servants in livery, and a good cook, and to keep a table open to all comers. You could ruin yourself at one of these camps, but you could make people talk about you. Whenever it was necessary to pay with your body,[1] these gentlemen did not spare themselves; they fought like gallant men as we have always done and will do when the occasion requires, but their military life was mostly roses without thorns — thorns being cannon fire and such drolleries.

For them, the camp was a distraction, a means of showing themselves off; you had hopes of being noticed by the king, or his mistresses. A word might be said at the king's bedside — and that word might make you colonel of a regiment. It was astounding what you could spend during three months in camp. Marshal Boufflers "ate" or "had eaten" millions [of francs] at the Compiegne camp in 1698; every day his couriers brought him the wines of every country, the best game, the finest fish. He had the honor of hosting a dinner for Louis XIV and the King of England — and that honor cost him dearly. In the poetical life of Versailles, one never calculated costs, but simply went along. "See my steward," said the great noble, "and settle matters with him. I concern myself only with spending — everything else is his responsibility."

In those times, when a month of campaigning had wearied you, you arranged a truce at the outposts and everyone went into quarters without bothering to inform your minister of war. "When it rains, stay put; we won't budge. It's very disagreeable to get muddy." Today, we march all the time in any weather, but the enemy does the same. We have huge mortars, so does he; we have *canons à vapeur*,[2] they have them. But luck will always play the same role, because ten to ten is no different from one to one.

In perfecting the art of destroying men we possibly may gain something; wars will be less frequent; everyone will stay quietly in his own corner and keep his feet warm. Perhaps we will again return to the times of the Horatii and the Curiatii; after having gone through a whole cycle, we shall return to our point of departure.[3] While two or three champions settle the quarrel for their country, the rest watch with folded arms. Agriculture, commerce, industry — those three great levers of civilization — will no longer suffer from the follies of certain kings.

Today, when an army is in the field, it bivouacs; one does not camp except during armistices or when peace has been made. When in cantonments[4] the troops are too

---

[1] Risk death.

[2] This probably refers to some experimental steam-powered cannon developed during the 19th century. They were unsuccessful.

[3] See page 92. Blaze certainly does not qualify as a prophet!

[4] See Chapter X.

scattered, it takes too long to reassemble them; also you can't keep close enough watch on them, so discipline suffers. In a garrison[5] you rarely have enough regiments for large-scale maneuvers. But in a camp you have all you need and always ready to hand.

Camp maneuvers are the school of the colonels and generals; it is there that they learn the art of ploying and deploying their troops,[6] as well as to judge distances or the opportune moment for a cavalry charge, and to gain that professional precision which is indispensable for major strategic movements.

As soon as a suspension of hostilities existed between the two armies, we camped by divisions. Since hostilities might be renewed at a moment's notice, we had to be ready to reassemble and march like one man.

There are also circumstances when, without an armistice or any agreement whatever, the two armies are not ready to go into the field — whether because of bad weather or some other reason — and so form camps while awaiting the order to attack. It was thus in the first days of May 1807, the Grande Armée left the cantonments it had occupied several days after the battle of Eylau, and formed camps near Osterode and Doringen. It remained there quietly until 3 June, when the Russians, bored by that inaction, attacked our first line, commanded by Marshal Ney. That campaign lasted nine days. We whipped them at Friedland and soon thereafter we began to set up new camps around Tilsit.

A camp is a town of wood and straw, sometimes of canvas,[7] carefully laid out, with its main and side streets, long and short. The whole is kept scrupulously clean. A camp is a very fine thing, but I maintain that it is much better to be stationed in a town.

Generally, to construct our camps we demolished the nearby villages. At Tilsit, each regiment was assigned thirty houses to take apart; one or two of these were given to each company. We had a large number of wagons and horses the soldiers had "found" to transport the materials. With such resources, you can easily believe that our camps were superb — those who haven't seen them really have no idea. Once the huts had been built to uniform dimensions, everyone goes to work decorating their own in an elegant fashion. Soon an order comes for everyone to take a certain company of such and such regiment as their model in certain aspects. The soldiers, irked by having to redo their work, invent some new variations to make the model decorators do some work in their

turn. There is no reason that competition should ever end. You might say that a camp is never finished: you work as much as you rest.

A regiment decided to cut several wagonloads of fir trees in a neighboring forest, and to plant them along the line of the arms racks.[8] This produced a fine effect because that species of tree retains its green color for a long time, even after it has been cut. The

---

5   Of a city or fortress. See Chapter XII

6   Forming from line into column, and from column into line.

7   Blaze's note: "Under the empire we did not have tents; our armies marched so rapidly that they were not able to take along all the necessary baggage without reducing the speed of their movements." I have seen only one mention of a tented camp.

8   Usually placed in front of the men's huts.

next morning the orders of the day directed all units to copy that regiment; however, the imitators, wanting something better, planted a tree at each corner of each of their huts. This was even better looking; consequently the order was given to imitate the imitators. Then, to outdo everyone, we laid out an immense rectangle, which was leveled and cleared to serve as a parade ground in front of our regimental area.

We then planted six rows of trees on each side of it, so that it looked like a magnificent promenade. All that was done as if by enchantment; when you have two or three thousand men at your disposition and they are willing to work, things really move. The other organizations were promptly ordered to do likewise, but all the nearby forests had been cut down. You can clearly see that war, flood, hail and fire are less dangerous than the presence of an enemy army. In its turn, France learned something about that.

The two emperors and the King of Prussia[9] came to visit our camp, and we performed large-scale maneuvers for them, General Mouton, Napoleon's aide-de-camp (later Count of Lobau), commanding us. We marched past the three rulers and an army of princes, marshals, and generals of the three nations. I doubt that such a mass of braided coats was ever collected anywhere else in this world. Napoleon, in his simple chasseur à cheval's uniform, dominated that multitude. Alexander and Frederick William galloped behind him, never letting their horses come abreast of his. Much later they made Napoleon pay dearly for the glory that he won from them at Tilsit.

While passing our huts, the King of Prussia halted to talk with us; our regimental mail box, which was placed beside our flag while we were in the field, really surprised him.

"What purpose does that box serve?" the king demanded.

"Sire, to receive the letters we write home to France."

"Do you mean that even in the field your postal system is capable of handling the letters of all your soldiers?"

"Yes, Sire — every day it leaves, every day it arrives, and we get the Paris newspapers fifteen days after publication."

"That's admirable! Besides that, gentlemen, it would be impossible to build finer camps than yours — but admit that you've left some wretched villages."[10]

The Queen of Prussia came to Tilsit. Napoleon treated her with courtesy. For a spectator it was a most unusual spectacle to see all these rulers gathered there, going out every day together, eating at the same table, seeming in short to be old friends — they who a few days previously had been tearing each other apart in their official gazettes — weapons more dangerous to rulers than cannon. Nevertheless, that new friendship between Napoleon and Alexander gave the impression of being sincere, and if one can trust to appearances in political matters, it is probably that at Tilsit they acted in good faith. The queen of Prussia was very pretty; I have seen her. People said that she was very amiable; I know nothing of that, but it is certain that she obtained many concessions from Napoleon.[11] That pretty queen, dining one day with the three sovereigns, filled a glass with champagne, and said with that perfect grace which she possessed to such a degree — a grace which she brought at that moment to the aid of Prussia's diplomatic endeavors, "To the health of Napoleon the Great. He has taken our provinces from us, and he will return them." The Emperor stood up, courteously returned her salutation and responded, "Don't drink it all, Madame."

---

[9] Napoleon, Alexander I of Russia, and King Frederick William III.
[10] Those wrecked to get materials for the camp. See page 120.
[11] In fact, few — if any.

The time in camp is ruinous for the officers. Generally they preferred the bivouac, every day in a new position. In that situation they lived as they could, without having to spend money, while in camp the idleness sends them to the sutler's cafe or even to the nearest town — and their back pay is spent far in advance.

After the armistice that followed the battle of Znaim [1809], all the army encamped until peace was concluded. We were in the area of Brunn and Austerlitz, on the old battlefields. When we did any digging, we often found broken weapons and human bones.

Napoleon wanted to give a reenactment of the battle of Austerlitz; one fine December day all the army took up the same positions and went through the same maneuvers as they had four years previously. All went off splendidly; the regiments which represented the Austrian and Russian forces allowed themselves to be defeated, as had been arranged in advance, and nobody was drowned in the famous Sokolnitz Pond,[12] which wasn't frozen.

Louis XV loved to give mock battles for the ladies of his court; one day he decided to stage a sham siege. The memoirs of that time speak seriously of the courage of the besiegers and the besieged, all of them inspired by the king's presence. An assault was made, mines were exploded; cardboard heads, arms, and legs went flying into the air — it would have been difficult to carry the imitation any further. However they did not stop there. The besieged were obliged to sign a capitulation which, surviving to this day, proves how much those gentlemen loved to play at make-believe and especially to play soldier.[13]

This was of no importance whatever, but the besiegers would not accept the capitulation as offered. They became difficult, and the king was obliged to intervene. The besieged demanded eight cannon, but were allowed only four and only two mortars. What a farce!!

The most favorable location for a camp is always near a fine chateau, which serves as headquarters; once the staff is comfortably settled in, everything goes better.

A regiment's camp should occupy the same area as it would when formed under arms. Ordinarily each company has six huts, arranged in three rows. Opposite the center of these huts and behind them are the company kitchens, built of sods, with walls and shoulder pieces designed to keep sparks from reaching the huts' thatched roofs. Further back you find the hut of the captain and those of the lieutenants; still further, that of the battalion commander, and, behind all of them, that of the colonel, placed opposite the center of the regimental area.

The colonel's hut is there, but ordinarily the colonel is not; those gentlemen prefer to live in the nearest village — be it understood that is only when one is far from the enemy or after peace has been made. In times of war, they are with their soldiers night and day.

In camp, officers either took their meals with the sutler, who would have a restaurant seating one hundred customers, or a group would get together to form a mess. In every company there always was a soldier who was at least a passable cook. And on occasions everyone pitched in to help and produced a delicious dinner.

---

[12] Properly, the Satschen and Menitz ponds. In 1805 these were frozen, but their ice was broken by the weight of retreating Austrians and Russians and French artillery fire.

[13] This is a digression, but an interesting look at the etiquette of war. U.S. forces at Ft. Bowyer went through the same routine in 1815. See appendix at the end of this chapter.

In the field the officers were entitled to receive rations — bread, meat, salt, rice, and the like. When eight or ten club together and know how to handle things, you can live very well, provided that you can find extra items in the next town.

In camp the day passes with inspections, parades, drills, and maneuvers — a life that is certainly very agreeable to those who like it. When you don't have them, you promenade and then in the evening you gamble and drink mulled wine amid pipe smoke. That goes on at the sutler's tent or in each officer's hut in rotation.

At the camp of Sochacew, near Warsaw, Laborie and I gave a party one evening in our hut; we drank, we smoked, we talked. Everyone told his best story, and then my turn came. At the most interesting point, I was interrupted by a young second lieutenant name Masson; he told me that a comet had been seen on the horizon and urged me to come out and look at it.

"Don't pester us about your comet," said Laborie, who wanted to hear the end of my story.

Masson pulled at my coat, but Laborie held me tight to my bench. To please him, I continued with an abridged version, cutting it short to reach its climax sooner. But just as I stood up to go outside, we heard a musket shot in the camp. "Good!" said Laborie. "That's a relief. Stay here and give us another story. Your comet's dead — someone just shot it."

In some regiments, the colonels prohibited gambling; in many others they tolerated it because — being gamblers themselves — they needed someone to play against. We played *bouillotte, impériale,* and twenty-and-one,[14] and you often lost your year's pay and allowances at these amusements. A dragoon officer whom I knew very well never budged from the tent of our favorite sutler. Always ready to be the first to join in any suggested game, he carried a well-stocked purse, the contents of which he displayed to tempt amateurs' cupidity.

One evening all those gold coins changed masters. Though he played skillfully, he lost every time. Fortune is fickle — she is not considered a woman for nothing. This officer, in a thunderous voice, called the sutler and demanded a knife.

"What do you want it for?"

"None of your business! A knife! Right now!"

The sutler gave him one. Immediately, he gave himself a great slash over the heart. Shocked, we threw ourselves upon him to wrench the knife from him.

"What are you doing?" he laughed. "Sit down and give me my revenge."

"But you're wounded!"

"Wounded? My faith, nothing so stupid! I have cut open my vest, that's all. It was necessary to liberate these unfortunate prisoners."

And in fact gold coins poured by the hundred from the gash that had frightened us so badly. He began playing again, and soon recovered all that he had lost.

This officer claimed that, of all the world's pleasures, gambling was the greatest. "You dare not admit that you love gambling," he said. "Others lose confidence in you; everyone says 'He's a gambler.' On the other hand, merchants and ship owners are honored. However they run great risks and are really gambling — sometimes with other peoples' money, which is not good. The Emperor Napoleon is the greatest gambler I know; four times at least he's shot the works, and he is always ready to try again. As for me, nothing makes me appreciate life like the varying luck of gambling. If I couldn't

---

[14]   *Bouillotte* is also known as *brelan; impériale* as piquet and twenty-and-one as blackjack.

gamble, I'd be dead in two weeks. Every morning, every evening, I say my prayers like a good Christian, and I end them with these words: 'My Lord, let me always gamble and always win.'"

A philosophical office told him one day, "Even when you lose nothing but time when you're gambling, it's sheer waste."

"You're right — we do waste a lot of time shuffling the cards."

If the officers gamble with money, the enlisted men use fillips.[15] Nothing is as amusing as seeing an old *grognard* receive these snaps on the end of his nose. Sometimes they are administered by a young Johnny-Raw; the old-timer takes them without complaint, but not without making decidedly funny grimaces. And afterwards, to vary their amusements, they play *drogue* — a card game in which the loser has to wear a wooden clothespin on his nose. You will often see such scenes in passing near a guard room or in leafing through the portfolios of Charlet.[16]

In the Italian regiments and in those which had large numbers of Piedmontese,[17] for example the 111th Line Infantry, every evening you heard thousands of cries constantly repeated; these soldiers were playing *Murra*. Murra is a very ancient game, the *micare* of the Romans. Two men facing one another simultaneously extend a hand, either closed, or with one or more fingers extended. At the same time each gambler utters a number from zero to ten. If the number of extended fingers on both hands corresponds to the number you uttered, you win. This game, though very simple in appearance, requires a certain skill: the Piedmontese play it with incredible speed and love it with a passion. Since they always chant their numbers, the result is a racket, a cacophony beyond all description.

They have a very amusing proverb based on *murra*; to describe an absolutely trustworthy man, they say that you could play *murra* with him in the dark.

Mankind has always gambled, and probably will go on gambling until the end of time. Some gamble to amuse themselves, others in the hope of winning large sums of money — something that appears easier and move convenient than gaining it by hard work. I have known very rich men who gamble to stir up their blood and emotions. I once said to one of them, "What's the point of gambling for money when you have an annual income of 200,000 francs, and don't spend half of that?"

"My dear fellow, it's only for the fun of it."

"You could find another better diversion."

"And what would that be. Come on — tell me. I'd really like to know."

"Become a benefactor, make people happy. It's a fine part to play in this world. How many tears could you dry! How many old people go hungry! How many girls need a dowry! Become a second Providence for them. We know great ladies who do fine work which they sell or offer as lottery prizes to raise money for the unfortunate. The queen, her sister, and their girls spend their evenings sewing and embroidering.[18] Everyone is eager to purchase their work, and the poor profit from it."

"Those ladies are doing the right thing; I approve of them. But myself — my dear fellow — I don't know how to embroider."

---

[15] A strike with the nail of a finger snapped from the end of the thumb.

[16] Nicholas T. Charlet, (1792-1845). French artist and humorist-caricaturist.

[17] Napoleon annexed Piedmont (northwestern Italy) to France in 1802.

[18] Since this is obviously post-Waterloo, this would be the wife of either Louis XVIII or Charles X.

Appendix

Blaze's note: Here is that curious document:

The governor of this place had the chamade [drum beat signifying a request for a parley] beaten, and a white flag raised on the flanking angle of a bastion. An officer promptly approached and demanded what this signified. He was told that the place was ready to surrender and that an exchange of hostages was proposed. Arrangements were made to carry out this exchange. The fortress sent out two officers; the besiegers sent in an equal number. This was the proposed capitulation:

We, the governor of this place, having considered its condition, the superior force of the besiegers, the impossibility of being relieved, have assembled a council of war, which, after having considered our situation, has decided to surrender this place under the following conditions, to wit:

1. That the citizens of this place are not molested for any reason, that they are left free to exercise their religion, and that they are not deprived of any privilege which they have always enjoyed and which our kings have always authorized.
2. That several public buildings, such as hospitals, churches, and the town hall which have been destroyed by the besiegers, will be rebuilt at their expense.
3. That no deserters will be reclaimed.
4. That all the prisoners, taken by either army during the sorties, are released without regard to their respective numbers.
5. That the sick, whatever the nature of their illness, are cared for by the besiegers.
6. That the besieged will be allowed four covered wagons to carry the personal property and other effects of the besieged [meaning the governor and his senior officers] and that these will not be searched. [A wise condition, if you have some easily identifiable loot on hand.]
7. That four carriages be furnished for several ladies of rank who were caught in this place during the siege, and who were not allowed to leave though we had requested it.
8. That we march out, accompanied by our garrison with all the honors of war — drums beating, matches burning, flags flying, muskets shouldered, thumbs on the hammer, musket ball in the mouth, eight cannon, eight mortars, weapons and baggage.

We promise, on our word of honor, that the commanding officer of the detachment which escorts us will be furnished a properly signed safe-conduct so that he may return in perfect safety into territory controlled by the victors.

Signed: Chevalier d' Allemant, Governor
Charles de Bourbon, Count of Eu.

X

The Cantonments

Cantonments are the soldier's favorite way of living. The bivouac finally becomes tiresome; it rains and turns cold. Life in camp is too laborious — he has to be a mason, a carpenter, and a roofer all at once. In garrisons, the service is hard; he is too often on guard, drill comes regularly every day with its oppressive monotony; and — to use an expression perpetuated in the squad rooms — he is too "sullen in the service."

In cantonments, there is none of that; he does nothing or very little. The companies, scattered through several villages, are not often assembled. Each soldier finds food and a bed with his host; he strolls with a switch in hand,[1] jokes with the men, flirts with the women, and sometimes everyone gets along famously.

A German lady told me one day, "Your Emperor resembles a shepherd who moves his sheep to a new area every morning, so as not to overgraze anyone pasture. But if he leaves a little grass anywhere he keeps it in mind for later use."

That dame understood our method; for years the French army was maintained by the Germans. The most economical method for the Germans, and the most agreeable for our soldiers was this system of cantonments. Each peasant fed the soldier billeted on him; the burden was equally distributed and there was no waste. The German contractors and the French supply personnel disliked this method of feeding the troops, for it left them no opportunities for graft, and so caused them serious financial losses.

The officers also had a great liking for cantonments. Billeted in the best houses of the villages, they usually found good company and an agreeable leisure, free from the petty details[2] of garrison service, with nothing to do but keep an eye on their men and woo the ladies. The German way of life is generally patriarchal: take away half of their old-fashioned genealogical notions and pride of place and rank, and German nobles are the best people in this world. They never could believe that any officer who was educated, polite, and well-spoken was not also of noble birth. In speaking or writing his name, they would always give it the aristocratic particle.[3]

Before the campaign of 1809, we were in cantonments around Bayreuth, and — to be less of a burden on the inhabitants — we were distributed over a wide area. Billeted in little villages during that winter, we had no other recreations than to hunt and to visit among ourselves. One day Rougé called on his nearest neighbor, Montro, and dined with him. When the dessert arrived Rouge expressed astonishment at seeing his friend so poorly fed.

"What the devil," he said. "They're treating you like a corporal. When these scoundrelly peasants see a young officer without moustaches they take advantage of him. Every drummer in my company is better fed than you are. If I hadn't known what

---

[1] For a swagger stick. This can be translated "ramrod," but sketches show a small branch or cane.

[2] With us, chicken, Mickey Mouse or less polite terms.

[3] Thus our author would become "Elzear de Blaze" or "von Blaze."

to do on my arrival, my host would have treated me as yours does you, but I set him straight the first day. Now everything goes splendidly."

"And what did you do?"

"I commenced by taking a stick — that's an argument these Germans always comprehend — and giving my peasant twenty wallops with it. Then I promised him I'd begin again any time that he failed to serve me according to the menu which I hung on his kitchen door. From that moment, everything changed. I have three course meals like all respectable second lieutenants should — good wine, coffee, liqueurs, and champagne on holidays. Try my recipe — you'll find it effective."

Poor Montro took all that for gospel, never suspecting that Rougé was playing a trick on him. Once his comrade had left, he drew up is own menu and presented it to his host, who received it with loud protests, declaring that such a bill of fare would quickly bankrupt him and that, as he might, he could not do better than he was. Thereupon, our second lieutenant, attempted to apply Rouge's recipe, but the peasant — a big fellow with broad shoulders — immediately seized hold of Montro's stick, wrenched it out of his hands, and thrashed him thoroughly.

Hearing Montro's cries, soldiers ran to rescue him. The host escaped, went to our general, and made a complaint against Montro — presenting, for convincing evidence, Montro's proposed menu. To complete his misfortunes, the general didn't think the business at all funny: he condemned Montro to fifteen days of close arrest[4] with a sentinel, whom he had to pay three francs a day according to military regulations, at his door. That last part of his punishment really hurt — and God alone knows how many jokes were heaped upon Montro — he was ridiculed! Rougé spent the fifteen days going from village to village to tell about his joke. Like La Ramée,[5] he did not rest until every officer in the regiment knew all about it.

In the cantonments, our military duties left us long hours of leisure, so we hunted. Masters of the country, the game belonged to us by right of conquest. If that manner of enjoying ourselves was disagreeable to the barons and great landlords, the owners of the forests through which we roved, it really pleased the common citizens on whom we were billeted. To begin with, by bringing the contents of our game bags to their kitchens, we compensated them for expenses they incurred because of us. Moreover, they were not troubled to see their lords and masters — so jealous of their hunting rights — troubled in their turn, after having kept everyone else from hunting for so long.

In Germany, once my host learned that I was a hunter, he would take me aside and show me the best localities, the local nobles' preserves! I was never misdirected, and often I needed a vehicle to bring back the products of my work. Not being able to hunt himself, because of the severe penalties for doing so, he got even by sending me in his place.

The great barons complained to our marshals, and sometimes hunting was prohibited. In that case we were careful, but we always hunted. In any case, if you were caught, the punishment was never more than two or three days under arrest — and a true hunter would never let a little thing like that stop him.

Around Breslau, we were in cantonments at Oels, in the territory of the Prince of Brunswick-Oels, who later showed himself so great an enemy to Napoleon. The

[4]   Confinement to his quarters
[5]   See page 40 In Marches chapter

marshal had forbidden hunting, and we did very little of it.[6] One evening, the prince declared in his salon that — if all Prussians were like him, in three days there wouldn't be a Frenchman left in Prussia. Thereafter, elaborating that subject, he spoke of Sicilian vespers, daggers, poisons, and the like. All this being reported, the next day the marshal withdrew the veto he had issued against hunting, and let us march against the prince's hares, roe-deer, and stags, and fall upon them.

What slaughter followed that order of the day! Between Oels and Bernstadt, you heard nothing but the baying of hounds and gun shots. Once, the price attempted to disarm one of our officers — fortunately we arrived to rescue the prince.

At one of the prince's country houses, between Oels and Breslau, I have seen the most bizarre avenue in the world. It was formed by around a hundred ancient yew trees, trimmed in the shapes of dogs, horses and hunters; at the far end another yew, in the center of the avenue, formed a galloping stag. All that, which was very well done, required continual care. These trees had to be trimmed every eight days because their growth constantly tended to destroy their proportions. During a brightly moonlit evening, when the fantastic shadows of these creations are set moving by the wind, you could think yourself among Virgil's heroes in the Elysian Fields.

When we weren't hunting, we visited back and forth, and for that important business the mayors were required to furnish us a carriage, or else a sleigh. Our trips became so frequent that all the local horses were kept busy serving our whims. These perpetual visits hindered agricultural work, trade was blocked, and — the markets being unable to replenish their food stocks — famine threatened. An order of the day accordingly prohibited, under pain of the most severe punishment, the requisition of any vehicle for such purposes.

Apparently I never knew about this order. Every time the desire for a change of scenery struck me, I'd simply, and without ceremony, order out the buggy of the mayor on whom I was billeted. He complained, and I was put under arrest. The honorable corps of second lieutenants sided with me; I received many visits from the most distant villages in our cantonment area. In these meetings we planned a shattering vengeance against that spoil-sport mayor, and this is what we beardless areopaguses[7] adopted.

During one fine night — I say "fine" because it was raining heavily — we took that buggy, the innocent cause of my arrest, apart. At the risk, a hundred times over, of breaking our necks we patiently hoisted it piece-by-piece to the ridgepole of the house. When everything was up there, the buggy was reassembled between two chimneys, all ready to go again, once it was hitched up.

At daybreak, the mayor — having a trip to take — went out to the stables to hitch up, but couldn't find his buggy. He cried out that it had been stolen — everyone ran in all directions; they searched, but found nothing. Finally a child saw the vehicle in that peculiar coach-house where we had placed it. Imagine, if you can, the anger of that unfortunate man — it would make you die laughing. He swore hard enough to blow his house over. Our soldiers' jokes made him still angrier. One said that as long as it was up there, he wouldn't have to worry about it being stolen; another, that all he had to do was to get his horses up there and everything would come down in a hurry. In the end

---

[6]   This was probably Marshal Davout — you did not argue with him. Also he always had a first-rate intelligence/counter-intelligence system.

[7]   The Areophagus was the high tribunal of Athens — more of Blaze's classical education.

the whole village assembled and went to work; it took them three days to undo what we had done in one night.

Even if there are good cantonments, you sometimes find bad ones. When the countryside has been ravaged by both armies and no longer provides any supplies, you need to be a genius to find your daily bread. For example, in the area of Osterode after the battle of Eylau, those "scoundrel peasants" (to borrow a term from our soldiers) hid their provisions in the woods or buried them. But they hadn't done it too skillfully; every day we found a new hiding place.

Our foxy old veterans walked along, ramrod in hand, probing any freshly disturbed earth. The products of these excursions were stored up in each company for equal distribution to all. We had not known the art of feeding an army in the field — at least no one had ever put it into practice.[8] We had a flood of supply service employees with the various headquarters, but that gentry were busy getting rich. Their principal concern was to look after the Imperial Guard, and everyone else had to look after themselves. When the Guard had been issued rations for four days, the talk in the Emperor's antechamber was that the whole army was well supplied; the newspapers repeated, amplified and exaggerated this and everything went splendidly in the best of all possible worlds.

One day our soldiers found several sacks of oats in one of those caches. This was good fortune indeed, for our horses had nothing to keep them alive but dirty straw, taken from thatched roofs. Officers of our regiment billeted in the neighboring villages, having learned of this, came visiting in order to get a feed of oats for their horses. Since they did this repeatedly, our supply dwindled visibly. Laborie devised a really expedient way of handling the situation. He told the soldier responsible for putting their horses into the stable to carefully observe his signal: If he said, "Give him some oats, you understand," the horse got none; if he said simply, "Give him some oats," the horse was fed.

Thus, a few exceptions aside, when an officer said to us, while dismounting, "You can give my horse some oats, can't you?"

"Certainly we can," Laborie would reply. Then, turning to the soldiers, "Give him some oats, you understand?"

"Yes, my lieutenant."

The officer would depart and discover that his horse — not having been fed — would not respond to his spurring. Later on I told this anecdote to everyone's amusement; the words "you understand?" even became proverbial. Whenever we ate a good dinner, we always said, "That was without 'you understand?'"

We often went fishing in a lake near Peterswald, for we had to employ every possible means of finding food. One day when, our lines in our hand, we carefully watched our floats bobbing on the surface of the water, one of our fellow fishermen saw that his fish hook was snagged on some sticks he could see on the bottom of the lake. He tried to move them with a pole, when suddenly a corpse surfaced. Astonished, we continued probing and more bodies appeared. In short, we counted thirty-eight, one of them a woman's. They were naked and all appeared to have been killed with hatchet blows.

Our report went swiftly to the colonel, the general, the marshal. The village was encircled, all its inhabitants made prisoners. An examination was launched; we

---

8 Quite to the contrary: The armies of Louis XIV and XV and earlier kings had certainly known how to peel the countryside — in fact, far more brutally than the Grande Armée ever did.

searched the place thoroughly and found uniforms and weapons. It was established that a French detachment, which we had thought captured by the enemy, had perished in that village, all in the same hour of the same night, victims of a new Sicilian Vespers. Thirty-eight inhabitants of Peterswald were shot and the village burned to the ground for good measure.

As autumn approached, food became scarcer. You might say that in certain circumstances, and especially during the period of which I speak, the potato saved the French army. We have often seen soldiers bring their muskets to the marching salute while passing a field planted with those precious tubers. And consider how strange men are; they immortalize those individuals who get them killed, and forget the names of those who kept them alive. We have detailed histories of all possible conquerors; you can learn what they said and did almost every day of their lives — and the name of the sailor who first brought the potato to Europe remains unknown.

Yet what services did that man not render? Were the gold mines of Peru worth as much as the potato? Heap up the glory of a dozen kings, that sailor's would still outweigh the lot. What remains of most conquests? Nothing! Voltaire tells us that during the wars between the Bulgarians and the Abares, 20,000 men were killed on both sides. The Bulgarians captured two villages which they had to return when peace was made.[9] That is generally the history of all conquests; and — if you increase the number of dead and of villages taken and returned, it is exactly the same as our recent [Napoleonic] ones.

What makes military life so agreeable is that it is always changing. When you find yourself in an uncomfortable situation, you can readily console yourself with the knowledge that things soon will be different. One day, up to your knees in mud, without food or straw for your bed; the next day in a fine chateau, inhabited by pretty ladies and containing a perfectly equipped kitchen and wine cellars full to their ventilators.

All these things together provide a pleasant diversion, but it is necessary that they all be together — *sine Barcho et Cerere friget Venus*,[10] which signifies in French that it is difficult to woo the ladies when your belly is empty.

When our lucky star brought us to one of these blessed chateaus, especially the day after a miserable bivouac, we young *paracheres*,[11] (as Rabelais put it), experienced those pleasures which mere men of the world can never know. Actually happiness is relative, and it almost always is a matter of comparison that makes us find things bad or good. When, on Sunday, the corner messenger[12] eats a pork chop, his gullet finds it deliciously pleasing; when the pheasant of the Holy Alliance [Restaurant] is not cooked to perfection, the sybarite dines very badly.

If you have read *Hunting With a Pointer*, you should know of the Prince of Zeil-Walbourg Truchsses; the one who did not want anyone to kill his foxes. If you haven't read it, I advise you to do so — it is a book which I particularly recommend. I have excellent reasons to do so, which you perhaps have guessed.[13]

---

[9]   Voltaire's "history," especially when dealing with events outside France, is generally dubious.
[10] "Without Bacchus [god of wine] and Ceres [goddess of agriculture], Venus freezes."
[11] This translates in modern French as "achievers" or "finishers".
[12] In European cities, these "commissionnaires/commissioners" (often ex-soldiers) served as free-lance messengers, porters, errand boy, etc. They usually waited at strategic corners for possible customers.
[13] This was Blaze's first book.

In the chateau of Zeil, you could easily forget the miseries of the bivouac. The exquisite courtesy of its master, the comfort which you found with him, were an ample compensation for the poverty of Poland. I was billeted with a Count Ferdinand, the prince's brother and parish priest to a small neighboring village; almost every day he took me to dine at Zeil.

The German language is very rich in ceremonial expressions. It requires several lines to embellish the shortest title with all its accessories. You repeat them, you proclaim them on each occasion without omitting a syllable. If you took all the obligatory expressions out of a conversation between two titled Germans, nothing much would be left. That's why French has become the diplomatic language of Europe; if you used German, you'd never get to the point. When I was present, the two brothers spoke French, thereby saving at least ten pages in a quarter of an hour.

On the princess's saint's day,[14] Count Ferdinand was up early in the morning; his servants were in ceremonial dress, horses in their best harness. He himself wore the insignia of his office as canon of Augsburg. I put on my full-dress uniform, and we were off.

"It will be splendid today at Zeil," he told me en route. "Everybody will be there, and in the evening we will have the Turkish music."

"What do you mean by such words?"

"Every year, on this same day, it's the same thing."

"But what is that Turkish music?"

"You'll see. I want it to be a surprise to you.".

All the minor gentry of the area were gathered at the Zeil chateau; there were introductions with all the ceremony required in such a case; finally a splendid luncheon. While leaving the table, the princess proposed a walk, but it was so hot that the prince preferred a game of *tarots*. That game is played by groups of four, like boston:[15] the prince, the princess, Count Ferdinand, and I had played together frequently, which I found amusing enough, but this day I would have preferred to be free, for among the Frauleins[16] which this special occasion had attracted, I could see an extremely good-looking one with whom I wanted to strike up a conversation. There were plenty of groups of fours, but the prince politely asked me to join his as usual, and I had to accept that honor which, incidentally, made many people jealous.

In the past, when our card party had dragged out too long, I had had an infallible method of ending it. I would tell some comic story of garrison life; the prince laughed and laughed until he wept and could not see his cards. One story led to another, the laughter continued heartily; and finally we'd leave the table. When the princess was wearied by a run of poor hands — though our game usually was quite lively — she would signal me to use my recipe, for she would not want to simply leave a game which her excellent husband enjoyed so much. This day, I wanted more than ever to quit playing: The pretty Countess of Ill__ was seated facing me; her beautiful eyes kept me from studying my cards, absorbing all my attention. Accordingly, I tried to do as I had previously, but the prince remained grave and imperturbable. Count Ferdinand

[14] The day consecrated to her patron saint — in parts of Europe considered more important than birthdays.

[15] Card games.

[16] Blaze's note: "That is what ladies of noble origin are called in Germany; the others are all simply *frauenzimmer*."

signaled me to stop, the princess lowered her eyes; I pretended to see neither and went ahead. A hundred times I had gotten my audience laughing with much less trouble, but this time nothing promised me my usual success. Many spectators crowded around our table, looking at one another with obvious astonishment, as if they could not believe the excess of my audacity. I therefore realized that I was violating court etiquette; I promised myself that I'd make them forget it. I continued bravely; I embroidered my story, I warmed to my subject; ideas came crowding in and I really caught fire. I looked at the prince: he was pinching his lips to keep from laughing, but two big tears forming in his eyes betrayed how much he wanted to. Therefore I mustered my forces, really outdid my usual performance — and the bomb burst. The prince laughed even more heartily than he had restrained himself previously, and everyone imitated him — for a prince is always imitated. The scene reminded me of the ending of *The Trial of the Fandango*,[17] when the judges no longer able to retain their dignity — begin dancing on their bench. Thereafter the card games broke up, several groups formed, and we no longer were the target of all eyes. I approached the beautiful countess, but her husband, like a vulture that defends its young, reached his wife at the same time that I did. I was obliged to talk about the great heat, how a heavy rain would help the wheat crop, and what a pleasant evening we were having while waiting for the Turkish music.

Conspicuous among the nobles gathered in the salon was a man in a red coat, embroidered with silver, who wore the broad blue cordon of some Bavarian order and a handsome badge on his left breast — when he turned, I saw it was the key insignia of a chamberlain.

"Who is that handsome gentleman?" I asked Count Ferdinand.

"He's a French emigre,[18] my cousin's husband. He lives in a village near here and is a most likeable person. Would you like to make his acquaintance? I'll be happy to introduce you."

"With pleasure."

"Also, since he is your neighbor, you'll be able to see him frequently, and you'll enjoy his society."

We approached Monsieur the Count of F__; his south-of-France accent showed that he was one of my countrymen. In 1791 he had emigrated like so many others but, managing better than they had, he had the talents to make his fortune. From a French second lieutenant, he had become a Russian colonel, had earned the Grand Cross of the Order of Bavaria, had been chamberlain to the king of Württemberg and grand master — of his kitchens. He asked me to visit his chateau and promised to soon extend the same invitation at my home — which is to say Count Ferdinand's.

At dinner I was very happy to find myself seated next to the pretty countess; all the time while eating, while drinking the detestable wine from the Lake Constance region, I talked sweet nonsense to her; the lady gave every indication of enjoying it, but seldom answered because her husband never lost sight of us. That unfortunate man! As you will see later on, it was not I whom he should have suspected. To foil the count I therefore said very little more to his wife, but I carefully continued my conversation with my feet;[19]

---

[17] A now forgotten play of some sort.

[18] One of the French nobility who "emigrated" (fled) from France during the early years of the Revolution.

[19] In full dress for social occasions, Blaze would have been wearing light pumps, not boots.

you can say very pleasing things in that fashion. That day I must have been very eloquent, for she responded most charmingly. Go find me a husband, the most jealous in the world, who can tell what is going on in a case like that. The Count of Ille__ saw no more than anyone else did, and when we got up from the table we were already in full accord.

"The devil," you're going to say, "you certainly are a proud conqueror; when necessary, you certainly work fast. You've hardly had time to get in four words[20] and already you've won!" But gently: don't hasten to congratulate me — I was not as lucky as these preliminaries would had you to believe. We were taking our coffee in the drawing room, when all of a sudden a frightful uproar broke loose under the windows.

One day some time previously I had asked Count Ferdinand, "Who is that little man with the mustaches who seems so pleased with himself?"

"He is the officer who formerly commanded the contingent the prince sent to the Emperor's army. He is now the court gentleman-usher and historian."

"Historian?"

"Yes. In our family we have a book in which every day we write the acts and deeds of our prince."

"Every day! But when there is nothing worth entering?"

"There's always something. This book was begun at the time of the Crusades and has been kept up without interruption — you can understand how valuable it can be for us. There, we see what our forefathers did, we imitate them, and our offspring will do the same. All those customs which our ancestors have handed down to us, we shall pass to our posterity. In that book we protest against the unjust pillaging of our territories.[21] Our prince is always presented as a sovereign; as for the king of Bavaria, he gets no more attention than if he had never existed."

"Then isn't your book only a romance?"

"That may be all it is, if it pleases you to call it one, but my brother is sovereign; he should always be, in any event, come what may. It is essential that our descendants never suppose there was a gap in our history."

"But the facts?"

"What do they matter!"

Poor posterity! They'll be thoroughly bamboozled.

But now Monsieur the Historian was the maestro of the Turkish music. He added that job to those he already accumulated and, beyond all that, he also played the clarinet. The childrens' tutor played the flute, the game keepers blew their horns, and all the servants, armed with cymbals, triangles, tomtoms — and also, I think, casseroles or something that look very much like them — joined in the most horrible din that ever scorched human ears. All of them were dressed Turkish fashion, in old tawdry finery, captured doubtlessly from the Saracens in the times of Richard the Lion-Hearted.

I turned to the Count of F__. "How could anyone make such an uproar in a country like Germany where everyone they say is born a musician? How is it possible that the prince, a man of intellect, finds that pleasing? Just look at his face — it's radiant with joy. He's jubilant!"

---

[20] *"Couchez-vous avec moi"????*

[21] These small German principalities were always been gobbled up or gradually absorbed by the larger ones — especially Prussia and Austria.

"These questions you're asking me are those I've asked myself a hundred times," replied the count. "All that I know about it is that from time immemorial they have made Turkish music at this chateau on major holidays. That should date back to the time of the Crusades; some ancestor of the prince doubtlessly came back from Palestine with instruments captured from the Saracens. He had them played on his Saint's day, and — because in this country everything is continued — that was continued. Just look at those instruments; their antiquity proves their origin — you couldn't find anything like them anywhere. German nobles have the mania for reenactments; here, posterity's principal care is to imitate its ancestors. I'll wager that a thousand years from now, on another saint's day, they'll be making Turkish music at this chateau with the same casseroles."

The prince was a good musician, and yet that crazy music enchanted him. "Why?" you might ask me. It was because that in that music he found something entirely different from the music itself. He saw the acts and deeds of his ancestors, the crusades, the long sword of his grandfather, the cuirass of his great-grandfather, the helmet of his great-great-grandfather. When he played music with a few intimate friends, he was a musician; but at that moment he was no longer a musician — he was a prince. He preferred that terrible cacophony to the smoothest harmony of the finest orchestra.

Since everything comes to an end in this best of all possible worlds, even the most agreeable things, that music ceased. I had seen the pretty countess leave the salon and walk toward a little grove at the bottom of the garden. Darkness had fallen. I thought the hour of the shepherd[22] had come, and I hastened to seek adventure. I went at first to the right, then to the left, listening, peering in all directions as best I could in the dim light when, on turning into a pathway, I glimpsed two figures who tried to avoid me. I walked faster; they began to run; I ran faster — and found myself nose-to-nose with the pretty countess in a tender ___ with the historian, who was still wearing a turban and carrying his clarinet.

I left with a loud burst of laughter, and that was my sole revenge. "Ah, Count Ill__," I thought while heading back to the chateau, "take heed to your offspring. Apparently everybody here wants to do your work for you."

The next day I was in Count Ferdinand's drawing room, intent on a game of chess, when I heard the guard's drum beat *"Aux Champs."*[23] I looked out the window and saw the soldiers in formation, at "Present Arms." An open calash[24] rolled into the courtyard; my philistine[25] warned me that Marshal Davout was coming up the steps to visit me. The door swung open, and Count Ferdinand's valet — who had hastily pulled on his grand ceremonial coat — announced the Count of F__.

---

[22] The favorable moment for a lover.

[23] The ceremonial salute drum beat or trumpet call. This is interesting, since it indicates that — even when in cantonments — a guard was kept on duty at all headquarters, apparently down to company level, for emergencies.

[24] A light, 2-wheeled carriage, usually with a rear seat for two passengers and a front one for the driver.

[25] Blaze's note: "That is what we called our enlisted orderlies. The term "domestic" [properly a civilian servant] not being in harmony with the military uniform, that of "philistine" had been adopted." (Editor's query: Was this inspired by the Philistine bodyguard King David enlisted, not trusting his loving Hebrew subjects?)

He was six inches taller since yesterday, and was radiant because of the honors my soldiers had rendered him. He really believed that the guard had turned out for him; it would never occur to him that he had been mistaken for someone else. He was covered with embroideries and cordons, as he had been the day before. The sentry, seeing such a fancy coat had shouted, "Turn out the guard!" — and the corporal of the guard, like a greenhorn, had received him with the same honors that Napoleon would have received.

I left the count, free to believe that all that had been intended for him, while making a mental note that one incident would not become a custom.

By golly, I thought, looking at the magnificence of his court costume, the count really has no reason to make fun of his cousin, the prince, for the latter's love of display when he himself, going from one village to another to visit an unimportant second lieutenant, puts on a coat which he wouldn't wear — even at court — except on major ceremonial occasions.

Mankind's great desire is usually to appear superior to his neighbor. If not, you often let yourself be dominated by someone who has more money or is higher in the social hierarchy. Our species is essentially sheep-like. Put two men, previously unknown to each other, in a post carriage and send them down a highway — they will hardly have gone four leagues before one of them has got his hooks into the mind of the other — and the latter will be neither hungry, thirsty or sleepy except when his fellow traveler wants to eat, drink, or sleep.

Everyone knows what influence wealth and social rank have on the minds of fools; and, since their number is infinite, everyone can be admired by a certain number. If you're admired in one place, do you doubt that you can become an admirer simply by crossing the street?

"An eagle in one house is a fool in another."

Consider all the men you know: put them into a salon among persons they're meeting for the first time. They will display all possible skill while talking to those people to tell what they are or what they have been. If occasionally a mischievous interlocutor trips them up to get them onto a new subject, they come right back to their old one. You rebuff them; they come back again and always finish by telling you what they said at Court, that they belong to the Institute,[26] and are associated with notable financiers. You're trapped until they finish.

This practice is even more frequent among women. See that beautiful lady come to the ball in her superb private carriage — she will choose to sit beside another one who must always come in a hired hack. Take out your watch — I will bet you a hundred to one that in five minutes the first lady will be telling about accidents she claims happened to her carriage and her horses because of her coachman, who certainly is the most awkward of her servants. None of that is true, but it gives her a pretext to talk about her servants, her coachman, her horses, and her carriage — just to make the other lady, who has none of those things, pine away from envy.

There was a captain in my regiment who, every day as he sat down to dine, put a 40-franc under his plate. After the dessert, he picked up that gold piece, put it in his purse, and left. We often asked him why, and he would tell us to wait. Finally we learned the reason for that odd habit. "In officers' messes the conversation never gets beyond either

---

[26] A national society, founded 1795, to "advance the sciences."

military regulations or females — two subjects I find supremely boring. I promised myself to give this coin to our waiters, if some day I had the happiness to hear you talk about something else. I have never been that fortunate, and so I have kept my forty francs."

Today, after the first conventional compliments, I asked Count F__ the name of the order, the cordon and badge of which he wore.

"It is that of Saint Michael of Bavaria, the order which enjoys the highest privilege in Europe."

"What is that privilege?"

"We have the right to take Holy Communion with drawn sword in hand on St. Michael's Day."

"*Risum teneatis, amici;*"[27] for my part I managed to keep down the laughter which that superb privilege had aroused in me, and it was only with some difficulty that I kept a straight face. Several days later I returned his visit; he took me through his garden which was full of little thatched houses, kiosks, and buildings of all sorts. In a little gothic temple there was a mechanical hermit who answered all questions; unfortunately, this sorcerer understood only German. Next to the hermit was an altar with this dedication: "DEO IGNOTO (to the unknown God)."

"Is this where you take communion on St. Michael's day?" I asked the count. He gave the impression of not having heard me. I repeated the question. "No," he answered, "that is in the chapel of the chateau."

I collected information, and I learned that on 29 September the count, in full ceremonial dress, with sword unsheathed, took communion in the presence of his edified vassals. He gave that ceremony all the solemnity possible, and if he had any sort of a historian under his authority, he would not have failed to have the minutes of his proceedings duly drawn up for the great advantage of posterity. It no doubt is very well to take communion sword in hand, especially when one has the unchallengeable right to do so, but I must confess that the *Deo ignoto* has always shocked me. Here, do we not see two men in one body? The *Deo Ignoto* was a conception of the count himself;[28] the other a privilege he wanted to enjoy. For nothing in this world would he forego it. A privilege, whatever it is, is always a fine thing. For the gentlemen of the "boots off"[29] the important thing was to stand out from the rest of mankind. They wanted that distinction, cost what it might; if the king had accorded them the privilege of not eating on a certain day of the year, you can be certain that they would not dine — and that they would have a great scorn for all the common scum who went happily to the table while mocking their foolishness.

That reminds me of a certain duke who always wore his *cordon bleu*.[30] Every one of his costumes included a broad blue ribbon; he wore one to bed at night and — an extraordinary thing, and nevertheless true — he went so far as to have a cordon made of corrugated iron to use on those days when he took a bath.

That's impossible, you say! Well, if you don't believe my anecdotes, I'll give you straight history. The son of the "Great Condé"[31] while he was dying did nothing but

[27] Roughly, "Don't laugh at a friend."
[28] Apparently Blaze did not go in for Bible study. See Acts XVII, 23
[29] See page 39.
[30] Probably the broad, light-blue ribbon of the French Order of the Holy Ghost.
[31] French prince, traitor, and general, 1621-1686.

specify the details of his funeral rites. "At the death of my father, serious mistakes were made — the pall was carried by so-and-so, which was wrong. The bearers should be princes of the blood[32] and not mere marshals." He specified the shape of the bed where he was to lie in state, the arrangements in the chapel, the etiquette of the entombment. He died while deciding the number of candles to be placed around his bier.

All that is easily understood: on our death beds we still have the thoughts that have filled our heads all our lives. Haller, the great physiologist, felt his own pulse, and thinking he was visiting a patient, said: "That man has no more than five minutes to live; they have brought me here too late." He died five minutes later. A pawnbroker instead of kissing the crucifix his confessor held out to him, took it, weighed it in his hands, and exclaimed. "It's mighty light. I can't loan more than three francs on that."

Among those cantonments which have left me the happiest memories, that of Zeil certainly takes first place, and Ratschiltz comes right behind it. You should know my worthy baron, the man who persuaded me to grow a mustache,[33] We lead a joyous life in his country seat; during the day we hunted; in the evening, gathered in a big room with a half-dozen very pretty ladies, we did our very best to be friendly. The old baron told us marvelous stories concerning the knights who had inhabited his fine manor house in days gone by. They were noble men, his ancestors, whose origin was lost in the waters of the Flood. We came to know all their deeds and conquests. I knew them so well by name that when going along the halls of an evening, I felt that at any instant I might meet a certain Conrad of the Iron Arm or Othon of the Head of Steel.

One evening, by a bright moonlight that threw the fantastic shadows of the towers on the ground, I peopled the silent courtyard with knights competing for the prize of valor.[34] The beautiful ladies, excited by fear and hope, revived the courage of their almost-defeated lovers. They tore away their ribbons; the pages ran in all directions to carry these favors[35] and promises of favors still more precious. I heard the neighing of horses, the din of broken lances and cuirasses, and sounds of trumpets, and the acclamations of the crowd. The herald-at-arms proclaims the victor; a handsome knight, his visor raised, covered with dust, received from an adored hand the gage of victory, which will leave so many jealous — when I was plucked from my dream by the most matter-of-fact man who ever wore a uniform.

"My lieutenant," said the fourrier,[36] "I have brought you a requisition for three pairs of leggings for you to sign."

May the devil fly off with the shoe and linen fund![37]

---

[32] Members — uncles, cousins, and nephews — of the royal family.
[33] Blaze's Note: "See my *Hunting with a Pointer*, the Chapter on Saint-Hubert."
[34] A tournament.
[35] Blaze's Note: "that was the reason why one type of narrow ribbon is still called "favor." Besides, the ladies were not content just to give their ribbons to knights who fought in the tourneys. They tore their robes and threw the pieces into the area. One was seen who, at the combat's end, had only the one indispensable garment left. Was that for love or really from coquettishness? I will leave the solution of that question to my beautiful countrywomen."
[36] Combination company clerk/supply sergeant.
[37] See *Swords Around the Throne*, p. 584-585.

XI

The Surgeons

Most surgeon-majors were expert practitioners. They amputated an arm or a leg as easily as they drank a glass of water. I have even known some who made the uglier face over the latter operation. These gentlemen were full of zeal; you often saw them on the battlefield, risking their necks while they cared for the wounded. Many of them had both training and practical experience; a good many had to rely on experience alone, but from having to constantly treat wounds of all sorts they had learned as much as they needed to know.

However we were always getting young men from France who — through patronage and to avoid joining the army with packs on their backs[1] — had obtained, I don't know how, an appointment as a *sous-aide* surgeon after a 3-months course at the School of Medicine. Thereafter they learned by on-the-job training in the Army, at the expense of their patients. Woe to the poor devils who fell into their hands; escaping the cannon, they faced their scalpels — and— Believe me, that was very much like being between Charybdis and Scylla.

Monsieur Varno, one of the "Æsculapius-by-the-dozen,"[2] was a sous-aide of my regiment. The soldiers, who always have a nickname ready for everyone and everything, called him, "the doctor for salty soup." Laborie had asked him for several days to extract a tooth which was causing him much suffering, but the doctor kept putting off the operation under various pretexts — he did not have the time, a dangerously ill patient was waiting for him, he had forgotten his case of instruments, and the like. One day *aide-major* Margaillan,[3] a capable man, came by our hut. Laborie told him his troubles, and the tooth was extracted. Five minutes later, Master Varno appeared. Laborie, a natural-born joker, called to him: "And my tooth, when will you pull it?"

"Tomorrow, without fail."

"Why not today?"

"I don't have my instruments."

"Here is Monsieur Margaillan — he has his, and he'll loan them to you."

"Since Monsieur Margaillan is here, why don't you get him to pull your tooth? It's his responsibility and he's my superior, and I wouldn't think of interfering in his cases."

"I would be interfering in yours," the aide-major responded. "Lieutenant Laborie has confidence in you; he has been asking you to perform that minor operation for a long time. Here's my extractor — get to work."

Our doctor could not put it off any longer; he must show his skill. Laborie sat down and opened his mouth; Varno took the extractor — but he had barely inserted it into Laborie's mouth when Laborie spat out the tooth — which he had hidden under his

---

[1]   They used family influence to avoid being conscripted. *"Sous-aide"* translates as "deputy" or "under" assistant. See *Swords Around a Throne*, 281-286.

[2]   Æsculepius — Roman god of medicine and healing.

[3]   The second grade of surgeons — "assistant surgeon."

tongue — and proclaimed our beardless Æsculapius the most skillful dentist in the world. Never, he said, had he had a tooth removed so quickly and moreover without pain. We all chorused compliments on the doctor's dexterity. Varno thought that he really had extracted the tooth; but nothing pleased him as much as having Margaillan ask him, with grave imperturbability, for the method by which he had performed that operation so quickly and, especially, painlessly.

"It's very simple," answered Varno. "As soon as I touched the tooth, I turned my hand and — crack — it was done."

When we were in camps, to prevent fire, the soldiers were forbidden to have lights or fires in their huts. Consequently as soon as the sun disappeared they had nothing better to do than to go to bed. When the nights are long, you cannot always sleep, and in each room a story-teller takes it on himself to entertain the others. But this story-teller, who is

(JOB)

139

sacrificing himself for everyone's pleasure, wants to have their attention; you can understand that is right, nothing could be fairer. He therefore checks from time to time to see if his audience is still awake, and this is how he does it. In the course of his story, he occasionally slips in the word *"sabot;"* his listeners must respond at once at the top of their voices, "cuiller à pot."[4] Everyone checks to see if the man next to him has replied; if he hasn't, a can full of cold water, thrown into his face, will always awaken the most determined sleeper. You can easily imagine what an uproar all this *"sabot, cuiller à pot"* produces, since there is a story-teller in every hut. This lasts until nine o'clock when a roll of drums imposes silence on everyone. We often walked around the huts in the evenings to listen to those tales. It was most amusing, and we have heard some really funny ones which I would like to repeat here, but —. It is useless for me to tell you why I can't; you can easily guess them. One day, I don't know why, I tried to put one soldier's story into bad verse. Since I was obliged to leave out the interjections which give so much color to their speech, this story has lost much of its effect while passing through my hands—it is practically a translation. I really would rather not give you this specimen of my forgettable poetry, but it is necessary for the rest of this chapter.

The Marvelous Cure

"A certain doctor, passing across a battlefield
Found, that evening, a dead soldier;
Not exactly a rare find,
A saber blow, delivered by chance,
Had cut off the brave man's head.
Which lay there beside him. The Æsculapius halted,
And considering the extent of his skill,
He decided to reattach it to the old soldier's neck.
   He slashed, he clipped, he plied his instruments.
   The dead man endured it all, without a word.
   The surgeon carried him to his tent.
Although the dead man was heavy, he managed it by himself.
Like a thoughtful host he made him
   A bed from whatever he could find.
   The dead man had the best of characters
   As he proved then and there.
   Though his bed was harder than the rocks
   He did not complain. The next morning
   Our Aesculapius or our carabin[5]
   On getting up, went to see if his treatment
Had joined the head to the body. Good Heavens! What could one think?
   The corpse — what an admirable cure!
The dead man — he was no longer dead, he spoke, he shouted, he swore,
And he complained that he had been poorly bandaged.
To clear up the situation the surgeon examined him

---

[4]   A large cooking ladle.

[5]   Army slang for a *sous-aide-major*, since they customarily were armed with carbines. Spaniards, Cossacks, Austrian irregulars, and guerrillas/marauders in general considered hospitals easy pickings.

And saw that, inadvertently,
He had put the head on backwards –
The nape of the neck to the front and the nose to the rear,
In short, everything had been reversed.
"Oh what misfortune," he said, "And what remedy to apply."
"My faith, I don't know." He assembled a council
of all the skilled surgeons. He removed the bandages,
And consulted them, one after the others
And collected the opinions of them all.
Their judgement was unanimous
That, without losing any more time,
To properly replace his face,
That the soldier should be re-decapitated.
That decision reached, the surgeon prepared
To execute it immediately.
But the soldier rose from his bed,
"Monsieur, I shall keep my head
Just as it is now," he said with a shout
So loud that it could be heard a mile away.
"If I no longer can see where I'm going —
I now do have the advantage
Of seeing how to braid my queue properly."

Several days later we were gathered at the sutlers around a bowl of mulled wine, and I told that story to several officers, in the presence of doctor Varno. It would be difficult to be stupider than that aforesaid doctor; he was born to eat corn,[6] as you will judge. You could honestly say that he realized it, for he always wrote out his requisition for forage as follows: "Requisition for [so many] rations of oats, of corn, of straw for the subsistence of the undersigned." While I told my yarn, he listened with an icy seriousness: I can see him now, both elbows on the table, his head supported by both hands, apparently absorbed in the most profound meditations. Everyone laughed, talked, and drank about him, but the doctor heard nothing, saw nothing. After having passed several minutes in that position, he shouted in a thoroughly convinced tone: "NO! THAT IS NOT POSSIBLE."

We all knew that the doctor was a fool, but we hadn't suspected that he could be that badly off. Right away I received significant looks from everyone present and — seeing what sort of man I had to deal with — decided to have some fun at his expense.

"You think that's not possible?" I said to the doctor. "Don't you know that surgery has made astonishing progress during the last few years? The war has furnished so many subjects for their experiments that — after many unsuccessful trials, Larrey,[7] Dubois, and a number of less celebrated surgeons have learned how to restore a head as easily as they formerly fixed a broken leg."

"Well, this is the first time I've heard about it."

"When did you leave Paris?"

"Almost three years ago."

---

[6] To be a perfect ass.
[7] Dominique Jean Larrey, Surgeon-in-chief to the Imperial Guard.

"Oh — I see how you wouldn't know about it, since it's been barely eight months since the first successful experiment. Monsieur Dubois performed it on a criminal decapitated by the state executioner, and the fellow is now in perfect health. The Emperor has pardoned him, since it would have been really brutal for the poor devil to have been executed all over again. They are busy informing all army surgeons of this operation and the exact method of performing it, which will be quite useful. However we hear that one minor difficulty often complicates the operation: it is essential to stop the bleeding. To do that, the arteries must be closed with a certain cement, the formula for which is appearing in all the newspapers. Once that is accomplished, the rest is no problem at all. Perhaps they will discover the secret of replacing the blood when the doctor arrives too late to stop the bleeding. But until those experts can solve that problem, which will complete this sublime discovery, all our generals are to be assigned a surgeon who will follow him like his shadow and will be responsible for giving him first aid by stopping the flow of blood if a saber cut between his head and his shoulders should separate them. Later they doubtlessly will send enough surgeons into the army to watch over the heads of all its soldiers. That will be a great savings for France, since its soldiers will last a lot longer."

At once, ten officers interrupted me, giving examples to back up my statement. One had seen the operation performed; another knew a grenadier who had had his head reattached by that operation. Another added that, thanks to Larrey, the finest surgeon in the army, he now had the pleasure of talking with us, after having been decapitated by a big, six-foot devil of a Russian cuirassier. For three hours he had lain among the dead, and he congratulated himself every day to have been brought back to life among such good company. By way of proving his statement, he displayed as evidence a great scar around his neck, speaking all that time with utter seriousness.

"You've made a convincing case, gentlemen," said the doctor, "But — supposing that a head could be replaced and life restored — I still am not convinced that could be done if the head were replaced backwards."

"And why not?"

"Because the veins, the arteries, the nerves, and all the muscles which support the neck would not find themselves in the same relative positions which they had formerly occupied — instead, a nerve would be opposite an artery, a vein opposite a muscle, and nothing would work! I have carefully studied all that — if you knew anatomy, osteology, and pathology as well as I do, you would realize that it was impossible."

"I wouldn't pretend to argue with you, doctor — I lack the knowledge, and I must admit my lack of experience. But permit me a few suggestions. It seems to me that the parts of the human body are practically homogeneous; and you must have come to realize that this almost-homogeneousness — if I may be permitted to coin such

A PHYSICIAN, 2ND CLASS
BY KNÖTEL

a term — could result under certain circumstances in their being able to modify themselves and join together despite some differences — really too minor for us to consider — in their nature. Listen now and follow my reasoning carefully. (By now, I was having trouble following it myself.) Isn't it true that a rooster's spur is composed of horn and that his comb is made of flesh and cartilage. These two parts are really different, composed of different materials, and at opposite ends of the bird. However we all know and have all seen that a rooster's spur can be grafted onto his comb; all poultry-keepers have had that strange experience. If we hadn't seen it ourselves, we wouldn't have believed it possible. We see every day that a man who has lost a leg continues to enjoy life and get around easily enough; he has trouble only in certain movements, though he has lost arteries, muscles, nerves, and bone. Yet nature is so generous to us that one wheel the less does not stop the machine's movement. When you treat a broken leg, and the two ends of the bone do not fit together properly, what is the result? A callus forms, but — though you may limp — you've kept your leg. I understand very well that the parts of a head reattached to its body backwards would not all reconnect with parts of the same type, but it would suffice that a few are placed close enough to their original connections for life to be restored. The failure of the others to reconnect might cause a sort of callus and a crick in the neck that might be quite painful at first, but to which the patient would soon become accustomed — you know how we can get used to anything. You may even claim that his brain might not be as active or that he might lose his memory, but those minor inconveniences are nothing in comparison to death, which is always the inevitable consequence of decapitation."

As soon as my harangue was finished, the officers who had supported me continued in the same style, in a way that suggested neither the slightest doubts on their parts nor the least indication of connivance among us. The doctor hesitated: he did not want to appear ignorant, as he would be denying an established fact which he should know, or play the fool by believing a preposterous story. The risk was equal either way: he stared at all our faces, searching for some hint of irony or suppressed laughter, but we were all as impassive as a judge on his bench. Not wanting to risk either total repudiation or total belief, he took a middle course, saying as he left. "No on can persuade me that a cut-off head could be replaced unless the surgeon adjusts it exactly as it had been previously."

As soon as the doctor was gone, there was a storm of laughter, and everyone agreed that there was plenty of reason for it. Within days everyone knew the story; the doctor became the laughing-stock of the regiment, the target of endless jokes. Everyone made fun of him, even the little drummer boys who talked of cut-off heads whenever they passed him. His position became impossible, and the colonel was obliged to ask the minister of war to transfer him. He left. I have never heard anything more about him.

We were in Spain, at Soria, near the ruins of ancient Numantia.[8] A surgeon-major, who had a great interest in antiquities, employed all the laborers he could find to excavate them. From break of day until dark, he was among his workers whom he paid quite generously. This worthy man felt himself thoroughly compensated whenever an ancient potsherd or a medal, corroded by time, could be added to his cherished collection. He took his meals at his diggings, which he never wanted to leave. However, he neglected his patients — which may have been the best thing that could have happened to them.

[8] Soria is in northern Spain, west of Saragossa. Numantia was an ancient Spanish city, famed for long resistance to Roman rule, later a Roman garrison town.

One day the workers discovered a vase having the shape of those which we today have the habit of using to satisfy certain minor night-time needs. Chipped and cracked, it had the appearance of great antiquity. Our worthy surgeon-major took it up and examined it thoroughly; imagine, if you can, his extreme glee when he saw on its bottom, in still-legible letters, the name SERTORIUS.[9] A gold mine could not have given the good doctor that much happiness. Overcome by joy, he came back to his quarters to deposit that precious vase in a safe place. Looking at it, displaying it to the curious, was thereafter his sole occupation. He declared that his discovery would throw a new light on Roman history; that, so far, no one had found anything like it in the excavations of Pompeii and Herculaneum; that the best-stocked museums could show nothing comparable to this treasure he possessed. "For, in short," he would add," You can find weapons, utensils, and every sort of vase in all of them, but we do not know the names of their owners — while I, by unimaginable good luck, I possess a chamber pot unequaled today in any collection, and that chamber pot was owned by Sertorius."

We quickly learned that his antique vase was very modern, that two second lieutenants had buried it the night before in the area which was to be excavated the next day, and that they themselves had marked its bottom with the name of that famous Roman general. All that was said and repeated in whispers; it soon was a sort of comedy — all the army knew it except the good surgeon-major. He was so happy that no one wanted to have the act of disillusioning him on their conscience. He always believed that he possessed Sertorius's chamber pot. If I myself knew that good and respectable man were still alive, and that he might see my book, I would have suppressed this story. But that being doubtful, I shall not do so since it would really be unfair to keep it from my contemporaries.

[About 1 ½ pages dealing with a non-medical, non-military fuss in 1825 over faked antiquities has been omitted.]

I was visiting a sick officer at the moment that our antiquarian-surgeon came to visit him. The patient was in bed and had difficulty explaining how he felt. After each of his responses to the doctor's questions, the latter always said. "Good, very good, you couldn't do better." When he had learned all the circumstances of the sickness, he wrote two prescriptions.

"Listen carefully," he said. "The first is a potion of which you must take a teaspoon-full every half-hour; the second is a herbal infusion; swallow a soup spoon of it every quarter-hour. If you feel the effects of the teaspoon dose passing away quickly, you can take the soupspoon dose sooner. If, however the soupspoon dose upsets your stomach, you may delay the second teaspoon dose. This remedy is infallible and is indispensable for a patient in your condition. Everything depends on the regularity with which you take it. Remember now what I've told you."

"But, doctor, it's so devilishly complicated. I'll never be able to remember."

"Oh well," said the doctor, forgetting his role as a charlatan and reverting to his every-day self, "do it or don't do it, you'll get neither better nor worse — all that is good for is to keep up the patient's morale."

I met him one day, and he asked, "How are you?"

"Poorly. I have dizzy spells and a headache."

---

[9] Roman general (c.123-72 B.C.) who, left isolated in Spain after the defeat of the popular party in Rome's Civil Wars, established and long defended an independent Spanish state.

"You have too much blood. Tomorrow I'll have to apply a heavy application of leeches to it."

"With a pleonasm, doctor?"[10]

"No. With a hot cloth."

Captain L__ had been seriously ill. The doctor took great pains with him, but — seeing that all his prescriptions did not restore his health — he called in another doctor, and shortly thereafter the captain was much better. We often teased our antiquarian over the fact that this other doctor had accomplished what he himself thought impossible.

"Your colleague," we told him, repeating what we had overheard, "says that you treated Captain L__ backwards — you bled him when he should have been purged; you used emollients when it was necessary to use resolvents.[11] He also said that if the patient had remained under your care for another three days he would have been a dead man."

"Such conduct surprises me," retorted our doctor. "Between colleagues there should be mutual respect; and no doctor should ever state that his predecessor had been mistaken. It ill becomes Doctor R__ to come and take over my patients after I had them practically cured! But that isn't going to be the end of this; my honor will be too deeply committed. I shall have reparation for those proceedings. Yes, gentlemen, I shall meet him one of these days, I shall lead him before the commanding general, and I shall report his scandalous remarks. 'My general,' I shall add, 'here is a gentleman who vaunts himself as a better healer than I. You can reconcile our claims: station us in a hospital for fifteen days and put us each in charge of a ward of fever cases, and you will soon see which of the two of us kills the greater number of them.'"

You can imagine the pleasure those fever cases would have felt if those two characters, competing in their doctoring, had subjected them to every treatment that happened to pop into their heads.

I have said that not everyone in the army is brave. A good many soldiers, to avoid the inconveniences of bullets, pretended an illness in order to have a good excuse to enter the hospital. The doctors recognize them at first glance; they give them several doses of an emetic and one or two purgatives, and put them on a very strict diet: very soon our fine fellows, facing starvation, decide to behave themselves.

Soldier who have been in the hospitals for an extended stay come back to their regiments with a large number of medical recipes which they would try out on anyone. If they cured someone, that settled it; the surgeon-major lost his customers — and truly, whether by ability or simple good luck — they were sometimes successful.

While fishing in troubled waters, you often could catch a fish. In every village, you might find a local wise woman whose treatments put the service doctor out of business.

I had had the fever for three months. All the remedies prescribed by the regimental medical staff had failed. They had me swallow the contents of an apothecary's shop, and the fever remained firmly entrenched. "My lieutenant," a soldier of my company said to me, "if you're willing to take what I give you, you'll be cured. Believe me, doctors are blockheads. Follow my advice and if you don't get over that fever, you have my permission to have me shot."

---

[10] "Pleonasm" — The use of more words than are necessary to express an idea. Blaze apparently was strutting his education, hinting that "apply leeches" would have been sufficient. The doctor wasn't impressed.

[11] Emollients softened/relaxed tissues; resolvents caused swellings to disappear without festering.

A GENERAL RECEIVES VITAL MEDICAL ASSISTANCE (JOB)

Though I had neither the right nor the desire to so punish my alley Æsculapius if he weren't successful, I accepted his offer. I fully realized that I was going to take something that might kill a horse, but being an invalid had wearied me to the point that I did not hesitate to play double or nothing. The next day I swallowed the potion without asking what was in it — and I was cured.

"But what did you put in that drink," I asked my Aesculapius while thanking him.

"Oh — well, many things, my lieutenant; a little of everything — coffee, rum, sugar, lemon juice, pepper, salt, cloves, cinnamon, and, to top it off, a cartridge."

Gunpowder was a principal ingredient of all the remedies which the soldiers made up for themselves. Our surgeon-major to whom I told this story, claimed that medicine could have killed an ox; possibly he said that out of jealousy.

But don't make too much fun of the army doctors: I owe my life to one of them. I had fallen sick at Valladolid — cerebral fever, nervous fever, putrid fever — every variety possible — and more than enough to kill a man.[12] I knew that because the surgeon-major who attended me said every evening when leaving me, "He won't live through the night." The regiment left Valladolid and the doctor with it. I was left alone in a house where twenty to thirty officers of different outfits were billeted; none of them knew me and they did not even know that one of their comrades was in such a pitiful state.

One fine morning, my domestic[13] took all I possessed, put on my uniform, and went off to join the Spanish insurgents. I don't know if he thought me dead, or if, knowing me still alive, he had the cruelty to abandon me. However it was, I remained fifty-six hours in my bed without anyone suspecting it. At the end of that period a chambermaid came into my room to get it ready for a new occupant. Approaching the bed, the girl saw a corpse — me. Going down the staircase four steps at a time, she screamed out , "Un muerto! Un muerto!" The officers who were quartered in the house appeared at the doors of their rooms.

"What's going on? Why all that noise?"

"Upstairs — there is a man —"

"Well?"

"He is dead."

"We should seize the opportunity to bury him."

"Did he bite you, to make you yell so loudly?"

"No, but he really frightened me."

"Let's go see this dead man."

All of them climbed the stairs and gathered around my bed. "He's dead," said one. "No, he's not," said another. "He won't get any better," said Monsieur Krasniki, a Polish surgeon-major who happened to be among them, "but that's not important. I'll do what I can for him." That honest Æsculapius applied a half-dozen vesicants[14] to me, and the next morning I had regained consciousness.

As soon as I got my wits together and understood my condition, I fell sick again. However, though the only thing I had left in this world was my shirt, I strengthened my resolve with the aid of philosophy — I thought of Gil Blas[15] who had been robbed by Don Raphael and amiable Camille in Valladolid. "Gil Blas recovered from it," I said to myself, "why shouldn't I?" And I got well.

---

[12] These medical terms are almost impossible to identify; a horseback guess would be that Blaze had acute malaria, and/or typhoid fever, complicated by pleurisy or other afflictions.

[13] Civilian servant.

[14] To raise blisters, as a means of stimulating the system and taking the patient's mind off his other troubles.

[15] From the *Historie de Gil Blas de Santillane*, a 4-volume picaresque novel (1715-1735) by Alain R. Lesage. Set in Spain, it was really a satire on French society.

XII
Garrison Life

The priest must say his Divine Office every day; for the officer, drill is what the Divine Office is for the priest. There are few things more entertaining; after having done it, for thirty years, you must keep on doing it unless you retire. When you don't know it, you must learn it — which is only natural. When you've learned it, you must teach others — which is only fair. When all the regiment maneuvers expertly, it must keep on doing so to show how expert it is. The result is that you are always drilling. An officer is always going to drill or just coming from it. If his first sergeant approaches him, he is certain to hear these ritual words: "My lieutenant (or, my captain) we will drill today at such-and-such a time, if the weather permits."

Whenever I saw a man with a double stripe on his sleeve[1] approaching, I always expected the customary phrase; instead of letting him speak, I would interrupt him with, "If the weather permits, isn't it?"

"Yes, my lieutenant," he would reply, and we understood each other perfectly. Thanks to my forethought, I saved the poor first sergeant enough useless words to fill up four fine octavo volumes.

Captain G__ of the Imperial Guard had a passion for drill. I have seen him, sick enough to be in bed, drill men he extracted from his unit's guard house in the manual of arms. One day the time came, but no one appeared; he sent for his first sergeant.

"Well," he said to him, "where's my punishment squad?"

"Captain, the guard house is empty; we don't have a single man under punishment."

"That's your responsibility; punish some."

In ten degree weather,[2] he held those poor devils at "shoulder arms" in the courtyard, and woe unto anyone who made the least movement. Sometimes, frozen to their bones, they fainted and fell face down on the cobblestones.

"Is the musket damaged?" the captain would demand.

"No."

"Lucky for him."

Sergeant Roussel was an able instructor; no one knew better how to teach a soldier the manual of arms or to explain how to hold their shoulders while executing the oblique step. Being naturally good-natured he never sullied his prudish mouth with gross expressions, those guard-room oaths which other sergeants always employed. When he was really angry, he called his recruits *candidates.* "Look at those candidates — they are as limp as rags; they move like seamstresses who have dined on cabbage."

You understand that in marching a soldier should step off with his left foot. One day Sergeant Roussel, having his unit formed, commanded "March!" One soldier stepped off with his right foot, the next man with his left. Sergeant Roussel was in the rear of the

---

[1] The insignia of the company sergeant-major (US topkick) was 2 half-chevrons in gold (line infantry) or silver (light infantry) worn on the forearm above the cuff.
[2] Probably Rénumur or Centigrade measurement — approximately fifty degrees Fahrenheit.

column; this lack of harmony in those lines of legs shocked his exact mind — but in seeing the effect, he mistook the reason for it. Arriving angrily at the head of the column, he demanded: "Which of you candidates has both legs in the air?"

He did not have much knowledge of the art of spelling, even of the simplified version. One day, in making his guard post report, he gave the strength of his 4 man detachment by writing in large letters KATROM.[3] Sergeant Roussel was thereafter Corporal Roussel.[4]

Strictly speaking, he did not have to know any more. But consider Laborie, who had entered the service in 1780, made corporal in 1789 (doubtlessly because of the great events of that time),[5] then sergeant in 1794, and second lieutenant in 1806. Having supervised an issue of bread and wanting to report that it was not good and had not been baked sufficiently, Laborie wrote all that out as one word in this manner:

"Pinpaboninepaasecai"[6]

Well, why shouldn't I mention some colonels and generals who weren't any more learned. One said to Napoleon, "Monsieur, Sire, I don't know any *matics*, but I f__ well can use by saber" — and he was a general in the Imperial Guard and certainly no brigade ever was commanded by a braver man.

And there was that general in the Army of the Eastern Pyrenees who wrote his commander-in-chief. "We have no bread; no bread, no rabbits;[7] I have written to your headquarters; the coconut[8] has not answered me, wake up."

And there was another general who received the order to move his brigade up to Linz and take up a position *à cheval* [astride] the road to Vienna, and who—much like Don Quixote — was found actually *à cheval* [on horseback] in the middle of the highway, and would still be there, if new orders hadn't made him dismount.

And that colonel, commanding a fortress, who received an order to redouble his vigilance, so as not to be surprised by the enemy — the equinox was approaching, the nights would become longer, he should keep alert, and so forth. He checked his outposts, and his artillery, and when he was certain that everything was in proper shape, he reported: "When that bastard of a General Equinox shows up, we'll f— him with cannon balls."

But remember that these men had conquered all Europe; besides, you don't have to know everything to get yourself killed.

And also you can be a genius and still not know how to spell. Marshal Villars did not know how to write — or, if he wrote, nobody could read it, which amounts to the same thing. Yet that did not prevent him from being a member of the French Academy.[9] That Academy also invited Marshal Saxe to occupy one of its forty armchairs and got an illiterate refusal, declaring that he feared the ridicule his presence would invoke.[10]

---

[3] For "quatre" — four.

[4] Noncommissioned officers were supposed to know how to read and write.

[5] Beginnings of the French Revolution

[6] "Pin" (pain) = bread; "Pa" (pas) = not; bon = good. The rest is more difficult – possibly "inepa" is inapte (unfit) with "as" for another "pas" and "ecuri" for "cuire" (baked or done).

[7] Slang for "soldier."

[8] Apparently, at that time, a term of insult.

[9] Académie Française, established 1635 by King Louis XIII and Cardinal Richelieu, supposedly to consist of 40 of the most distinguished French men of letters, dedicated to the protection and perfection of the French language.

Let us return to Sergeant Roussel; he was good and respectable; he loved to pose as an educated man. When he found a rare stone, he put it in to his pack; if he found a book, a map, or a mathematical instrument in our bivouac (you might find almost anything in a bivouac), that too went into his pack. The good Roussel was loaded like a pack mule, but he compensated for that by explaining the uses of all those items to his fellow soldiers. Did you need a pen, a pencil, a compass, or a ruler, you could be certain of finding all that in Sergeant Roussel's pack. He even had a long telescope which he used not only to look at the enemy, but also to describe the weaknesses of the Russian or Prussian positions and the manner for which we might envelop them and end the war in one day.

When he was on duty at the outposts, he never limited himself to looking at what was near at hand. Perched on a high point with his telescope, his view reached the enemy's bivouacs. He could see very far, but one day he did not see what was going on nearby — a dozen enemy cavalrymen swooped down on him unexpectedly and the poor man and his detachment were made prisoners. That adventure reminds us of the story of the astronomer who fell into a well while studying the moon.

Drill bored me considerably, but I understood the reasons for it: When you had mastered it you had to do it, whether to teach it to others or to make sure you did not forget it. But one thing which I never could stomach, which was always disagreeable to me from first to last, is the guard mount parade.[11] How can one conceive that in real life reasonable men would be required to form up every day at noon in a public place, just to watch fifty-some heroes at thirty-five centimes[12] pass at ordinary marching step en route to the guard room, which they will occupy for twenty-four hours. All that is done with imperturbable seriousness. I have known officers who dedicated themselves to it with a truly admirable sincerity, to whom guard mount was as necessary as bread; who are ill at ease all day until they have taken part in one. Then, when it is finished, the colonel or the general turns to you and says, "That's all, gentlemen," and everyone goes his own way — until drill time.

On Sundays, they make the business much more striking and especially more entertaining. They add three or four companies who march past as if they really were part of the guard, and you can imagine the fine effect that produces. Sometimes they use the whole regiment, but then there is no one left to see them pass.[13]

After drill and guard mounting, you must count the theoretical instruction among the pleasures of our profession. This *"theorie"* consists of reciting every day some part of the school of the soldier, of the platoon,[14] or of the battalion for a senior officer who questions you. You can see old, gray moustached officers with thirty years of service stammering over their answers like young college students. (For regiments are like colleges in many respects: there are the same worries, the same emotions, the same rivalries on a much larger scale.) Because you have to read and recite that theoretical instruction, you end

---

[10] Hermann Maurice de Saxe (1696-1750), bastard son of Augustus II of Saxony, famous French general, victor of Fontenoy, author of *Mes Revéries* on the art of war.

[11] For absolute amateurs, this is the ceremony during which the old guard detail is relieved by a new guard.

[12] Reference to their pay.

[13] Blaze leaves out the local citizens, for whom this would be quite a show.

[14] Actually company. "Platoon" had become an obsolete term, but was still used in the drill regulations.

up knowing it; you have mastered it as thoroughly as the man who invented it. In that case, if your senior officers favored you, you might be excused from the periodic recitations, but at guard mount and drill everyone had to be present and nothing got you out of it. You spent four to five hours a day on those duties; count up how many hours you would have thus employed in thirty years' service.

During garrison duty, billiards were very popular. It was thus that officers frittered away their lives, wasting almost all the time they did not devote to their military duties. I say "almost all," because ladies claimed a part, and that certainly was the best employed time of all.

In France, an officer often has some difficulty in gaining acceptance into society; in Germany it is very easy, especially in fine weather. The fashionable people gather in the public gardens to pass the afternoons. The ladies bring their work; you see small groups of them everywhere, embroidering, sewing, trimming, talking over their coffee. All that goes on to the sound of music, amid an atmosphere of smoke from the pipes which the local gallants always have in their mouths. From the moment you become acquainted with a member of one of these groups, you are soon introduced into others, and within a few days you become a fellow citizen of their town. The Italians do their visiting in the evenings at public spectacles, from one box to another. The Germans do it in their public gardens; it is there that you meet everyone, that you begin love affairs, that you get out of them, if you can.

Germans are always smoking; they have pipes for every moment of the day.[15] A German has pipes of every value and every quality which he offers to strangers according to their social position or the degree of friendship he feels toward them. There are elaborate pipes to smoke in the public gardens while courting the ladies; there are others to smoke at home in his dressing gown. Finally a true German smoker must have a museum of pipes in his home. It is a drawing room which, from floor to ceiling, is so thickly hung with pipes that you can't make out the color of its walls. You will find pipes made entirely of metal, of wood, of all sorts of materials. It is a great favor to introduce strangers into this private place. You are served streams of beer, you are offered pipes, and the height of good taste is to ask for more before the other guests are half finished.

At Charlottenburg[16] I have seen the most singular historical painting.[17] It showed the young Frederick the Great making his first visit to the smoking room of his father, the King.[18] The courtiers are smoking; the king smokes; everyone has an enormous pot of beer. The scene takes place in a cloud of smoke. The young prince, just fifteen years old, advances timidly: The king hands him a pipe, the prime minister offers the stein of beer. Behold him recognized as a grown man, behold him, entirely German. The Romans gave the "virile robe";[19] the Prussians gave a pipe. Customs change with the years. The courtiers applaud joyfully, looking as if they are about to burst out in a hymn of praise. But you should see those square heads[20] and those square-cut coats! The creator of the painting must have used a T-square.

---

[15] It is not tragic, to think of these millions of people, growing up and flourishing without ever having experienced the tender ministrations of our present-day anti-tobacco zealots?
[16] Frederick the Great's royal palace, outside Berlin.
[17] Blaze used the word "tableau" which might mean either a painting or a diorama.
[18] Frederick-William I, 1688-1740, a careful ruler and thorough Prussian.
[19] An adult's garment, given to Roman youths as a symbol that they had reached manhood.
[20] Actually, a French nickname for Germans, adopted by the AEF in 1917.

We would gather at a cafe before going to guard mount and drill or on returning from them. It was there that we talked over the news concerning the army and our regiment and the barracks scandal. There we gambled, we drank, and smoked; there was always on officer ready for a game of billiards, a cigar, or a little drink. The little drink was something which newly commissioned officers did not dare refuse, for fear that they might be considered mere fops. Having a little drink is essentially a military custom; it gives you a certain "old campaigner" aspect, when — after having swallowed the blessed dog[21] to the last drop, you argue over some good reason for getting drunk. "If so-and-so makes corporal after length of service, he'll have to wait a while yet, Hey, down there—leave some room. You'll soon have lots of company,"[22] "My captain always knows when I am drunk, but he never knows when I'm thirsty." These habits are very harmful to the health; we knew that, but we wanted to do what the others did. For a long time I took my little drink because I thought it really necessary; for the relief of my conscience I regularly took my three or four little drinks every day.

These pleasures — if pleasures they are — are the result of idleness and very expensive. It isn't unusual to see officers who, because of that, use up their monthly pay and allowances well in advance. I have often been one of them; what I received was not sufficient to pay up my open account at the garrison cafe.

A second lieutenant whom I knew had been a sutler during the first campaigns of the Revolution, and in accordance with established custom, he had married Margot, a female sutler. On receiving his epaulet he had quit the profitable trade of selling drinks to other people, but he retained a very decided liking for taverns. Every evening he and his wife went arm-in-arm, she in a plumed velvet hat, he in uniform, to a cheap pot-house. There, while emptying a bottle, they sang at the top of their voices. Nothing was nicer than to see this loving couple bawling in chorus, "As soon as daylight," and that seriously, without laughing. Every day they started all over again; they couldn't sleep unless they had sung their drinking song clear to its last couplet. Whether the tavern was crowded or they were the only ones there made no difference; they paid no attention to anyone. Enjoying themselves as they did, you could say that they were very happy. Happiness! It is wheresoever you think to look for it.

In times gone by, when the regiment of Champagne[23] arrived in a town, it posted a notice on the door of the best cafe. On that sign "CAFE DE MESSIEURS LES OFFICIERS DU REGIMENT DE CHAMPAGNE" was written in large letters. Any nobly born individual could dine without payment. That latter was compulsory. Whenever a stranger, ignorant of the customs of those gentlemen, insisted on paying his own bill, they told him haughtily that the officers of the Regiment of Champagne were well pleased to give, but disdained to receive. Sometimes these strangers were offended, and often the resulting quarrels ended in expert sword thrusts. Such aristocratic customs were too high for our tastes and for our purses. In our plebeian cafes, everyone paid for his own meals, except when we invited one another.

Sometimes our casual love affairs ended very badly. Quarrels broke out with her parents or your rivals. Swords were drawn — a disagreeable thing because the results,

<hr>

[21] Apparently one's last drink.
[22] The reader may decide as to whether this is addressed to comrades already under the table or in hell!
[23] One of the six "Old" infantry regiments, organized in 1575.

whatever they might be, are always a painful memory in the life of an honorable man. And then the business of betrayals and infidelities...

Note particularly that you never are forsaken by any woman except the ones you love. The others pursue you desperately, for life. "When they love you — they love you," said Count Almaviva.

When we remained for a long period in a garrison, we had two major means of having a pleasant time. If there was a local lodge of Free Masons, we all joined it; otherwise we formed a lodge of our own. Everyone knew that, while seeking the philosopher's store,[25] the Masonic brothers loved to laugh and to dine. Many regiments formed their own lodge, with their colonel as its head.

At Stettin, almost all of the "profanes" — non-members — saw the light and joined us. French and Prussians, we were the best friends in the world, except that we had to exchange cannon shots whenever the circumstances required it, which was fairly frequently. Every fifteen days however, we held a meeting; nobody talked politics, and everything went very well. One of our comrades was still "profane"; he mocked us free masons and freemasonry every chance he had. Our initiation ceremonies, he declared, were good only to scare little children; when we dared him to face them, he would answer with a sneer that he was, "too big a boy to play games in church."[26]

However our entertainments were always held in our lodge. Not only could he not attend, but the next day he had to listen to highly exaggerated accounts of what had gone on the night before. That stirred him up; he was weary of taking his pleasures all alone, and so he demanded admission into our happy group. We told him therefore to prepare himself for the most drastic initiation in the memory of living man. He defied us to frighten him for a single moment.

The great day arrived. All our plans were ready; our man duly entered the "room of reflection,"[27] when the building where our lodge met caught fire. To end the day in proper Masonic style, we had prepared a lavish dinner. The kitchen was a magnificent sight: the stoves were lighted, the kitchen boys ran in all directions to carry out the orders of the head cook. A chimney, which doubtlessly had been too long without the services of a chimney-sweep, caught fire. The fire spread to the upper stories and set the roof ablaze. The drums beat the *Generale*,[28] the garrison turned out under arms, the firemen arrived and poured out torrents of water to put out the fire.

However our poor candidate was still in the "room of reflection." We had forgotten him — or if someone remembered him, they thought the fire would chase him out. Not at all, firm at his post, he did not budge. Luckily, his side of the building did not catch fire; if it had he certainly would have been burned alive. But if he wasn't roasted, he really was baptized — the hose of a pumper, striking him squarely on the head, gave him the finest shower bath that ever cooled the brain of a lunatic.

"You can't scare me," he shouted. "You can't frighten me with your straw fire.[29] I've seen bigger ones at Hohenlinden, at Austerlitz, at Jena." And our man continued, amid

---

[25] Since Masonic rites are secret, Blaze has used this ancient alchemist's expression as a substitute.

[26] Too mature to belong to any clique.

[27] A room, generally scantily furnished, where the candidate awaits summons to his initiation.

[28] The "long roll" – "To arms". Used as a general alarm.

[29] Which would blaze up quickly and brightly, but soon go out.

the smoke, the litany of battles he had seen. The firemen had to literally drag him out — if they hadn't I suspect he still would be there. "You never frightened me with your stupid initiation," he said, as they brought him our, "but you've certainly smothered me — I'll probably come down with a bad cold. Gentlemen, this went too far beyond a joke; I'm as soaked as if I'd fallen into the river." It took quite a while to get him to understand what had happened, to get him to realize that the fire was not a joke, and that we did not ordinarily roast our candidates in order to persuade them not to reveal our secrets.

After freemasonry came the theater. Acting is still a happy way to pass your time while you are young. At Magdeburg, the town play house was being used by some wretched German comedians; since they did not want to let us have it, we improvised another out of a forage[30] storehouse. The garrison numbered 25,000; each officer gave one day's pay a month for lighting, costumes, and decorations. Our theater soon was perfectly organized, equipped with scenery, and completely furnished. Since admission was free, we were always applauded. Tickets were distributed in the town, there was always a full house; in other words, we had all the pleasures of an actor's life without any of its inconveniences. Moreover, the wives of officers, commissaries, and ration service employees who acted with us were very friendly.

Marshal Villars always had a party of comedians with his headquarters; they played in barns, tents, or stables. As soon as the army halted, the scenery came out of the wagons and the theater was put up. Often, between two acts, the leading actress came out into the middle of the military audience. "Gentlemen," she would say, "tomorrow the theater will be closed because of the battle the Marshal will wage; day-after-tomorrow, we present, *Village Loves* and *The Rogueries of Scapin*."[31]

At Magdeburg the officer-actors did no other duty. Since the plays they presented amused their comrades, the latter took care of the guard details and drill, and everyone was satisfied. We played all types of theatrical works — tragedy, comedy, opera, and vaudeville. The orchestra, made up of the best bandsmen from all our regiments, was perfect. We put on certain plays in our Magdeburg show house as expertly as in the best French theaters. We received the new plays from Paris and had them rehearsed and ready as soon as in Lyon, Rouen, and Bordeaux. The poor German actors could not compete with comedians who worked for nothing, and so left to try their luck elsewhere.

At each performance, a number of tickets were distributed among the enlisted men. One of those worthy fellows had seen the *Citizen of Guadeloupe* twice; in leaving the theater the second time, he discussed it with one of his comrades. "It's obvious," said he, "that those people are really stupid to allow the same man to swindle them twice in succession. Well, I may be only a buck private, but I've got more sense than my captain — I'd have remembered that dirty trick from the first time."[32]

We often argued over the roles we were to play and — as usual — everyone wanted to have the most brilliant one. But nobody would accept a part which merely required them to deliver a letter; we would have to get an enlisted man for that.

All these little disagreements sometimes caused comical divisions among us: we separated, we were reconciled — just as in the Paris theaters.

---

[30] Forage — oats, hay, straw, and the like for the army's horses.

[31] The first has left no history; the second was a famous (1671) comedy by Molière. European practice at that time was to have two, usually contrasting plays each day.

[32] Obviously the gallant soldier was somewhat confused as to the difference between drama and real life!

One day, one of our young actors had the curtain raised for his own purpose: that done, he bowed three times to his audience.

"Gentlemen: My white cashmere breeches, which cost me forty francs have been ruined — someone poured all the oil in a lamp over me. You can imagine how angry that has made me. Certainly the thought of it will distract me while I act my part. I ask your indulgence if I do not perform as well as usual."

In the army some men wished to impose the military hierarchy and its subordination everywhere. One claimed the role of Alceste because he was a battalion commander; another, to that of Scapin or Mascarille[33] because of his position as a *commissaire des guerres*. One captain of grenadiers would never take the part of Trissotin because that character was treated as a villain by Clitandre, without being able to demand satisfaction.[34]

These pretensions were much stronger among the wives of the colonels and generals. They demanded a sort of subordination and shows of respect from the other women. Each one had a following, composed of officers of "her" regiment. You often saw them, like Achilles, go off to sulk "in their tent," taking with them a crowd of the discontented. But they soon became bored, diplomatic negotiations were begun, and all the dissenters would soon be back, with two or three rehearsed plays to enrich our repertory. It was like a hen which for a long time you think lost, but reappears one fine day, escorted by her happy family which she has raised secretly.

What fussing, rivalries, tittle-tattle, and gossip went on backstage! If we had been fortunate enough to have had some little newspapers in Magdeburg, their columns would have been crammed with spicy intrigue, but there were none; there was plenty of future opportunities for one, but that future never arrived. From all that I saw in our ludicrous affairs (I could even say from all that I myself had done), I have developed an aphorism that I advise all husbands to keep constantly in mind. This is it: "When a wife takes part in theatricals, the more she enjoys it, the greater the danger to her husband's honor (or whatever honor he may have)."[35]

The wife of a general, whom I shall not name, had been an actress at the Montansier Theater in Paris; now that she was a baroness of the Empire,[36] she was careful not to mention her former occupation. All those ladies who made fun of the noblewomen of the Saint-Germain suburb[37] were anxious to imitate them. This comely comedienne behaved in the same fashion, giving herself grand airs, which much displeased the captains' wives.

Though those malicious ladies whispered about why the general had married her and her behavior before her marriage — nay, even after her marriage — we did not listen to that bad-mouthing. The lady was pleasant and attractive; the women alone exulted over her indiscretions. She wished to play light comedies, she chose her parts (a general's wife could choose), and she played them wonderfully well. Her natural feelings took over; she forgot that she was a baroness. The desire to take charge seized her womanly heart, and in the hope of ruling our theater she admitted that she had been a comedienne in Paris. Nobody could have directed our work better than she did. Whatever she lost

---

[33] Alceste was the hero of Molière's "*Le Misanthrope.*" For Scapin, see note 31. I have not identified Mascarille.

[34] Character from Molière's "*L'Amour Medecin,*" 1665. Here again "satisfaction" means a duel.

[35] The greater the chance of her cuckolding him.

[36] The average general was made a baron in the new nobility Napoleon created.

[37] A strongly royalist district, favored by the "old" nobility.

in the way of social esteem, she gained as much in the matter of authority, and for women such compensation is always satisfactory. What they want, every time, everywhere, is to rule the roost. If you don't believe me, read the works of Voltaire.

The other ladies consoled themselves with loosing a flood of satirical verses, which the general's wife ignored. She was the arbitress of our pleasures; we all schemed to obtain a part opposite the one she played; some even intrigued to play two.[38] Her words created reputations and became veritable decrees and destinies. We called her the Geoffroy of Magdeburg.[39]

Her success in light comedy encouraged the general's wife to try greater roles. She wanted to "put on the buskin,"[40] and so played Phaedra[41] and similar parts. Unfortunately —

"Those who shine in the second rank are eclipsed in the first."

There is a world of difference between the "fol-de-rol" of Desaugier's[42] and the eloquence of Racine. Nevertheless, people who never had seen a tragedy played in Paris admired the general's wife as Phaedre. Laborie affirmed that the finest moment of that play was when Phaedre said to the nun, "It is thou whom you have named."

The citizens of Magdeburg, who did not exactly love us, were quite pleased when we invited them to our plays. I believe their city was never more sparkling than at that time. We also gave very fine balls, and of all possible balls, a garrison ball is the finest. The variety of uniforms produces a charming effect, especially when the garrison includes regiments of all the different arms.[43] Look at a Paris ball: the women compete among themselves as to the elegance of their finery; they have gowns of the most beautiful and varied colors. Gold, silk, lace, and gauze — all are lavishly displayed. The men, by contrast, dressed those everlasting black outfits, all have the appearance of returning from a funeral. We really should have a different style of dress for such different occasions, but until the English set us an example, we dare not get out of our old rut.

The French have a singular mania. They usually make fun of the English. When they have an Englishman in their plays, he is almost always a ridiculous character. John Bull is the ludicrous subject of an infinite number of cartoons — and yet, as soon as a fashion is imported from England, our fops and fine ladies always adopt it. Why they even imitate their style of dining. What good has it done us to have carried the gastronomic art to the apogee of its glory, to serve as a world-wide model of how to eat, if — returning to our original style — we chose to revert to the meals of Ajax and Diomedes[44] and devour an ox roasted whole? My dear fellow countrymen, I beg of you, let us go back to our pleasant, simple French dishes: abandon these huge meals, fit only for the Greek heroes of antiquity, or draymen of today. Let the English soak themselves in tea; above all, leave to them those glasses of warm water in which, after the dessert, each one

---

[38] To seduce the lady.

[39] Possibly the bloody-minded Baron George Jeffreys (1648-1689), chief justice of the King's Bench under James II.

[40] To play tragedies.

[41] Character from Greek mythology, heroine of Jean Racine's (French playwright, 1639-1698) tragedy, *"Phèdre"* (Phaedra).

[42] Marc Antoine Desaugier (1772-1827), French popular playwright and composer.

[43] Various types of infantry, cavalry, artillery, and engineers.

[44] In Homer's "Iliad", Greek heroes of the Trojan War.

performs his disgusting ablutions — almost as bad as vomiting — before his neighbors.[45]
Let us be French, and take care that we do not, from imitating imitators, end up ignobly
in the chamber pot.

"But it is the fashion! It is fashionable!" someone might say. It is not a matter of
amusing yourself; it is necessary that people think you are amused. You could have a
happy evening by gathering sixty people in a drawing room, but fashion requires that
you invite 400 to have a "rout."[46] Everyone suffocates, but that's of no importance. One
must be fashionable. We need ordinary pleasures, but it seems that high society is the
judge of whether our pleasures really are pleasures; if you amuse yourself quietly, you
are not really being amused. An amateur said to one of the most famous gourmets of
our times, "I have had an excellent dinner." The latter responded with admirable
composure. "That is not necessarily so. Tell me what you have eaten; I shall tell you
if you have had a good meal."

But let us return to our garrison balls. As in Paris, we marched a good deal, but we did
not dance as much. Our usual plan was to gather as many people as possible: in that way,
the lovers (there were many of them in our regiments) could be with the objects of their
affections, and the mothers — separated from their daughters by a wall of uniforms —
could not see what went on. Love notes were passed, hands pressed; glances and
thrilling hints replaced the dancing, and everyone found the ball delightful. Alfonso,
King of Aragon,[47] surnamed "The Magnanimous," once said, "The only difference
between a lunatic and a dancing man is that the latter doesn't remain crazy." Alfonso
was right, concerning those who go to a ball to dance. But, with the exception of certain
imbeciles who conscientiously, seriously, and in good faith caper through the affected
measures of "the hen" and "the cat's tail," most officers never danced except when
seeking a chance to begin a liaison — or to get out of one.

It's all the same with the women; the ball is nothing more than a pretext, a chance, to
see the lucky mortal whom they could not hope to meet otherwise. And, while an
affectionate conversation would be too conspicuous in a drawing room, at a dance the
music, the movement, and the crowd tend to conceal it. At a ball the ladies appear at
their greatest advantage, without counting their evening gowns; they can walk, skip,
come and go instead of remaining seated firmly on their haunches, straight as a stalk of
asparagus — a tiresome and unattractive position. Look at a woman face to face; an
instant later she will turn her head so that you can admire her profile.

Watch several young ladies gathered in a drawing room; they embroider, talk, read
— all very seriously. A young man enters, and they suddenly begin whispering; they
seem to be talking about something very pleasant because they laugh frequently. Their
countenances become animated, which brings out the brilliance of two beautiful eyes.
If, before the young man has appeared, the young ladies are wearing shawls, be certain
that, five minutes later, without fear of catching cold, they will have discarded everything
which would have kept him from being able to admire their slender figures. I have had
that experience a hundred times, and always the shawl has slipped behind the armchair.

Since we are talking about balls, I am going to take you to Spain for an instant, to tell
you about the fandango. We won't remain there long and soon — recrossing the
Pyrenees and the Rhine — we shall take a look at Vienna.

---

[45] Blaze apparently is referring to "finger bowls"!!
[46] Contemporary English term for a large-scale reception/evening party.
[47] (1385-1458), King of Aragon, Naples, and Sicily.

When Saint Anthony was alive, if the she-devils, to tempt him, had danced the fandango, I doubt that he would have resisted their friendly seductions for two hours. He would have needed triple sainthood to have kept from losing his self-control against all the lascivious positions contrived out of voluptuousness itself. And it's very certain that a hermit probably would be easier to overcome than a man of the world; when you have been deprived of everything, you are more easily tempted; when you have succumbed frequently, it takes much more to interest you.

Father Marti[48] once wrote a somewhat jocose description of the fandango. The austerity of my morals prevents me from giving you a translation.

The fandango is danced every evening in the theaters between the two plays. The audience gets an unspeakable pleasure from that spectacle; you see them squirm in their seats; they wave their hands; they stamp their feet in delight. Pliny[49] mentioned the fandango in his writings, but I don't know if they danced it with castanets in his days. The castanet is Spain's national musical instrument; everyone plays them. See that servant sweeping a staircase; she sings, and her song is improvised from everything that passes through her head. When she has finished a verse, she lays down her broom, waves her hands in the air, and sings a flourish while pretending to accompany herself with castanets. In Spain nobody can sing four notes without waving their hands and twisting their fingers. Everyone has that habit, from the old men to four-year-old children.

Nothing is as paltry as the typical Spanish play. Our worst melodramas are masterpieces in comparison. The most improbable affairs, the most bizarre adventures really please our neighbors. As playwrights, they were once our masters, but we have left them far behind us. To make them laugh, the author must insert some gross nonsense into a trivial, bombastic speech; to keep them interested, he must give them a matamore captain who kills everyone except the prompter.

Their *Saynetes* and *Tonadillas* are short works, full of songs, which they have instead of operas. They present them during the intermissions in such a way that a foreigner never knows what's going on. It's rather like reading two books at once, changing to the other book at the end of each chapter.

There is an unusual abnormality in Spanish morals. No country puts as much emphasis on the external aspects of religion as Spain. And possibly none permits a greater license in its theaters. To begin with, they dance the fandango everywhere — to stormy applause from priests, monks, and churchmen who openly admire the lascivious wigglings of the current favorite dancer. And yet in all the plays the ridiculous character, the thief, or the traitor is always a churchman. He is the scapegoat who is sacrificed for the laughter of the pit. In Spanish theaters they posture and kiss with a lewdness that makes hussar trumpeters blush.

We are not very devout in our good land of France but if the most decent of Spanish plays was presented in Paris, unless especially for the literary element, it would be greeted with whistles.[50] And yet these Spaniards, who every day applaud these indecencies, believe themselves perpetually damned if they eat a pork chop on Friday. Really, with all their pretenses, the Spanish are not more devout than other nations; possibly they are less. They don't comprehend the Christian religion; they reduce it to

---

[48] Unidentifiable.
[49] Roman naturalist/writer, AD 23-79.
[50] The European equivalent of booing.

a genuflection, to "Our Fathers" recited absentmindedly, to the statue of a saint who has done more miracles than the others.

At all the church doors they ask you for alms for the souls in purgatory. Your offering is destined to pay for masses which will be said — or may have already been said in spare moments — for their deliverance. This habit has passed into our [French] southern provinces; when you hand over a coin the collector thanks you with a "May you rest in peace." For that duty they select someone whose voice is sad, dismal, and monotonous; you get the feeling that he himself has been in purgatory several centuries and wants to get himself released.

All of these affairs did not keep us from amusing ourselves. We attended the theaters. The hall at the Corinthian Gate (in Vienna) was used alternately by French and Italian companies of actors. Though that hall was large, it was far from large enough for all the people who wised to attend. Besides an army in a capital helps mightily to fill up the seats of the theaters. We were not always able to find a place, but the green room[51] offered us a sufficient compensation. We weren't in the least interested in the play or the actors — we preferred to talk with the ladies.

[51] Room where actors/actresses gathered while off-stage.

XIII

The Official Visits

Official visits are really something so entertaining, both for the visitors and the visited, that it is a shame not to devote a little chapter to them.

A Chinese proverb rightly states, "When a man has ten steps to take, and already has made nine, he is halfway there." We others, who are not obliged to comprehend the language of the Celestial Empire, say it in prosaic speech of a cook. "The tail is the most difficult [part of a beast] to skin." When a regiment is changing stations and has completed its daily march, the soldiers can rest themselves in their billets, but the officer has not finished his travels. If he has arrived in a large city, he must spend two or three hours striding along the streets to visit the prefect, the general [commanding the garrison], the bishop, and the mayor, as required by the Regulations of 1791 — without any doubt a very wise law, but very annoying to those who must execute it.

Whatever time it takes, you must get on with it. We arrive, and the colonel speaks. "Monsieur Prefect, I have the honor to present to you the officers of the ___ regiment. I am glad that the orders of the Minister of War have stationed me in your city [or have routed me through it], giving me the opportunity to meet such a distinguished administrator as yourself."

"Colonel, I myself am very flattered to meet the officers of such a fine regiment. (Regiments are always "fine.") I was at the window when you marched in, and must say that your grenadier companies are superb. (Grenadier companies always are "superb.") "You have had bad weather today?" (Sometimes the prefect says that we have had good weather.)

"Yes, monsieur, but the roads of your department are so good, so well maintained." (The prefect bows.)

"Your voltigeur companies are composed of shorter men, but to me they seem strong, vigorous, neat, and full of spirit." (The colonel bows.)

"I have been struck by the appearance of affluence and happiness among all the inhabitants of the villages we marched through today." (The prefect bows.)

"As to your center companies, I cannot believe, after seeing them, that they had been picked over to form the elite companies." (The colonel bows.)[1]

"We have seen laborers along the road — young, broad-shouldered men, brisk and spirited. They sang while they worked."

"They were rejoicing that they would be selected by the next conscription; they're ready and willing to march. Your profession is so appealing, gentlemen, in this time of glory in which we live."

"Yours, Monsieur Prefect, is not less honorable."

"From which departments do you draw your recruits?"

---

[1] A French line infantry regiment of this period had 5 battalions, one at their depot and 4 "war" battalions. Each of the latter had 2 elite (one grenadier, one voltigeur) and 4 "center" (fusilier) companies.

"From the Ardennes, Finistere, and Calvados."[2]

"Those departments provide fine men." (This response is the same for all departments.)

"Yes monsieur, they are slow to accustom themselves to military life, but from the moment they catch on —"

"They're really good, I know that. Your regiment has proved it." (All regiments have proved their valor.)

"In the service of Napoleon the Great, that is nothing unusual."

"You are fortunate, gentlemen, to serve him on the battlefield. If I were younger, I would be marching with you." (And the prefect raises his head, stiffens his leg, and claps his hand to his sword.)

"If the Emperor has need of good soldiers, he has equal need of intelligent and conscientious administrators." (And the prefect bows.)

"Let us work together for the glory of the hero who rules us; gentlemen, we shall seek to imitate you."

The colonel bows, the prefect bows, everyone bows — it's all very touching. You then go visit the other authorities, where the conversation differs in certain minor respects. With the general, you "talk shop," with the bishop, you talk of his cathedral, which you have seen from a distance and which appears to be a superb edifice (something that colonels seldom bother to verify by visiting it.) But the grenadier and voltigeur companies and the fine type of your soldiers are always discussed. All this sometimes end with invitations to dinner which make for an agreeable diversion.

Speaking of dinners, I must not forget to tell you about those of Marshal Davout. This estimable general, for all his outstanding military talents, had one serious fault which made him many enemies among the army's epicures. When he invited us to dinner it was a dirty trick, not because his meals were unceremonious, but because they were hopelessly brief. You sat down and ten minutes later you had to get up because your host had set the example. The first time that I had the honor to sit at the marshal's table, I was caught. Hardly had I cut my bread and cracked a few jokes by way of getting acquainted, when people began getting up.

"What's going on?" I asked.

"We're finished."

"The dinner?"

"Yes."

"But I've not even began."

"That's your hard luck."

"This is an abominable trick — a regular ambush!"

"Right you are! But the marshal imitates the Emperor."

One should not always follow the example of great men.

However, when I was invited the second time, things went differently. I maneuvered quickly, my attacks were swift; everything within my reach was gobbled up. I finished well ahead of the others, and I remarked to those same table companions that I though the meal lasted much too long.

Marshal Turenne[3] also had that mania for quick meals. In the lives of great men you always find some extreme contrast, a deep shadow, and "I-can't-name-it," which cries

---

[2] Ardennes in modern Belgium, Calvados in Normandy, Finistere in the northwest corner of France.

[3] Marshal of France, 1611-1675. Louis XIV's greatest general.

out against them. The foreign officers, volunteer amateurs, attached to Davout's headquarters, did not in the least appreciate his antisocial manners. As they said, "These [French] gentlemen no sooner have left the table than they start asking one another, 'What will we do now?'" "Heck! We were enjoying ourselves, we should have kept on eating. You tell us that you have the most important business[4] in the world to take care of, and here you don't understand how to go about it. Why not continue this most important business — or at least let us do it by ourselves?"

These worthy officers reasoned very logically.

We should not imitate the Spartans.[5] They knew only how to die — truly a virtue when you never can dine properly. We are far from the sumptuary laws of Philip the Fair,[6] who prohibited serving more than two sorts of meat with any meal. Later, Charles IX[7] permitted three courses, each of six dishes. This was all very well, but he also ordained that the soup would be considered the equivalent of a dish, and there he was wrong. As everyone said, this was a heinous heresy by so orthodox a king. He ruled also that only one thing could be put on each plate — for example, one capon, one rabbit, or one partridge. If you ate two partridges, that was two plates — all of that under the penalty of a fine of 200 *livres*. If the offense were repeated, the cook was publicly whipped and then banished from France. A regulation truly worthy of the hero of Saint Bartholomew![8] Really, long live the Charter! Hurray for representative government!

Let's talk about the Emperor Geta.[9] He was really a different man than Turenne, Davout, and Napoleon. He would remain at the table for three consecutive days; his foods were served in alphabetical order; the names of the dishes served in each course began with the same letter, and that honored man's dinners always consisted of six courses!

In the *Grande Armée*, almost all the generals had a soldier-cook. Since the conscription covered all classes of society, cooks were no more exempt than anyone else. But once their talents were recognized, we were very careful to guard this gentry from the hazards of war and their precious health from sentry duty in bad weather. They had no other responsibility than to perfect the art of good living and they always developed a high military reputation by exhibiting the skills they had acquired in the schools of Véry, Beauvillers, or the Frères Provencaux.

But these artists did their best work only on campaign, in the bivouacs or certain cantonments occupied in time of war. Then, receiving the necessary raw materials from all sources, they had only to prepare them in ways inspired by the genius so often found under a chef's cap. Under those fortunate circumstances, the generals and colonels would invite their officers to dine; on all sides you could hear the clinking of forks. Everyone held open house; the peasants supplied the where-with-all, and nobody troubled themselves about it. But the moment order was reestablished, when we went back to garrison duty, many of these cooks became unnecessary. Reduced to producing a modest pot-au-feu, their skill was useless; they got of out practice.

---

[4] Eating.

[5] Famous in ancient Greece for the simplicity of their diet.

[6] King of France, 1285-1314, and a hard, grasping man.

[7] King of France 1560-1574.

[8] "Saint Bartholomew's Day," the massacre of Huguenots during a proclaimed truce in 1572.

[9] Briefly co-Emperor, 211-212 AD with his brother Caracalla, Blaze's story probably is mostly myth.

"Oh, my lieutenant," one of these artists said to me one day, "Yesterday I made stew; today two eggs on a platter — what a lousy job I have here! Can't we have another war pretty soon?"

I seemed to see Corneille and Racine fallen to the role of public scriveners, drafting letters for the wives of the neighborhood. When that cook I mentioned was on a fat farm with plenty of livestock and had a free hand, God knows what a frightful massacre followed. That man could ruin a province in three months. A week's sojourn by him and his master was as bad as a hailstorm and a conflagration combined.

This master had the world's most adaptable stomach. When his cook was functioning, or when he was billeted on a rich man, he ate everything and lots of it; he devoured enough to feed a company of drum majors. He claimed that when one was worn down, it was necessary to replace what one had lost by nourishing food. But when he was in a town where he had to expend his own money every day to keep his stomach functioning, he cut his consumption to the quick — the pot-au-feu, omelettes, and ration bread became his usual menu. "To keep in good health," he would say, "one should live simply." I really believe he would have eaten the Spartan black broth[10] if someone had offered it to him free.

How he loved money! If you gave him some good news, he would immediately exclaim, "That please me as much as if you had given me money." The word "money" was always strongly emphasized; when he uttered it he extended his hand with his fingers crooked; as if ready to seize it.

Harpagon[11] fired his servants before New Years, to avoid having to give them the customary gifts. My miser, without ever having read Moliere, did almost the same thing by instinct. The day before 1 January he put his colonels and battalion commanders under arrest, to avoid giving them the usual dinner the next day.

You can see how, by such methods, it is not difficult to get rich. Spend nothing, have a large salary and so forth and so on — that's the way to keep your fund quite full, as the soldiers put it.

The Emperor gave his generals endowments and gifts since they had many expenses. Some of them spent too much, but most sinned excessively in the opposite direction. General L___ arrived at the Tuileries one evening. Napoleon shook his hand and noticed that drops of water sparkled on the gold lace [of his coat]. He turned and ordered the first available chamberlain to go find out what sort of vehicle the general had arrived in. The chamberlain soon reported that he had come in a public hackney-coach; since these licensed cabs were not allowed into the Tuileries courtyard, the general had to come some distance on foot, which explained the presence of the rain drops.

The next day, a chamberlain arrived at the house of the general with the damp coat.

"The Emperor has ordered me, monsieur, to offer you this carriage and these horses; all are of the best that could be found in Paris. The coachman and the footmen have been paid for one year. Here is an account of the cost; it will be deducted from your pay."

The Emperor had his reasons: he wished you to spend freely and to have faith in his star.[12] [In earlier times] the Duke of Montmorency, passing through Bourges, saw his nephew, the Duke of Enghien, who was attending a school in that city, and gave him 100

---

[10]   A broth made with pork, cooked in blood, seasoned with salt and vinegar. Only Spartans ate it willingly.

[11]   Principle character in Moliere's comedy, *"The Miser."*

[12]   Not to hoard up money against a time of troubles.

pistoles[13] for minor expenses. Some time later he returned, and asked Enghien what he had done with that money. "Here it is," said the young prince, showing his full purse. Montmorency took it and threw it out the window. "Learn, young man, that a great noble does not hoard money Spend, gamble, or give!"

General Friant was not only a very brave man, but also a very worthy man whom everyone loved. When we paid him a formal visit he did not harangue us; there was not the least bit of phrase-maker in his character. He said little, but what he said always impressed us because it came from his heart. His features tanned by the Egyptian sun, his alert and brilliant eyes, his naturally martial posture combined to give his words a pungency which many orators longed to add to their high-flown bombast, such as "Welcome, my comrades. When ones sees you, one wants to fight. Would you even think of making peace when we have such regiments?" Friant said what he thought. Even when he simply said to us, "Come in, gentlemen. I'm very happy to see you," you could see that he was speaking the truth. General Friant was an estimable and deserving man. No officer was afraid to go to him; none left him discontented. That which I say concerning officers also applies to sergeants, corporals, and buck privates. That man had the ability to make himself loved by everyone. That talent is rare.

Other generals had adopted aristocratic habits, savouring of the times of Louis XIV; when you visited them, you were received with ceremony: you would have thought yourselves at Versailles in the days of the old monarchy. Some of them even scorned the title of "general," preferring "your highness" or "excellency." Turenne considered his title of viscount, which came to him by chance, more important than that of "marshal of France."

It is surprising that in the imperial army, daughter of the armies of 1792, the change was so rapid from republican rudeness to servility. The patriots of the revolutionary levies quickly adapted themselves to the manners of the old royal court, and that without any objections. Leaving their cottages for chateaux, they were not embarrassed to take up the trade of tyrant. The foremost of them became princes, dukes, and counts; their subordinates barons and knights. None of them happened to think that they might be losing something by abandoning the glorious title of "citizen." Those who remained "merely monsieur" said nothing because they feared it would delay the day when a Westphalian patent of nobility[14] would make them members of the privileged castes. Nevertheless, these new nobilities were honestly earned; won sword in hand, they were reward for bloodshed all across Europe. Friant had three horses killed under him at Austerlitz, and so put three horses' heads on his coat of arms. I do not know of a nobler blazon.

The French officer, along with his pride and his shining bravery, is a bit of a courtier. His habit of obedience to his superiors, combined with a thirst for promotion, leads him to adopt a flattering attitude toward those who might help him along. At that time, a line written by your commanding general would mean a promotion, possibly a title;[15] your name inserted in the after-action report would make your military reputation and assure your future.

---

[13] Bourges is a city in central France; a pistole was a gold coin equal to approximately 10 francs.

[14] This may be a bit of sarcasm: King Jerome Bonaparte of Westphalia was wildly lavish with awards.

[15] All generals more-or-less automatically became barons.

When we marched in Spain the officer commanding the advance guard would summon the mayors of the villages through which we passed and order them to ring their church bells when the commanding general arrived. He had learned that speech in Spanish by heart, but that was all the Spanish he knew. Sometimes the mayor replied, "Senor, we have no bells." The officer, not comprehending that reply, did not answer but went on his way, repeating his set speech.

When we were in Posen, the king and queen of Saxony and their daughter, Princess Augusta, arrived, en route to Warsaw to visit their new subjects in that Grand Duchy.[16] The garrison received them with military honors, and before us passed the biggest collection of old carriages that I have ever seen. I don't know where that good prince found all those old wrecks that carried him and his entourage. Certainly they must have dated from 1515 when the first carriages were built in Germany. And you should have seen all the officers of his court and his personal servants. Their get-up, their coats, and especially their wigs, which terminated in a queue a yard long. It outdid anything you've ever seen even in a burlesque show.[17]

The next day, 1 January 1808, all the French and Polish officers had the honor of being presented to their majesties. During that visit General Dombroski[18] provided us with a really comic interlude. He stood next to the king and queen, introducing the Polish officers one by one — stepping back and forth, speaking, saluting, and clashing his spurs in the Polish fashion. In turning, he caught one of their rowels in the queen's gown; the floor was slippery and he lost his balance and fell. The queen's dress was ripped from top to bottom; she would have fallen too if someone had not caught her. Everyone there was gripped with the urge to laugh, but no one dared and we stifled it. Nothing was funnier than the sight of the bronzed face and moustaches of the old general. He confounded himself with excuses, he could not find strong enough expressions. I believe that he never, in all his campaigns, found himself in such an unhappy position. What did the king do? The king started laughing, the queen joined in. Their example was contagious; everyone really roared — even, finally, the old general. Probably no sovereigns reception was ever so joyful. Everyone laughed until it hurt and went on laughing, even out on the street after we left.

Since I have told you about General Friant, I must also tell you of how he maintained law and order. His method was somewhat rough and ready, but his common sense solved problems faster and better than all the mysterious workings of diplomacy, ancient or modern. Of all the Jews in the world, the Jews of Poland are the least Christian. Under the pretext of buying or selling, they would visit the billets of our officers; if no one happened to be there, they stole everything they could get their hands on. In Posen one fine night they carried off the horses and wardrobe of a battalion commander of my regiment.

The next day, General Friant sent grenadiers to bring the twelve principal Jews of the city, led by their rabbi, before him. This is the speech he made them on that solemn occasion. I was there, and can repeat it, word for word.

[16] In 1807, Napoleon created the Grand Duchy of Warsaw out of Prussia's former Polish provinces and placed it under the nominal rule of King Frederick Augustus I of Saxony.

[17] If you can, read the description of this visit in *"In the Wake of Napoleon, The Memoirs of Ferdinand Von Funck,"* London, 1931.

[18] General Jan H. Dombrowski, 1755-1818. Organizer of the Polish Legion in Italy, 1797.

"Gentlemen," said the general, "you are all thieves."

"But—"

"Silence! Last night you stole an officer's horses and clothing. Here is an exact list of what you took."

"We didn't do it, general."

"Shut up! If it wasn't you, it was your brethren, but it is you whom I hold responsible for recovering everything. To get that done, I'm sending you to jail. You can write to your thieving friends. Implore them, or command them. I don't care which, but everything must be returned within twenty-four hours. Everything! Do you understand? If the least thing is missing, the Jews of Posen will pay a fine of 6,000 francs, which I estimate to be the value of the stolen objects."

"But — however —"

"Silence! Not one word more. And — if everything is not returned tomorrow, I shall billet ten grenadiers on each of you. Take them out and lock them up!"

During that night the horses were brought to the battalion commander's door; on their backs was his clothing. Not even a handkerchief was missing. In place of his old epaulettes, the officer received new ones, proving that the old ones had already been melted down. General Friant's speech produced excellent results; from then on the thefts stopped.

The officers whom the Jews had robbed previously had hoped that a severe vengeance would smite the children of Israel. They were disappointed when everything was returned, claiming that such reparation was not enough and that — to satisfy their collective anger — some Jews must receive physical punishment. The honorable society of shavetails took up that cause. Full of bright ideas, we discussed it at our mess (that was where we considered all important questions) the next day. We laughed and we drank deeply; after developing, discussing, and rejecting several plans, we all signed a petition to General Friant, requesting that he grant us a special allowance of one Jew, who would serve as a scapegoat for the sins of all his fellows. Later I often heard that the general had said that he never laughed as much as he did on receiving that singular request.

"You'll be robbed," I said one day to an officer I knew "You either don't close your door, or else you leave the key in the lock, which amounts to the same thing."

"Don't worry," he replied. "If someone robs me, I'll be able to smoke him out, because I always carry a list of everything I own with me."

"That's a bright idea — at least you can be confident that nobody will steal your list."

French soldiers have disagreeable memories of those Polish Jews. The Polish Jew is not a Pole. He is Jewish, always openly at war with the whole universe. He does not at all resemble a French or German Jew, but is a unique species. In short, he is a Polish Jew.

One day when I was absolutely without a sou, a state in which I sometimes found myself, I tried borrowing from my friends. Montro, one of them — or a pretended one — resembled the ant in the fable.[19] He was by nature adverse to lending money, and refused me, claiming that he himself was penniless. I believed him — or at least pretended to.

Several days later we were eating and — unlike his usual habit — Montro was the last to appear. He was pale, choking with anger, anxious to speak but unable to do so. He had so many things to say that his words, pushing their way out all at once, jammed up

---

[19] Aesop's story of "The Ant and the Grasshopper."

in his throat. We heard, by bits and pieces, several interjections — very expressive no doubt — but not enlightening.

"What's the matter with you? Are you sick? Do you have a fever? Are you crazy?" Those questions and twenty more appropriate to the situation, were directed at him from every corner of our table. At last our man, getting a grip on his emotions, told us he had been robbed during the night; that a wallet containing fifty beautiful louises, saved up one by one by denying himself everything, had vanished — that he suspected his host, a Jew, of being the thief — and that, if he could gather enough evidence, he would see him hanged.

Montro was not liked by his comrades; he lived like a bear and a *grigou*, to use a barracks room expression.[20] At first glance I could see that his misfortune amused everyone — that, far from being sorry for him, they were saying to themselves, "So much the better. Good for the Jew." I decided to use his loss to avenge myself a little for the rebuff I had experienced. Assuming a mock-tragic expression I lectured our happy group. "Gentlemen, our comrade certainly has the fever: his obsessive hoarding money while he was in good health has so affected the fibers of his brain with the words "money," "pay," "golden louises," that today when he is sick they continue to dominate his mental functions. The craze to accumulate fifty louis which possessed him when he was well, makes him believe today that he actually had them; his fear of losing them once he did have them has been changed, by this attack of fever, into the certainty that they have been stolen.

"God forbid, gentlemen, that I should suggest something of which I am not certain! I would not do that, and you all know that. Recently I needed 100 francs, which one of you most obligingly loaned me. Our comrade, from whom I asked that sum earlier, told me that he was in the same state as me. I believed him because he gave me his word of honor. Now, gentlemen, an officer's word of honor is an inviolable thing; we must all believe that. We must believe his statement, and whatever he has said since then in his fever-delirium should not cause the slightest suspicion in our minds. I have concluded that his word of honor was entirely correct and complete — and that what our poor, sick comrade has said just now must be considered meaningless. And, in view of his present condition, we'd better get him into bed right away, without supper."

Mirabeau,[21] thundering from rostrum never made a greater impression on his listeners; applause broke out everywhere; the ringing "Bravos" nearly shook the house down. Montro furiously attempted to reply, but was drowned out by shouts of "Go to bed! Go to bed!" Then Doctor Magaillan, who was among us, arose, said that the case was his responsibility, and prepared to take Montro's pulse. Montro resisted, but four big fellows pinned him to his chair. After he had counted Montro's pulse, the doctor announced with comic gravity that the sickness was "gastro-cephalic,"[22] and that Montro must be bled, put on a strict diet, and given a strong purgative to clear his mind — and, while awaiting that treatment, he must get to bed.

[20] "Like a bear" — solitary and unsociable. Grigou now means an "old screw," "miserable curmudgeon" — then it may have been even more expressive.
[21] Honoré Gabrial Victor Riqueti, Count de Mirabeau, French revolutionary leader and orator,1749-1781.
[22] An invented malady — "stomach-head."

Montro's eyes bulged; he foamed with rage. Every time he tried to speak he was drowned out by thirty voices from all directions, "You are sick!" — "You have a fever!" — "You are a gastro-cephalic case, the doctor said so."— "If you aren't sick, you certainly look it!"

"You will give me satisfaction," he shouted, leaving in a fit of fury almost beyond description. We told him that the insults of a man out of his mind from fever were meant nothing, and that he'd better run along to bed.

The absurd part of this incident is that Montro was sick, that he really had a fever, and that the doctor's whole prescription was applied. When he was cured, our man tried to pick quarrels, but we soon let him understand that he was outnumbered, and eventually we all were friends again.

I never have known anyone who loved money like Montro did. That passion is rare among young men in the army; their main objective is to enjoy life and not to hoard treasure. But when Montro received his pay, he rushed to a Jew and exchanged it for gold coins. These he stowed away in a leather money belt which — since that experience I have just described — he always wore. If this exchange left him with twelve or fifteen odd francs, he would borrow enough to enable him to get one more 20-franc gold Napoleon. While slipping that in among the others, he never failed to quote magniloquently:

> "Lusignan ended his career in chains
> Never again to see sunlight."[23]

However all of Montro's "Lusignans" did see daylight. The cossacks who killed him put them back into circulation.

But to return to our official visits; it was especially on 1 January that we really staged them. During that happy day, those who enjoyed them could have that pleasure, heaped up and overflowing. It began very early in the morning and lasted into the evening. If you were in Paris, you began again the next morning, which was even better.

All these visits were made in order from grade to grade; the second lieutenants, after having received the compliments of their sergeants and corporals, took them all to the first lieutenant, who took them to the captain. All three grades then went on to the battalion commander who, followed by his party, went to the colonel. The latter, with all his group, went to the brigadier general. There, other groups of officers joined in to wish him a happy new year, and then everyone went on to the major general's[24] where you met the delegation from the other brigade, with which the business recommenced. You can imagine how this snowball — always increasing, never diminishing — could end up getting quite big. That is why the Parisians are all astounded on 1 January when a horde of officers blocks the passage of the omnibus.[25]

At each stop, you talked shop a little so as not to get out of practice. That day, small offenses are pardoned; the guard house is emptied — but, since you consume a dreadful number of drinks, the next day sees it filled up again, which evens things up.

---

[23] Lusignan — one of the great French medieval noble families. One, Guy, was briefly King of Jerusalem.

[24] Here Blaze used the post-Napoleonic terms of "maréchal de camp" and "lieutenant general" instead of the Napoleonic "general of brigade/of division."

[25] The horse-drawn equivalent of the modern public bus system.

Most of the important people we visited officially while on the march would invite us to dinner the next day, if the regiment were going to pause there. At Fulda, half of our officers were invited by the ruling prince-bishop. He was a man of high intelligence and great learning, small and thin with a face that reminded you somehow of a monkey. Being a bishop, he received us wearing a violet cassock. He had a very cute monkey, dressed like a Versailles courtier — spangled breeches, plumed hat, embroidered coat, sword — nothing was lacking. The animal gamboled around his master, imitating the salutations it saw him make, and rendering them to everyone.

Soon a servant announced that dinner was ready; the bishop invited us to enter the dining room, and everyone hurried to obey those kindly words. All had left the drawing room except the bishop with his monkey and an officer who felt it poor manners to go first.

"I beg of you, sire — after you."

"But, monsieur, this is my home."

"At least let monsieur your son go first."

At those words, a crash of laughter, like the explosion of a gunpowder factory, burst from all around the room. The bishop laughed so hard we feared he might hurt himself. The officer alone remained solemn — the good fellow never comprehended what had happened.

I shall end this chapter with the story of a banquet in Berlin to which I was invited by one of the senior officials of the military administration. Our host did the honors with typical French urbanity, though from time to time he expressed regret that — his wife being in Paris — his bachelor's home could not give us the reception he would like to, etc., etc.

Those oratorical precautions were really unnecessary for the dinner was splendid and very well arranged. Suddenly, and while we were assaulting the second course, a four horse carriage rumbled into the courtyard; we heard the postilions' whips; the servants scampered, shouted, and jostled each other. A lady swept into the dining room, and our host found himself in the arms of his wife. Because she could wait no longer to see her beloved husband, she said, she had braved the distance, the weather, and the bad roads. So strong was her wifely tenderness, the love that possessed her, the worries over her distant husband that tormented her, that she would have gone to Moscow, even to Tobolsk.[26] Paris without him was a mere desert; she had not wanted to warn him of her coming, believing that the surprise would please him as much as it did her.

Her husband made no response to all of this. He looked troubled and embarrassed, which contrasted sharply with his wife's joyful face, playful voice, and light-hearted manners.

"Set another place," said he to the servant standing behind him.

Those were the only words he uttered during the entire meal But in compensation his wife received the compliments of all the other guests. The conversation covered the vexations of a long trip and the pleasures of Paris. The lady appeared to pay no attention to the chill reserve of her spouse. She was very pretty, friendly, full of life and grace and she seemed to say, "I am cleverer than he is. I'll get all this straightened out tonight." But she really underrated him.

Just as we left the table, the husband spoke loudly to his loving wife.

[26] In western Siberia.

"Madame, your horses are ready, the postilions are in their saddles, and you will immediately take the road back to Paris."

"That's not a nice joke," said the lady, pretending to laugh heartily, but we could sense she did not think it was a laughing matter.

"I don't jest, madam. Go, and bon voyage!"

"But I want to spend at least a month in Berlin."

"You will not stay a day, not one hour."

"But, my love, I don't understand you."

"And I, madame, I understand you very well; you had your reasons for coming to Berlin, I have reasons for sending you back to Paris, and that at once."

"But I can't leave now. It's night, the weather is frightful, the roads are horrible."

"All that means little to me. You should have foreseen those inconveniences before you left. Gentlemen," and he turned to us, "I call on all of you to witness that madame arrived in Berlin at six o'clock in the evening, that she is leaving at eight, that during the short time she was here, we were always with you without being alone for a single instant. At present, madam, I leave you. Go. Say what you will about me, but you must realize at least that I am not your dupe."

Our position was most embarrassing; we guests looked at one another in astonishment. The lady was not happy, but she left that difficult scene with a certain aplomb. Women can rise to the occasion, and sometimes we blush more than they do.

Madame departed; some time later she brought a son into the world. I do not know if he was named Hercules.[27] Our host had planned well, but he nevertheless was declared the legal father of that interesting marmont.[28] He could produce thirty witnesses, but the imperial courts always gravely responded, "Hic pater est quem nuptiae demonstrant."[29] I shall not give a translation of that legal principle since I am certain that all the ladies understand it thoroughly.

---

[27] The Hercules of Greek myth was a bastard.
[28] A little monkey/brat.
[29] "The father is whomever the wife says he is."

XIV

The Reviews

A review is sometimes an amusing spectacle for civilians whether seated or standing in the pit; but for the actors it's something else entirely.[1] The first can leave whenever they want to, the second have to stay until the end of the show.

When the Emperor ordered a review at noon, the generals inspected their commands at eleven o'clock; the colonels had their regiments under arms at ten. The battalion commanders want to assure themselves that everything is in proper order and so begin checking at nine o'clock. And so it goes on downward until you reach the corporals, who turn their squads out at five in the morning All these successive formations weary a French soldier more than a day of combat. He knows that the battle has to be fought, and he goes into it willingly. As for the rest, he sees clearly that it could be dispensed with.

A colonel of my acquaintance galloped up to his regiment. "That's good — very good," he shouted, "but I'll bet that the file closers aren't aligned yet."

A sergeant answered, "Bet on it, colonel — you'll win!" We never learned the name of the guilty party — I say "guilty" because, from the military point of view, such a remark was a serious offense.

When the troops come on to the review ground, how many marches and countermarches are necessary to get each unit into its proper place! How many times must we "dress" to get into the proper alignment before the Emperor arrives. Finally, the drums beat "Aux Champs"[2] all across our line. There he is! His little hat, his green chasseur à cheval's coat distinguish him amid that crowd of princes and generals with gold lace on every seam of their coats.

Everyone talks today of the soldiers' feelings toward Napoleon, how their cheers — a thousand times repeated — always rang out as he passed. It is perhaps really wrong of me to contradict something sworn to by so many famous persons, but I can and do state that those occasions were really rare. In the Grande Armée, we fought hard, seldom cheered, and always bitched.

We were encamped under the walls of Tilsit; there was talk of peace and an interview between the two emperors, so we went to walk along the banks of the Niemen River to see what went on.[3] When we arrived the conference had just ended, the two boats carrying the emperors were moving toward the opposite banks. Emperor Alexander landed first and was saluted by a general hurrah from his troops. Then Napoleon appeared at our shore; Talleyrand[4] gave him his arm to help him disembark. Not one cheer came from our soldiers. However certain officers took the initiative: we all told those near us that it would not do to have Napoleon less well received among us than

---

[1] Blaze is using theatrical comparisons.
[2] The drum "battery" (beat) used as a salute.
[3] In 1807, after Napoleon had routed the Russians at Friedland, forcing them to sue for peace. He and Alexander I of Russia met on a raft anchored in the middle of the river.
[4] Charles Maurice Talleyrand-Perigord, Napoleon's able, immoral and always treacherous foreign minister.

Alexander had been by his Russians, and we raised here and there some volleys of "Vive le Empereur!"

"His Majesty is coming," said our colonel just before a review. "I hope that this won't be like the last time, and that your soldiers will shout, 'Vive l' Empereur!' I shall hold you gentlemen responsible if everyone doesn't really sound of." We went back to our companies to deliver an amplified version of the colonel's exhortation—and this is what we heard the men in the ranks murmuring.

"If he'd give me a furlough, I'd cheer all he wanted."

"We don't have any bread. When I've nothing in my belly, I can't cheer."

"I enlisted for six months and here I've been in the army for twenty years. I'll cheer when they send me home."

"We haven't been paid for six months. Why not?"

"You don't know? Well, I'll tell you — they're waiting until all those he got killed are paid."

The Emperor arrived; the colonel and some officers shouted their heads off and the rest were silent. I have not seen soldiers shout "Vive l' Empereur" whole-heartedly except in 1814 and 1815—and that was when they were told to cry "Vive le roi."[5] I should say that then they really cheered themselves hoarse. Why? Because the soldier is really a fault-finder, either because every now and then he wants to get even for his usual sheep-like obedience, or because he is secretly envious of those who command him, just as a servant is of his master, and a scholar of his instructor.

In 1815, in a regiment marching through a city in southern France the soldiers' talked themselves into shouting "Vive l' Empereur," all together and as loudly as they could. The uproar was enough to rupture eardrums and break windows. After each "chorus," they'd laugh quietly, saying, "Good! That will scare the solid citizens."[6]

How many times has it been written that the soldiers fought for the Emperor? That is still a sort of obligatory formula, which many people have said and repeated without knowing why. The soldiers fought for themselves, to defend themselves, because Frenchmen never hesitate to do so when the choice is between danger and disgrace. They fight because it is impossible to do anything else; because it is necessary to fight; because, when they join the army, they find that fighting is its business and that it intends to keep on doing just that. They fought under the old monarchy with Turenne, Villars, and Marshal Saxe; under the Republic with Hoche, Moreau, Kléber, and many others; they fight whenever their country calls them. Show them Prussians, Russians, or Austrians, and — whether it is Napoleon, Charles X,[7] or Louis Philippe[8] who commands them — French soldiers will always do their duty.

Nevertheless, I know very well that the presence of the Emperor produced a great effect on the army. Everyone had complete, blind confidence in him; experience had taught us that his plans brought us victory. Accordingly, the moral effect of his appearance was equivalent to doubling our number.[9] But unending combats[10] and

---

[5] King Louis XVIII.

[6] Southern France was full of royalist sympathizers.

[7] King of France, 1824-1830. Younger brother of Louis XVIII.

[8] King of the French, 1830-1848.

[9] This curiously resembles the Duke of Wellington's remark that Napoleon's appearance was equivalent to a reinforcement of 40,000 men.

[10] "Combats" were bigger than "skirmishes" but smaller than "battles."

battles bored old soldiers, the old officers, and the old generals stiff, and they did not hesitate to say so — which didn't keep them from doing their duty whenever the occasion required it.

Under the Empire the soldiers dreamed of nothing but furloughs, peace, and their return to France, just as today they dream about nothing but war, campaigns, bivouacs, combats, and battles. They are back in France, they have peace and furloughs. What are they doing? — They are regretting the days gone by. Why? Because a man's heart and mind are always reaching out for a future which — when it becomes the present — does not please him because it is all at once a matter of hard facts, no longer veiled by his fancies. "How nice it would be," they said then, "if we could have peace!" Today they say, "We really could use a good war now!" And besides, I say again, soldiers are soreheads. Many of them, while they enjoy the ease of peacetime life, don't hesitate to pretend that they miss the bustle of camp life. Each of them knows very well that all their murmurs won't affect the course of events, but meanwhile it gives them a certain heroic air among their associates. Meanwhile, lithographs, showing old soldiers with huge moustaches weeping as they read the word "Discharged" on a document, decorate all the boulevards of Paris. The numberless journals of our capital deplore in melancholy words the fate of our gallant soldiers who are unmercifully sent home from the army, as if France has not always openings for anyone who wants to enlist as a private.

One day I discussed this business with a lithograph printer, attempting to prove what I have been telling you. "You are preaching to a man who's already converted," he told me immediately. "I know that all that stuff is baloney — but it sells! In business that's all that matters I recently worked up a lithograph showing ten of our grenadiers forcing two whole English battalions to surrender. The names, the time, the place — I invented all that. But that's not important! The public really like it, and I sell hundreds of copies every day. Go to a music hall and notice which songs get the most applause — they're those in which "French" rhymes with "success," "glory" with "Victory," "warriors" with "laurels." See all those excited shop-clerks applauding with a sort of frenzy — and yet, if you wanted to check up on them, how many of those heroes of the pit[11] would you find had dodged the draft in 1814[12] and been saved from punishment for it by the restoration of Bourbon rule?"

The French have shown prodigious valor. To use an expression of Napoleon's, they have glory to throw away. But it would be better to let others say that than to burn incense to ourselves every day.

Napoleon was without doubt a very great general His Italian campaigns [1796-1797, 1800] bordered on the amazing, for then he did not have the immense resources which he had later. The battles of the Empire are more famous, but they will never surpass the glory of his earliest ones. They were all victories, you will say. True, but merit usually is measured by the difficulties overcome, and the glory of General Bonaparte will never be eclipsed by that of the Emperor Napoleon, for the resources of the Emperor were so much greater than those available to the general. When you can draw the last man and the last penny from a country like France, without having to be accountable to anyone, it is not surprising that — if you have a well-balanced mind — you can do great things. It would be surprising if you couldn't.

[11]   Used in its theatrical sense.
[12]   When France was invaded and Paris in danger.

But imagine Napoleon with a representative government such as we have today in France: it is likely that his victorious march would have soon been cut short. For today we conscript 80,000 men a year, but the numbers for each department are published in the newspapers and the total conforms strictly to the letter of the law. Under the Empire, when you apparently called up 100,000 men, you actually obtained 300,000; the prefects saw to that, being in constant competition for appointment to the Council of State.[13]

Or, what would Napoleon do with a poor little conscription of 100,000 men, leaving from France? Some 80,000 would actually report to their regiments; half of them, as usually happened, would be in the hospital eight days later. Only 40,000 could be put into line, and 40,000 men don't amount to much in times of heavy casualties. They would be enough for one day of battle; we can remember some that cost even more.

That's a mere trifle: Suppose that in Napoleon's day, the French government had two independent tribunes; that all the government's operations were controlled down to the last detail by an opposition party — even a conscientious one. Suppose the ministers [of war, etc.] were obliged to worry perpetually over keeping the support of a majority of the legislative bodies, and consequently could give only half their time to their administrative duties. Suppose a multitude of newspapers were publishing gossip about the government's inner workings, the positions of the troops, their movements, their equipment, the number of cannon and caissons, the number of soldiers down to the drummers for the enemy to read — I doubt if Napoleon would have won as many battles. But also his thirst for conquest would have been naturally reduced by that general state of things, and he, we, and all the world would be better off. Freedom of the press is certainly a fine thing, but it should show more patriotism in its everyday activities, it should not publish what our neighbors are so anxious to learn. Our enemies always have spies among us, but they could learn a lot more by subscribing to our newspapers.

But, I see that, without intending to, I am talking politics, and certainly I had no intention of doing that. Lots of people would say that I know nothing about that subject, and they would be right You shall see me happy to get off it.

All the same, while I am thinking of might-have-beens, I'll share an idea that often goes trotting through my head with you. During the Consulate [1799-1804] Louis XVIII[14] wrote to First Consul General Bonaparte to persuade him to give up his own rule and reestablish the Bourbon monarchy. "Choose," Louis wrote, "for yourself and your friends the posts that you would most prefer." I often amuse myself by calculating what would have happened if Napoleon had accepted that proposition. Imagine the Marquis de Bonaparte, Captain of the *"Garde du Corps."*[15] But would the proprietary captains of the other three companies deign to accept him? Any gentleman guardsman who got himself into trouble would be assigned to Bonaparte's company. What witty jokes would they share as to the appearance and awkwardness of that Corsican upstart, that *"officier de fortune!"*[16] Why the most impoverished back-country squireen — even the lowest-ranking servant of those noblemen — would have thought himself higher in the

---

[13] Napoleon's equivalent of our president's cabinet. As for the numbers of conscripts called up, the prefects were normally energetic in meeting the department's quotas, but Blaze's statement that one was called and three sent is incorrect.

[14] Then a refugee in England.

[15] Horse Guards. Their "captains" ranked as generals.

[16] A professional officer, often promoted out of ranks, with no fortune but his commission.

court hierarchy. Make no mistake, a nobleman's valet thinks himself far superior to a man without a title; he is as insolent to the common citizen as his is servile to a noble.

I send my Bonaparte from the Tuileries to Versailles, from Saint-Cloud to Rambuoillet,[17] galloping by the door of the king's carriage. I see him vexed by the sneers of the great nobles; I visualize them, pulverized by his glance, turning on their red heels[18] and saying, "That man is not born."[19] Would he have received the "Cordon Bleu"?[20] I can't guess. I laugh when I think of the catastrophe which necessarily would end the last act of that comedy. One fine day our newly created marquis would have called in several companies of veterans of his Egyptian campaign and then — Look out, everybody! Move over and make room! Nothing would be left of Louis' monarchy. It is really too bad that we, who have seen so many things, didn't get to see that.

An odd duck said to me one day, "At the Brienne Military School I was a friend of Bonaparte, but since that period I have not seen him again and don't want to see him."

"And why not?"

"Because all the world knows that he has not followed the same line as I have."[21]

At every review the Emperor announced promotions to fill vacant positions, and distributed crosses of the Legion of Honor and titles of nobility. The regiments he reviewed accordingly were lucky. But this way of doing things was extremely unfair; I could cite regiments which he reviewed four or five times in one campaign. Their officers got a promotion every month, while other regiments stationed six miles away got none of the imperial munificence.[22]

Sometimes Napoleon liked to question the officers; if they responded promptly, without hesitation, he appeared satisfied. After the battle of Ratisbonne, he paused before an officer of my regiment.

"How many men [in your company] are present under arms?"

"Sire, eighty-four."

"How many of them are this year's conscripts?"

"Twenty-two."

"How many have had four years' service?"

"Seventy-five."

"How many wounded did you have today?"

"Eighteen."

"And how many killed?"

"Ten."

"In bayonet fighting?"

"Yes, sire."

"Good."

---

[17] Various royal places.

[18] High red heels were an affectation of French nobility.

[19] His ancestors were commoners. (Actually Napoleon's family was from the lower fringes of nobility.)

[20] Insignia of the Order of the Holy Ghost, a major Bourbon decoration.

[21] The correct "line" (of conduct), as defined by Louis XVIII was to have fled France when he did at the beginning of the Revolution, and not return until he did in 1814.

[22] Possibly a touch of sour grapes here. The regiments Napoleon would single out for special favors were those that earned it.

To be killed properly, you had to be bayoneted. A coward could be killed at a distance by a musket or cannon ball; those who were killed by a bayonet thrust were necessarily brave. The Emperor had a special feeling for those who died that way. His questions might continue for quite a while, on all aspects of unit supply and administration; he did not appear to really listen to the answers, which often did not agree with previous figures. The essential thing was to answer promptly, without hesitation.

One often saw the Emperor detach his own cross of the Legion of Honor to fasten it himself on the chest of a brave soldier. Louis XIV would have asked first if the brave man were a noble; Napoleon asked if a noble were brave. A sergeant who had shown prodigious valor during a battle was brought before Louise XIV.

"I grant you a pension of 1,200 livres," said the king.

"Sire, I would rather have the cross of Saint-Louis."[23]

"I can believe that, but you won't get it."

Napoleon would have hugged the sergeant, Louis XIV turned his back on him. That is an example of the sharp difference between the two periods.

In 1815 a high and mighty noble of the court was named Grand-Cordon[24] of the Legion of Honor. He considered that an insult; twenty secret meetings were held in the most aristocratic circles to decide if he should refuse it. They did not wish to show lack of respect for Louis XVIII, but they sought some good compromise. It was decided that Bonaparte's decoration would be worn only on those special ceremonial occasions when etiquette absolutely required it. Louis XIV would have agreed entirely with that decision.

While we are on decorations, I'll tell you a story about General T___. He was returning to France in 1814 after having evacuated I can't remember which fortress.[25] He still was three days' marching east of the Rhine when a courier all a-flutter with white ribbons met him and handed him a packet from the minister of war. Curious officers quickly surrounded the general, all of them wondering what news he had received. Apparently it was excellent for the general smiled and his face relaxed. Then he read them the minister's letter:

"My dear general,
I am happy to inform you that, on my recommendation, the king has awarded you the decoration of the Lily.[26] You will find that favor from His Majesty a new reason to serve him with zeal.
I send you, with this letter, the insignia and the certificate of that decoration.
The Minister of War."

General T___ promptly displayed the silver Lily medal, suspended from its white ribbon, and the senior colonel requested permission to attach it to the happy general's button hole.

"Gentlemen," said the general, "I have received a very precious favor from His Majesty Louis XVIII. Doubtlessly it is your services that he rewards in my person.

[23] The principle Bourbon military distinction, founded 1693 (Cordon Rouge), you had to be both an officer and a Catholic to win it.

[24] Blaze meant "Grand-Croix", the Legion's highest grade.

[25] A number of fortresses in Germany and Spain held out through 1813-1814, until informed of Napoleon's first abdication.

However, be certain that when I reach Paris many of you will receive the same honor; I shall do everything possible to see that you do."

The courier galloped away, after having received a token of the general's pleasure and generosity. They reached Strasbourg, where they found two regiments of Guards of Honor[27] — and every officer, non-com, and buck private of them both had received the Lily decoration.

Napoleon had a splendid head; his glance was like a lightening-flash; his bearing was noble and austere. However, one day I saw that great man in convulsions of irrepressible laughter. An emperor can laugh like any other man; rulers would be really unhappy if they didn't have good occasions to laugh, which is so good for them.

Here is the story. We were at Courbevoie; the Emperor was reviewing a regiment of the Young Guard which had just recently been filled up with large numbers of conscripts. He was questioning these young men.

"And you — where are you from?" he said to the one standing to the left of one of my friends, then a second lieutenant, today a receiver-general of taxes. (Instead of cannon shots, he receives money, which should be compensation enough for his earlier service.)

"Sire," replied the conscript, "I am from Pezenas,[28] and my father had the honor of shaving your Eminence when you passed through there."

At those words, the Emperor became a man; decorum was forgotten. I wonder if Napoleon ever laughed so freely, even when he was a schoolboy at Brienne. The review ended happily for the laughter was contagious; the reason for it passed to left and right, from rank to rank. Everyone guffawed loudly, and the citizen of Pezenas was proud to have to have made everyone so happy.

In Berlin I was billeted on a Major Hansing, an old soldier who had brought home only a modest pension and the gout from his campaigns in Silesia with Frederick [the Great]. In his admiration for that Prussian hero the major was a Prussian-and-a-half; we argued without ever reaching an agreement; our usual discussion was based on the hypothesis: "What would have happened if Frederick had lived at the same time as Napoleon?" Such a comprehensive subject has seldom been open to disputation. Each of us preached for our respective saint, and our chattering ended like all political and religious discussions: neither of us could convert the other.

In Berlin, as in all of Prussia, the name of Frederick II is greatly venerated. You find his portrait everywhere, in rich men's homes and cottages alike. You see him afoot or on horseback on the walls of drawing rooms, lobbies, and kitchens; painted or engraved, carved, cast, stamped, or embossed. That portrait decorates jewelry, snuff boxes, and pipes. I don't believe the likeness of any man has been more frequently reproduced. The moment that we saw it, our host's eyes would light up; he always exclaimed happily, "Es ist mein alte guter Fritz." (That's my good old Frederick) And then he would add between his teeth, "Ah, if he were still living, you would not be here." "That's not at all certain," we answered sometimes.

The good Major Hansing often told me stories about the Prussian hero which I very much regret having forgotten. But however, here is one which I've recovered from a tiny corner of my memory.

---

[26] The lily (Lys) was a time-honored Bourbon symbol. The medal was instituted in 1791; during 1814-1815 it was hung on everything that couldn't run away.

[27] Over-sized light cavalry regiments, raised from sons of rich and/or noble families in 1813.

[28] Southwest France, between Montpellier and Narbonne.

Frederick's immense popularity among his soldiers owed more to his charlatanry than to his military genius. When he held reviews — and he held them frequently — he had a dozen notes concerning different officers, noncommissioned officers, and privates, giving their name, biography, and the number of their regiment, battalion and company. These were placed on a small square of paper which he could hold in the palm of his hand. Thus knowing the rank in which each of these men stood, and their place in that rank, Frederick would pass before his troops on his ambling white horse, counting off the men until he found the soldier he wanted and then halt.

"Hello, Private so-and-so. Have you heard the news of your sister's marriage?"

"Yes, sire."

"I received a letter from Breslau yesterday telling me about it. That marriage pleases me greatly. You will let your father know at the first opportunity."

"Yes, sire."

"He is a brave man, your father — one of my old soldiers at Mollwitz.[29] You will tell him in your letter that I have appointed him gate keeper at Potsdam; I never forget my old soldiers."

The king would continue his review and halt a good distance away before an officer, to whom he would speak of a lawsuit which his family had won, of the death of a relative who would leave a rich inheritance, and so forth. Frederick went into the smallest details of their private lives. Further along, he would rebuke someone for minor misbehavior; others would be praised. He spoke to all concerning little things, small peculiarities which they thought nobody but themselves knew. All the soldiers thought that the king knew them personally; all of them tried to catch his attention, and when he passed they all shouted, "Es lebe unser guter Fritz! (Long live our good Frederick!)" Later, the king would tell his friends, "That's the oil with which I lubricate the wheels of my machine."

Probably no ruler ever possessed the art of the quick put-down like Frederick did. He always had a retort, instant and sharp. Here is one example out of a thousand. Major Hansing told me about it twenty times. He had been on duty with the King's staff that day.

During the Seven Years War, England tired of paying subsidies to Frederick, and tried to break off its alliance with Prussia, while still continuing its own hostilities against France. Its fleet attacked Le Havre, but was repulsed with loss. This news delighted Frederick, who was always happy to hear of his allies being defeated by the French. Then the English ambassador arrived at the court.

"Well," said the king with a malicious look, "is it true that your fleet has been unsuccessful? Is it possible that the French have defeated it?"

"Yes, sire, it's true; unfortunately, very true. But we hope, with the help of God and our gallant navy, to revenge our loss."

"Oh ho! You count on the help of God? Don't depend on it. He is an ally who, like so many others, sometimes betrays you."

"That is so, sire — but He costs us nothing."

"Yes, but that's what He'd give you for your money."

Paul I,[30] whom I have no intention of comparing to Frederick, had a really strange fancy. When he held a review, he asked his officers the most unusual and ridiculous

---

[29] Frederick's first battle, 1741. Frederick ran away, but his infantry won it on their own.

questions, which it was impossible to answer seriously. Several officers of one regiment, very embarrassed by such demands, stopped short in their attempts to reply, and thereafter Paul declared that they served in his "I-Don't- Know-Regiment."

One day while riding across a bridge in Saint Petersburg, Paul saw an officer who stepped to one side and saluted him respectfully. The emperor recognized his uniform and said to his companions, "He's from my I-Don't-Know Regiment."

"Sire, I know everything," replied the officer.

"Oho! — so you know everything. We'll see about that. How many nails were needed to put down the planks on this bridge?"

"Fifty-three million, seventy-seven thousand, one hundred and twelve."

"Not bad! And how many fish are there in this river, from this bridge downstream to Krönstadt?"[31]

"Six hundred forty-two billion, eight hundred and one million, four hundred thirty-two thousand, three hundred and seventy nine."

"You are positive?"

"If I weren't, I would not have spoken to your majesty."

"That's what I thought. It pleases me when someone answers my questions; an officer should know everything."

"Certainly. And the Emperor?"

"He is never caught short."

"Will your majesty permit me one question?"

"Speak."

"What is my name?"

"Count of Balowski."

"My assignment?"

"Captain in my guard."

"Thank you."

I have that anecdote from a French emigre,[32] an eyewitness, who saw how one Second Lieutenant Krasanow became — by a moment of effrontery and an emperor's whim — a count and a captain in the Russian Imperial Guard.

All rulers love to hold reviews. Frederick II sent out invitations, and everyone was assigned places, good or bad according to the king's precise plan. Napoleon was not so formal; you came if you wanted to and took whatever place you could find. Certainly one of the world's finest reviews was that the Emperor held at Tilsit, with Alexander I and Frederick-William of Prussia beside him.

The queen of Prussia was present at that review; a few years later Canova[33] carved her statue atop her tomb in the Charlottenburg[34] mausoleum. I have seen that beautiful Queen Louise twice — the first time on horseback, shining with youth and health; the second time lying on a superb sarcophagus with robes of marble, and marble hair. She was still truly beautiful. If the living can prove their affection for the dead by a splendid

---

[30] Emperor of Russia, 1796-1801. Possibly somewhat unbalanced. Murdered with the assent of his loving son, Alexander.

[31] The island fortress guarding the sea approach to Saint Petersburg.

[32] A royalist who had "emigrated" during the Revolution. A good many took service in Russia.

[33] Antonio Canova, 1757-1822, Italian sculptor, famous for his almost-nude reclining statue of Napoleon's sister Pauline.

[34] Royal residence area near Berlin.

tomb, certainly the King of Prussia did everything he possibly could for his wife. You cannot imagine a tomb of purer style; it is a masterpiece of its kind.

The tomb of Frederick at Potsdam is simpler and also, you might say, without ceremony. But in fact the name "Frederick II" placed on a coffin tells you all you need to know. What does it matter whether that inscription is carved in marble or on gold? The name of Napoleon, placed on the rock of Saint Helena,[35] will last longer than the pyramids of Egypt, which hold bodies of unknown kings.

But see how you have trustingly let me lead you from the plains of Tilsit into the sepulchral crypts of Potsdam. Since we are here and still have the time, you and I, I will tell you the story of my guide there. He was an aged hussar, who assured me that he had served in Frederick's personal entourage; if he spoke of that great man, I responded with enthusiasm to get him (he did not need any greater encouragement) to talk freely.

My hussar had fought on the fields of Rossbach,[36] and that name was always popping up in his story. Every time he uttered it, a malicious smile twisted his white mustaches, and a sidelong glance at me would betray what satisfaction his vanity got from it. Rossbach was his key date, his point of departure. A certain thing had happened a year before Rossbach, or two years after Rossbach. You might suspect that repeating that word before Frederick's coffin would reconcile his ghost to the presence of one of Napoleon's soldiers. While we talked I though to tell him that Rossbach was not very far from Jena,[37] but I was sorry I did so because it thoroughly upset him.

"You see this tomb," he said to me. "I mourn constantly for whom it holds. Well, monsieur, if that great king were still alive, I would be in prison, yet I would gladly give my freedom, even my life, if it pleased God to have him still alive."

"And why were you in prison?"

"Because I was confined at the fortress of Spandau[38] for four years by his order. I was not released until his successor took over in 1786. Ah! I would rather still be within four walls and see from far off, between the bars of my window, my good old Fritz on his white horse, chasing your — Napoleon."

He paused slightly before pronouncing that name: he would have prefaced it with some insulting term — the first syllable of *verfluchte* (damned) was in his mouth, but he bit it off short.

"What had you done," I repeated, "that the king sent you to Spandau?"

"You shall know. For his personal service, Frederick had a hussar who lived in a small room located beneath his study. His duty was to deliver at any time, day or night, the king's letters; a bell placed next to his bed summoned him to receive the king's orders. That hussar was chosen from among veteran soldiers who were no longer fit for combat duty, for whom it was an excellent assignment. The king paid him nothing, preferring to let the people who received his letters pay the postage.[39] Each one was worth eight nice "groschen" (approximately a fourth of a franc). That was the rate; you could not

---

[35] Napoleon's body was not brought back to France until 1840

[36] At Rossbach, 1757, Frederick had defeated an overconfident French army and its German allies.

[37] Napoleon's great 1806 victory over Prussia.

[38] A fortress, arsenal, and state prison just west of Berlin.

[39] Blaze's Note: All letters and petitions addressed to Frederick, his ministers, and all his office holders had to be sent through the mail; this sale of stamps brought in 300,000 francs a year. Information for our government, present and future

request more. Whether from distrust or some other reason, Frederick insisted above all else that the hussar must be unable to read.

I had been badly wounded during our last campaign in Silesia — that was fifteen years after the battle of Rossbach, where you know how we beat the French. The king knew me; he knew the names of all his soldiers. At a review where Frederick was distributing rewards, he saw me. My colonel recommended me, and I was named hussar orderly First, the king asked me if I could read: I, knowing the requirement and wanting the position, answered, "no." You will see the result of that lie.

While I was in the king's service I made some respectable savings; sometimes I carried as many as a hundred letters a day, for you know that Frederick personally invited persons of distinction to his reviews, assigning each one the place he was to occupy. Receiving all those 8-groschen pieces, I became rich. I dreamed of leaving the service and getting married. I began to find my service unpleasant: when I was not trotting around the city, I had to be ready for that bell to ring. And when you feel that you have built up enough savings, you want nothing more than to be able to enjoy them.

I had a mistress then, and we were waiting for a favorable occasion to ask the king for permission to wed. There were days when it wasn't wise to approach Old Fritz, so you had to find the right moment to speak to him.

One day I had a rendezvous with my sweetheart, since the king was going away, but all at once he fell ill and returned. I began writing to my mistress to let her know, but just as I began, something — I can't remember what — distracted me and I left my room. The King rang — no hussar; he rang again — still no hussar. Then, behold Old Fritz, in his dressing gown, leaning on his crutch, leave his study, come down the stairs all alone, enter my room, find my letter, and read it. Here is what I had written — you don't forget such things:

"My dear love, I can't come to see you tonight because the old bear is sick—"

Frederick went back upstairs; shortly thereafter he rang and I came running.

"Listen," he said to me. "I have need of a man who is discreet and completely reliable. Can I count on you?"

"Yes, sire, What are your orders?"

"It concerns a letter of the highest importance. No one must be able to guess where it was written. All the world knows the handwriting of my secretaries; nobody knows yours. Sit down. I'll dictate it to you."

"Sire, your majesty should remember that I cannot write."

"Indeed! You said that to get this appointment; an innocent lie that helped one person without hurting anyone."

"Sire — I assure you —"

"...That you lied then, and that you're still lying."

"But —"

"Not one more word. Take that pen. Write."

"Since your majesty orders it —"

"My dear love,"

"My dear love," said I while writing it. I began to shiver.

"I can't see you tonight."

At those words I turned pale, I trembled. I had not one drop of blood in my veins. The King repeated:

"I can't see you tonight. Have you finished?"

"Yes, sire."

"I can't see you tonight because the old bear is sick." Frederick put strong emphasis on 'the old bear.'

"Pardon, Sire: Mercy!" I said and groveled at his feet.

"Sit down and write," he said. "Because the old bear is sick and I am in Spandau."

I had to write, sign, and seal that letter, then address it. Immediately I was sent to prison. I would be there yet if the king had not died, for he seldom pardoned anyone. I had deserved that punishment, and I do not complain about it After four years of captivity, my greatest regret was to find that I had recovered my liberty because Frederick was dead. I loved him with all my soul. Although I permitted myself to call him "old bear," that was only a name my mistress and I gave him to use between ourselves, and that would not have kept me from sacrificing my life to make his longer. Today I am old, I guide foreigners to the tomb where the great man rests; I never enter this crypt without shedding tears, and my only ambition — an ambition which never will be realized — is to occupy a space here when I shall be dead."

So spoke my old hussar of Rossbach. While leaving him I slipped into his hand an 8-groschen piece. It recalled memories that brought tears to his eyes. As for myself, on my return to Berlin, I carefully wrote down his story in my notebook, from which I have taken it today for anyone wants to read it.

FREDERICK II (MENZEL)

XV
The Barracks

The conscript whom the drawing[1] has plucked from his paternal roof, weeps as he leaves it; once at the barracks, he forgets everything. Fearing the jokes of his comrades, he has quickly dried his tears. We French people fear ridicule more than a sword thrust. Once the new soldier is measured, numbered, and clothed from feet to head, you might take him at a distance for a hero of Austerlitz. But close-up, he's something else: his figure is stiff, he doesn't know what to do with his arms and his legs embarrass him. When Jean-Jean[2] walks out from the barracks he always has a swagger stick in his hand to help him look military.

Then the instructor appears; he is a corporal with mustaches; a fast talker. During the rest periods which separate the hours of drill he never fails to tell the new recruit about all the mighty deeds in days gone by that have made his name famous. The conscript listens with mouth wide open, and can't comprehend why the corporal is not at least a colonel. This lack of promotion for a man so famous discourages him. Thus an author leaving a performance of *Tartiafe*[3] might throw the draft of his own comedy into the fireplace.

After leaving his plow the conscript expects to encounter all the miseries of human life when he enters the barracks. A hundred times people have told him, "You're going to eat like a crazy cow."[4] He is truly astonished to get good beef, flanked by a sufficiency of potatoes, and his everyday meals are better than what he got at home on Sundays. His bread is good, and whiter than that eaten in three fourths of the villages in France.

The soldier is a man who has an income of 1,200 francs, completely clear and free, without fear of bankruptcy, penalties, assessments, or bad debts. I have calculated that as the value of his housing, his food, his clothing, his heating, his furniture (which he always uses, but never has to replace). From all my figures, I have deduced that many *rentiers*[5] do not have as easy and carefree lives as the soldier. If he is sick, doctors and surgeons in embroidered coats are happy to take care of him, free of charge; the pharmacists give him emetics and Peruvian bark[6] for nothing; leeches,[7] brought at great expense from Hungary, lavish their beneficial bites upon him under the supervision of a medical orderly, who places them on the areas specified by regulations.

In our sickrooms they receive, over and above their pay, sweetened drinks, always copious, which they always empty; bottles of all sorts, and frequent bowls of broth —

[1] Frenchmen drew lots to determine who would be conscripted into the army; not so different from the proceedings of the U.S. draft boards.
[2] Country bumpkin, lout, idiot, God-help-me.
[3] Another of Moliere's comedies.
[4] In French, really have a rough time.
[5] People living on their income from stocks, bonds, rented property.
[6] Cinchona, the raw form of quinine.
[7] Used for drawing off blood, especially from bruised areas. When this editor was young, three quarters of a century ago, leeches still were being used to clear up "black" eyes.

and still they grumble from morning till night. They don't have to pay the medical orderly; to the contrary, if the soldier can handle it during convalescence, he gets the best soup, chicken wings, and a half-bottle of choice wine.

And then above all those advantages, consider again the blessings of the *sou de poche*.[8] This pocket money always arrives, always disappears; it is a rich, inexhaustible mine which furnishes all his pleasures, from the drink of brandy to the pipe of tobacco. A new wandering Jew, the soldier always finds that sou at the bottom of his pocket. What should I say? Let that pocket sou wait patiently for its brothers, which will never fail to arrive, and next Sunday after the parade beyond the city barriers, a succulent pork chop, washed down with delicious 6-sous-a-liter wine, will flood the gullet of the *tour lourou*[9] with pleasures that are as very real as they are very rare.

The soldier always lives in the finest house in the city. Go to Saint-Denis, ask for the finest residence — it is the barracks. At Vincennes, soldiers inhabit the rooms of our former kings; at Avignon they have the palace of the Pope. Well clad, kept warm, well fed, lodged in well-ventilated quarters, what more does the soldier need? This is what he lacks:

> Going along [the wolf] saw a bare spot on the dog's neck. 'What is that,' he said to him. 'Nothing.' 'What do you mean, nothing?' 'Very little.' 'But even so?' 'The collar that I am wearing, as you see, is probably the cause.'[10]

That collar, which we fasten around the soldier's neck, is broken only by his discharge, delivered on the final day of his service, or by a cannon ball. All the time he spends in his regiment is divided in a hundred different ways, hardly one of which is his own. If he sleeps, the drum wakes him up; if he's awake, the drum send him to bed. The drum starts him marching; it halts him; it leads him to drill, to combat, to mass,[11] to his off-duty promenade.

"I am hungry."

"You're mistaken, my friend. The drummer has not yet beaten that call, which is the only thing that should start your stomach muscles churning. The stew can't be ready yet, because the drummer hasn't said so."

"If only I had some bread."

"Imbecile! The *breloque* hasn't sounded yet."[12]

---

[8] See *Swords Around a Throne*, page 582. A small payment made weekly to give the soldier some ready cash.

[9] Old slang for enlisted infantryman.

[10] From some version of Aesop's fable of the wolf and the watchdog.

[11] This is indication enough that this chapter deals in part with the 1815-1830, mostly peacetime, royal army.

[12] Blaze's Note: a drum beat to assemble the fatigue detail which picks up their unit's rations. Soldiers might say, "This is a lousy place, they never beat the *breloque*," or "I was billeted on a peasant where the drum beat the *breloque* from morning to night."

In the morning, armed with a broom, the soldier sweeps the barracks, inside and out — and again it is the drum that summons him to that work. One day when Laborie was the duty officer,[13] and consequently in charge of the clean-up detail, he bawled out a corporal because a pile of sweepings had not disappeared, though the day before he had given a positive order to get rid of it.

"My lieutenant, we don't know where to put it."

"Dump it behind the barracks."

"Since the mayor complained, the colonel has forbidden that."

"Oh well, Dig a ditch and bury it."

"But where will we put the dirt from the ditch?"

"How dumb can a corporal be! Dig the ditch big enough to hold everything."

When the sweeping is finished, musket drill takes it place. Then it's polish the weapons and equipment, polish the cartridge box, brush the coat, black the shoes, polish the buttons — Get a move on; it's time for the parade. It's there that you must shine; come on, my heroes — distinguish yourselves. The least stain on your coat means trouble for the duty corporal and the duty sergeant, and an arrest[14] for the duty lieutenant, and they will resent the punishment they have received because of you for a long time. These men are responsible for the appearance of their soldiers. The colonel said, "If they are not clean and neat, I'll hold you responsible." This is very much like Monsieur de Poureaugnac,[15] "If someone tells me something, it will be his problem."

All the orders of the drum, the corporal, or the officers must be executed at once, without comments, without complaint. Just as the clock drives its pendulum, the soldier marches without asking why. Soldier! You are a pendulum: march, turn, halt, and — especially — not one word.

"But, Captain —"

"To the guard room for two days."

"If you would only listen to me —"

"Four days."

"But —"

"Eight days."

"This isn't fair."

"Fifteen days imprisonment. One word more out of you and you'll be locked up and facing court-martial."

That is the regiment's summary justice; it is administered like everything else there, so that, having experienced the hospitality of the guard room, the young soldiers learns a lesson from which he will thereafter profit. I always except the wrong-headed types who are incorrigible jail-birds and end up dragging a ball-and-chain or being shot.

That strict severity is necessary if one man is to control 100,000 armed men. Without passive obedience to the next higher grade, you can not have an army. The most foolish order, the most stupid, must be executed without debate. What could a commander do if everyone felt free to offer their advice. We all think that we're pretty smart; in our own minds we often consider an associate an imbecile — while he may very well think the same of us. A commander who asks his officers for advice, even one who may listen to

---

[13] We would say "officer of the day," etc. In France, this detail was for a week.

[14] Confinement to quarters.

[15] A French comic figure.

their objections, never can be sure that his orders will be executed. One subordinate will modify them; another decides that he can save the army by doing just the opposite.

We were near Berlin in 1813; our retreat was difficult for we had only to glance over our shoulders to see the pursuing Russians. One evening our general received a letter concerning that situation. I should explain that we had halted in a village with two battalions of infantry and four cannon, and that we were practically in the Russians' whiskers.[16]

> My dear general,
> Send one of your battalions immediately to the village of ____. Its commander must stay alert; he will send out patrols, which will maintain contact with yours throughout the night.
> Give him two of your cannon.
> Yours truly, General of Division ____

Certainly that order was positive, with nothing ambiguous about it. Our general sent off the battalion, he reread the letter, he reread it again, he meditated, and finally he exclaimed, "He doesn't tell me what to do with the other two cannon."

"You're supposed to keep them."

"That isn't in the letter."

"That letter doesn't tell you what to do with the other battalion either. Obviously you're supposed to keep it and those two cannon also."

Possibly the general was irritated to see that I had reasoned correctly. "He considers me a fool," he must have said to himself. "Well, I'll straighten out this young buck who thinks he's smarter than I am."

"Mount up, monsieur. Go to the division commander and get an explanation of this letter."

"But it seems to me that—"

"That the order I just gave you should be obeyed at once."

"My general, consider that there's no reason for this; I always have done my duty conscientiously, but at this moment—"

"Get going, monsieur. That's my order."

I had to go, to ride all night across fields and along horrible roads I'd never traveled before; the rain poured down, which I can assure you wasn't the least bit exhilarating. I had to pass along the French outpost line; in the darkness I blundered into enemy outposts two or three times — their shots got me going in the right direction again. French sentinels, sending me coming from the "bad" direction, shot at me and then shouted, "Who comes here?" as was pretty much their habit. I can only thank the bad weather — which I damned when I started out — that I wasn't killed that night. Finally I reached division headquarters.

"Where is the general? Wake him up; I have to speak to him."

"What's up? Are we being attacked?" asked the officers of the division staff.

"Wake up the general; I have to speak to him personally."

Worthy General ____ was in the delights of his first moments of sleep when I came into his room, letting my saber trail along the inlaid floor.

---

[16] Though Blaze doesn't say so, it's obvious that he now is aide-de-camp to a brigade commander and, as such, the brigade staff.

"Ah, it's you! Is there fighting in your direction? Have you come for reinforcements?"

"I have come to ask for an interpretation of your order."

"What order?"

"Our general wants to know what he should do with his two remaining cannon."

"Are you making fun of me?"

"I certainly would not take that liberty. I hope, my general, that you believe me incapable of such conduct."

"Then are you an imbecile?"

"Permit me, my general. I am here not as myself, but as the mouthpiece of my superior. He wishes to ask, by my voice, what he should do with those two cannon."

"Oh that! Are we staging a comedy, or is this a bet you hope to win?"

"My general, if I were staging a comedy, I would not take the liberty of casting you as the interlocutor, without your permission. If I were inclined to wager, I wouldn't dare bet on anything that involved waking you up in the middle of the night. I again repeat my question: What should we do with our remaining two cannon?"

"You can go f___!"[17]

"Good! So much for me, but for my general?"

"The same, both of them, together or separately! Now get out of here — I need some sleep."

My errand finished, I got back into my saddle, and arrived at eight o'clock in the morning, just as the battalion and those two cannon were ready to move out. The general was at the head of the column; I rode up to him, saluted, and waited to be questioned.

"Did you see the division commander?"

"Yes."

"What did he tell you?"

"Several things which I can not repeat."

"Say that again."

"Military subordination keeps me from telling you."

"Monsieur, that subordination requires that you obey me. What did the general tell you?"

"He told me that you could go f___!"

"Monsieur!"

"My general, twenty witnesses heard him; a hundred others here can say that you ordered me to speak."

That passive subordination, that necessary obedience sometimes has fatal results; but things would be still worse if it didn't exist. During the campaign of 1814, when so many excellent veterans had been left by the Emperor in fortress cities, along the Elbe and Oder rivers, as far as Danzig, if one general had dared to sally out from the city he was defending and then march on the other strongholds, gathering up their garrisons, what an immense diversion that would have been!

The thing would not have been as difficult as you might think.[18] All the generals had considered this idea, but all of them had recoiled before the enormous moral responsibility

---

[17] Apparently an abnormal form of self-copulation.

[18] This is one of the major myths of the Napoleonic Wars. Briefly, these garrisons were not composed of veterans; second, they mostly lacked the mobile artillery and transport for field operations.

they would have taken on themselves. Marshal Davout could have sortied from Hamburg with 20,000 men and marched on Magdeburg, when General Lemarois would have joined him with 12,000 more; together they could have marched to pick up the garrisons along the Elbe and Oder, thus gaining more reinforcements every three days.

Certainly they would have met opposition along their way, but they could have overcome it. They feared only one thing, and that was not to follow the exact order the Emperor had given them.[19]

The Allies' greatest efforts were directed against Napoleon; all their best troops were in France. It was troops from their last levies who blockaded these fortresses; the *landwehr* and *landsturm* who were making their first campaign;[20] who would have made way, willingly or unwillingly, to give the garrisons free passage.

Imagine the effect that news would have produced in France, after the battle of Brienne or of Montmirail! Picture to yourself a French army marching into Berlin the same day that the Allies entered Paris.

In a discussion between a superior and a subordinate, the worst mistake the latter can make is to be right. In the army I have known very intelligent officers who gave up all pretense of independence, agreeing with all their superiors' whims, to establish themselves as advisers to high-ranking persons without ever letting anyone know that they furnish them good advice. That is the height of the courtiers' art; not many people can do it.

Many generals would like to play the part of a prince.

"Every marquis must have his pages."

The uniform of aides-de-camp is a blue coat with sky-blue cuffs and collar. Almost all the generals' civilian servants are similarly dressed; the major difference is that they do not wear epaulettes. In that way a general has a well-mounted "household" of servants of all grades — captain, lieutenant, valet, groom, and so forth. These aristocratic manners have replaced republican austerity without any gradual change. I have known aides-de-camp who adjust easily to all this hierarchic servitude; they outrank the generals' valet and that is enough to satisfy them. On the other hand, I have known generals who were extremely scrupulous in such matters, never asking any officer under their orders to perform a service which was not strictly military.

I arrived one day with General P___ at an empty house. It was raining by bucketfuls and our coats were soaked through. We lighted a fire and warmed ourselves.

"Sit over there," the general told me.

"Why?"

"So I can pull your boots off."

"You're joking!"

"Not at all. Give me your foot."

"General, I can't let you do that."

"Your boots are soaked through; your feet are wet; you'll catch cold."

"But I can pull them off myself."

"I want to do it."

Willy nilly, the general got my boots off. I was really astonished; when he had finished, "It's my turn," he said. "One service deserves another Pull off my boots."

[19] Which were to hold the cities they occupied.
[20] Respectively, a national levy of all men, 17 to 40 capable of bearing arms (some had seen a year's service by 1814), and one of men over 40.

"With pleasure."

"To have the right to ask that of you, I had to do the same for you."

A barracks should be placed on an elevated area, so that it is not humid and so the air circulates around the mass of men gathered there. There are some very fine ones in the Paris area — at Courbevoie, Saint-Denis, and Rueil. Some have been built for that purpose; others are ancient convents where the virgins of the Lord chanted praises of God. If walls have ears, they should find a certain difference in what soldiers sing today. The barracks in Avignon, one of the finest in France, was inhabited by the popes in times past. A part of their palace has been converted into military quarters. Never did masons pile up stones with less good taste. This palace, on which the reigning pontiffs of Avignon toiled, one after the other, without ever finishing it, presents a really strange appearance — towers of a great height, immense halls, several churches tucked away within its eighteen-feet-thick walls — all that built without a plan or an established design. During the wars in Italy between the Guelfs and Ghibellines,[21] the popes took refuge in Avignon, and during the seventy years they lived there, each one added new stones to the stones heaped up by his predecessors.

When the popes returned to Rome, their Avignon palace became the home of a vice-legate who ruled the County of Venaissin in the name and for the benefit of Saint Peter's successors. All affairs, whether civil, military, or religious were handled by priests. Petitioners met a priest in the lobby, and then in the offices, the libraries, and the drawing rooms. Soutanes and clerical collars were everywhere.

To gain the favor of this gentry, it was wise to accompany your request with a little gift. They preferred confections, amazing amounts of which were consumed in that country. In the convents they did only two things — pray and make sugar-almonds, marzipan, and macaroons. Their ovens never had a chance to cool off.

These holy men were epicures and not gourmands; gluttony being a mortal sin, they carefully avoided it. Denied many worldly pleasures, they pounced on confections as a sort of compensation. A lady had solicited a certain favor from the vice-legate of Avignon and so wished to make him a small gift. She thought for a long time about what might please him the most. She did not believe that bonbons or preserved fruits would do — the Ursulines and the Benedictines crammed His Eminence with them from morning to night. She did have a very beautiful parrot; since such birds were quite rare, she sent it to the vice-legate.

Eight days later, the lady went to make her petition. Nobody thanked her. When you give something, you'd like to know how it was received. So the lady risked a few questions.

"Has the Vice-Legate received the parrot?"

"Yes, yes, the parrot. Yes, yes."[22]

"I had thought that the bird would please His Highness."

"So — so."

"How did he find that sweet little thing?"

"Tasty, but rather tough."

The vice-legate had eaten the bird.

---

[21] Respectively, supporters of the popes and the Holy Roman Emperor during the 12th, 13th, and 14th centuries.

[22] In Blaze's text, the priest here speaks Italian.

The delegates from Morieres, a village near Avignon, were to make a ceremonial visit to Vice-Legate Salviati. "What shall we take him?" they debated as they got ready to leave — for it was always necessary to bring him something and that something had better be good to eat.

"As for me, I have beautiful pears."

"And I have fine peaches."

"And I splendid quinces."

A large majority decided that they would take the quinces to Salviati. That decided, a new problem arose — should they be raw or cooked? A fast talker asserted that it would be more seemly to cook them, since, if the vice-legate wanted to eat five or six of them right away, it would be easier for him. Others suggested that it would be better to offer raw fruit; it would keep longer, and also that a pyramid of yellow fruit would be more attractive than a heap of scorched cakes which would collapse under its own weight. The fast talker's opinion prevailing, they cooked the quince.

Our worthy citizens arrived at the palace; when they entered the antechamber, the lackeys made fun of them; when they became angry, the lackeys laughed even louder. They took the quinces and threw them in the deputies' faces as they ejected them from the palace.

"Well," said the fast talker, "we really were wise to cook those quinces; if we hadn't done so we'd have been killed."[23]

Today part of that one-time palace of the popes is a prison; another was made over into a barracks. The rest is inhabited by owls, birds of prey, which have lived there for a long time. One of the most horrible incidents of 1791, known as the "Massacre of the Ice Tower," took place in that palace. There, several hundred prisoners were thrown into a deep chasm, and four days later some were found still alive amid the rotting corpses.

"The lists of those proscribed as outlaws were drawn up. Hate and vengeance wrote them in blood! The aged and the infirm were not spared. The virtuous Noilhac, an octogenarian priest, is dragged without pity by his venerable hair, whitened more by work than by the years, as if to give the unfortunate victims the aid of religion, and to find in this last act of apostleship, new rights to the martyr's palm. The gates of the dungeon swung wide; the executioners, possessed by the thirst for blood, whom a liquor invented in hell excited still more, entered in a fury. A dim light guided their staggering steps. They dragged their miserable victims to a pit dug to swallow them up and flung them in half-alive. In the midst of that scene of horror, while some fell under their murdering steel and others, inspired by despair, struggled with the executioners and by defending their lives only prolonged their torment, the virtuous Noilhac, ignoring all dangers, revived everyone's courage by the hopes and consolations of religion."[24]

And if we wished to write a history of all that has taken place within those 18-foot-thick walls, it would have to be a big book indeed.

---

[23] The raw quince is very hard, even when ripe.

[24] Blaze's Note: [From] *Julien, or the Priest*, published in 1805. My father, the author of that book, wrote this page the day after the Ice Tower Massacre." The Revolution saw rough doings in Avignon, graphically described in Thomas Carlyle's, *"The French Revolution."* The executioners were described as being soaked in brandy – of which Blaze, Senior, apparently had an unfavorable opinion!

Do not think that a soldier in barracks has nothing to do; his duties are so interconnected that he gets his main relaxation by shifting from one type of work to another. Fatigue details to keep the barracks and courtyards properly tidy, cleaning his weapons and clothing, drill, and guard duty all come around regularly, so that the soldier seldom finds himself with nothing to do for any length of time.

In the barracks they read a good deal in their spare moments; wild novels being favorites. You always can find a rental library near a barracks. Enter and you easily can tell the most popular books by the heavy black wrappers that protect them. One day I was standing in line near the lady cashier behind a young conscript, swagger stick in hand.

"Have you *Robert, the Bandit Chief*?"

"No monsieur, it's out."

"Have you *Rinaldo Rinaldini*?"

"No, monsieur, your comrades are reading it."

"Have you — but I don't know their titles. Find me some other book about bandits."

Five or six men, sometimes a whole squad, will club together to rent a book, and the cleverest one of them will read aloud to his comrades. It's a pleasure to see all those veteran campaigners listening open-mouthed to the marvelous stories of Cartouche, Mandrin, or La Ramée. Not that soldiers feel any sympathy for robbers, but the latter's adventurous lives have a certain resemblance to the experiences and dangers of their own pursuit of glory. They would rather read stories about robbers than heroes. They know the latter by heart. They can learn about all our campaigns, all our saber strokes, without have to spend a sou. In every barracks room there is a veteran who has seen everything and never misses a chance to tell of his mighty deeds. There is one of them in every company who has considerable moral influence over his comrades. He criticizes all of his captain's actions. "In my old regiment," he says, "we didn't do things this way." His old regiment is his hobby-horse; it is the example everyone should follow. If he transfers to another regiment, the one he just left becomes his model in its turn. Since he cannot cite two as models, the one he just left will always be the better one.

Barracks have a separate building which serves as quarters for a certain number of officers — you need some shepherds ready at hand for such a large flock. In the barracks area you also find merchants selling wine, brandy, and tobacco; sometimes a billiard parlor and eating places. The *cantiniere*, after having hiked the weary roads, her "keg" slung over her shoulder, sets herself up in a corner of the ground floor, pompously called a "restaurant." Later, it becomes a "cafe." Don't look for the luxury of gilt fixtures, mirrors, or crystal chandeliers — but who needs them? It offers second lieutenants one great advantage which more than makes up for their lack — it extends credit until the end of the month, which is a great help to some. I have often been one of them and so speak as an expert.

I have known cantinieres who, from serving a simple pot-au-feu, have worked their way up to a dinner for forty, perfectly served. They commence with four customers, then five, then ten, and soon, as their reputation grows in direct proportion to the excellence of their beefsteaks — they feed all the officers of the regiment.

There seldom is a time as agreeable as a meal at the officers' mess. The regiment is a family, its members are linked together by their honor. An officer who goes on leave is very happy, but he is even happier when he returns.

The officers' mess is where you talk over the affairs of the regiment and of the army; you sometimes also ponder the destinies of all Europe. You talk about drill and love affairs, those two subject always getting close attention. There is a separate table for each grade of officer; otherwise the familiarity which naturally develops between men eating together would undermine discipline. All of these diners have an open account in the proprietor's ledger, in which they are charged for all the "extras"[25] permitted them during the current month. Often this "lament" is very long, those extras costing more than the meals themselves.

And later over dessert you talk and, when your duties permit, stay a long time around the table. Those talks have furnished me with many of the tales I have told you — and here in one more to finish this chapter.

After the Restoration, we had a regimental chaplain[26] with a really queer habit; he used a sign language and spoke only when he absolutely had to. The soldiers said that this estimable priest had missed his true vocation, being really born to take part in the ballet or the opera. When he first climbed into the pulpit, we whispered, "Now he's really caught, because he'll finally have to speak. The Good God does not hear signs, so he needs words — clear, positive, well-articulated words."

One day we had him to dinner. The conversation turned to systems of sign language, such as those of the Abbe L'Epee, Abbe Sicard,[27] and others. Our chaplain claimed that you could make yourself better understood by signs than by speech. Signs, he said, were a universal language, comprehended by all races. Having traveled over all of Europe; though he spoke only French, he had found that his signs had been very well understood, from Rome to Berlin, in London and Saint Petersburg.

One of our waiters, who had listened to these claims and did not miss a word, came up to me, "Monsieur," he said, "This is really odd. Jacques, the peasant who takes care of the barracks garden, has precisely the same habit as Monsieur the priest. He talks only by making signs, so we think that he's deaf and dumb. It's the devil of a problem, because nobody knows what he's trying to say!"

I loudly repeated what the waiter had told me, and everyone agreed to bring the gardener and the chaplain together. Our good priest was excited by this lucky meeting, and soon the two silent speakers found themselves face to face.

The chaplain showed the gardener his closed fist; its four fingers were clenched, the thumb erect in a vertical position.

The gardener responded by the same sign, but with two fingers extended.

Immediately the chaplain extended three fingers.

The gardener showed a complete fist, all five digits closed.

"That's very good; one could not do better," cried the chaplain. "It would be impossible to answer more exactly and wisely." Thereupon he took an apple from the table and presented it to the gardener, who picked up a piece of bread, showed it to the chaplain, and turned to leave.

"Don't go, my friend, stay here. Your conversation pleases me, and you speak admirably. You are living proof of the correctness of my system, for if my signs did not make sense to everyone, certainly you would not have understood them."

---

[25] Such as a few "little drinks."

[26] These were a Bourbon revision to pre-Revolutionary practice. Except for its Swiss, Spanish, and Polish regiments, the *Grande Armée* had no chaplains.

[27] Abbe l'Epee apparently began systematic teaching of deaf-mutes in France; Sicard (1742-1822) took over and improved his methods.

"I don't know if Jacques really did understand your signs," I said, "but if he did, I can assure you that he's smarter than I am."

"What! You didn't understand them?"

"No."

"And you? — and you? — and you?" speaking to other officers.

"No." "No." "No."

"It's really very simple. In showing a single digit to our friend Jacques, I have said that there was only one God. By his two extended digits, he effectively indicated the double nature of God, the human and the divine. With my three digits I have continued the development of my idea, for these two natures belong to three persons. Thereupon Jacques, by his closed fist, has responded that those three persons are all one, thus clearly stating the mystery of the Holy Trinity. You see it is impossible to better comprehend the meaning of my signs. To confuse this worthy gardener a little — and I beg him to forgive my little trick — I took that apple; by showing it to him I wished to recall Adam, our first father, and the original sin, the consequence of the first mistake. Jacques, by presenting me with this bit of bread, has told us that the Son of God has taken away Adam's sin from us, and that the bread of Holy Communion has sealed the gates of Hell."

During that explanation Jacques' eyes had grown bigger and bigger.

"Aha!" said he, "Even if you are wicked, no one can say that you're stupid. I can see through you, though. After having insulted me, you want to be friends again."

"Insults? To you!"

"Yes, monsieur, you have insulted me badly. I am a married man; we are poor, but my wife is virtuous."

"What did our conversation have to do with your wife?"

"Just wait. Gentlemen, I take you as judges. This old crow told me that I had a horn.[28] I never pick quarrels, but I always defend myself when someone attacks me — so I showed him that he had two. He continued and told me that I had three; that made the mustard rise into my nose[29] and, except for the respect I have for all of you, I would have let him have my fist in his face. Then he tries to make it up to me with his apple, but as long as I have any bread in my house, he can take his apple and [censored]!"

---

[28] Been cuckolded.
[29] Lose his temper.

XVI

The Prisoners of War

Among civilized nations, it is ours that treats prisoners of war the best. In France, a disarmed enemy is no longer an enemy; not only does our government take care of them, but also private citizens provide them with all the relief that they can. When columns of prisoners of war cross French territory, in every town you will see charitable citizens take up collections for them. All Europe can bear witness to that truth, for we have had prisoners from all parts of Europe.

Certainly no foreign country comes close to giving us the same treatment. In Russia, our unfortunate comrades in arms have been sent into Siberia, where God alone knows what they had to endure. In England, not only did they suffer from official harshness, but individual Englishmen also treated them as enemies. The hate of one nation for another had become a hate of one man for another. The Spaniards are without doubt the most barbarous people. When our unfortunate comrades were not hanged, they crossed Spain amidst all sorts of insults: they suffered hunger and thirst; every day they were showered with stones and covered with filth. Those who survived such infamous treatment were imprisoned on the Island of Cabrera or the prison ships in Cadiz harbor.[1] I know of these horrors only by the reports of Frenchmen who survived them; they prove that a man can suffer much misery without dying — and also that there is a strong resemblance between Spain's old-fashioned Christians and the cannibals of the South Seas.

After that who would believe that there could be a race even more ferocious than the Spanish! One of my friends has told me of his life as a slave in Constantinople. The sufferings he endured would seem the stuff of fables if there were not plenty of people, still living, who can confirm the truth of his tale. He was captured together with 300 of his comrades; they were all fastened together by their necks, the chain to which they were fastened having the form of a long ladder which they carried horizontally on their shoulders. Each prisoner's head was between two iron cross-bars, placed so close together that they were barely able to breath. Since all these unfortunates were not the same height, the tall ones had to march bent over, while the shortest had to go always on tiptoe or risk being choked to death. Those who were too exhausted to keep up the pace or sick and soon to die were beaten pitilessly with clubs. When one of them died, their head was cut off and — incredible as it sounds — the next man in line was compelled to carry it. Since the Sublime Porte[2] rewarded its soldiers according to the number of enemies' heads they turned in, they didn't much care whether they brought in living prisoners or only that portion of their corpses. Imagine how those poor prisoners must have suffered under the boiling sunshine, marching a distance of some 600 miles, each one carrying a decaying head — some of them at the last being obliged to carry two.[3]

---

[1] Both hell-holes, but the island was far worse. See *Swords Around a Throne*, pp. 618-620.
[2] The Turkish government.

194

"Our fortunes soon will be the same," said Edie Ochiltree, Walter Scott's[4] beggar, facing the flood that was about to swallow up him and his companions. You might apply that same phrase to prisoners of war. From the moment they are in the power of the enemy, rank does not exist — that is to say that no one recognizes the old grades, but develops new ones.[5] You always run into a tough character who seizes authority and sets up a set of rules, which his companions soon accept. As soon as a few men are brought together, rules are developed. Some make them, and secretly laugh at them. That is the story of all human societies.

During our stay in Posen a column of Russian prisoners whom Napoleon was returning to Alexander, passed through that city; newly uniformed, armed, and equipped and organized into regiments. Several years earlier, Napoleon had used the same courtesy with Paul I, to whom he had thus returned the prisoners taken by Massena in Switzerland.[6] Our soldiers were furious to see them in new coats of good cloth while their own were so old that they were beyond repair. Napoleon wanted to woo the emperor of Russia, and the French prisoners coming home from Siberia, in rags, leaning on their staffs, crossed the path of these splendid columns, armed with French muskets.

Officers taken prisoner remained on the muster rolls as a matter of record, but were not promoted, and no one did anything for them. The Emperor was interested only in officers present for duty; you might say that no ruler ever treated enemy prisoners better, or those captured from his own army worse. He seemed to wish to punish those who allowed themselves to be captured, as if an enlisted man or junior officer ever were responsible for the capture of his unit. The regiments always did their duty; whenever one was captured in whole or part, that was because if had not been supported, or because it had been given an impossible mission.[7] The disaster always is the result of unforeseen circumstances or is the fault of the commander-in-chief, whether is in Emperor, marshal, or general. Since those gentlemen take all the glory of a campaign for themselves alone, it is only fair to hold them responsible for the blunders they commit from time to time. Besides, they have all the advantages; when the bravery of the soldiers and officers wins the victory, it adds to the fame of the commanding general. Our soldiers are brave beyond all description; every time that we called for a hundred volunteers, a thousand stepped forward from the ranks. The main concern of the officers is to keep them in hand, for they go forward swiftly. I need not say anything more; all Europe has seen them. All that can be written will neither augment or diminish

---

[3] Though Blaze does not mention it, Turks and Arabs frequently sodomized their prisoners. Their greatment was so brutal that even their Russian allies in 1798 finally could not tolerate it and intervened.

[4] From Scott's novel, "The Antiquary."

[5] As when junior officers took over from fearful seniors and led the seizure of one of the prison hulks in Cadiz harbor.

[6] Paul had been highly pleased and had promptly established close relations with France. Alexander however, was a far more devious character.

[7] Blaze's Note: "The word 'impossible' is not French," said some marshal of France or other. Such a retort is charming in vaudeville. Actors have repeated it a hundred times, with great satisfaction, to the frantic applause of their audiences, which proves only that the audiences are composed of imbeciles.

their glory. The story of so many high deeds, carved in stone or cast in bronze, will last longer than the Vendôme column and the Arch of Triumph. Their memory is forever.

Frederick II knew our army well; when Prince Ferdinand of Brunswick replaced the Duke of Cumberland after the latter had been defeated by Marshal d' Estrees at Hastenbeck in 1757, Frederick told him: "My cousin, you are going to fight the French. You will find it easy to vanquish their generals — but never their soldiers."[8]

While our imprisoned fellow-countrymen in Cadiz harbor, and on the Island of Cabrera endured every possible physical and mental agony, while they were pelted with filth, and every sort of ignominy was heaped upon them in each village through which they passed on their way to those horrible destinations, those Spaniards whom the fortunes of war made our prisoners were as well treated in France as French soldiers, and, in some localities much better. If there was a priest among them, the pious Catholics of the area took particular care of him: pampered, coddled, stuffed with sweetmeats,[9] the holy man would have no desire to return to Spain.

In the little town of S___, in Limousin,[10] a Spanish officer prisoner was billeted with a wealthy and very devout lady. He conducted himself with the greatest propriety, was always at his prayers, and talked only of religion; in short, his hostess soon regarded him as a minor saint. He also was a man of mystery; he carefully concealed some papers which he seemed to think of great importance. One day, while talking with the lady as he left the house, he pulled out his handkerchief and a letter fell from his pocket. Pretending not to have noticed it, he continued on his way. The letter was addressed to "His Eminence, Monseigneur the Archbishop of Toledo, at the home of Madame ____ at S___."

Immediately the demon of curiosity clutched the devotee. How could she not read the pages which she held open in her hands? Her good angel counseled discretion, but the devil rapidly won out. That's the way it is with women; and has been since time began. The letter advised His Eminence to remain strictly incognito; his friends were active and shortly would send him a large sum of money. Some carefully picked men would rescue him and bring him back to Spain — and so forth, and so on.

When this "archbishop" returned, the lady threw herself at his feet and asked his holy blessing. He pretended to be astonished; she showed him the letter and begged forgiveness. Thereafter our rascal played his part very expertly; he pretended to be concerned that his identity might be revealed; the lady promised to guard it; and he accepted her assurances. However the lady could not bear that such a dignitary of the church should continue in his modest room; she moved him into the finest one in her house, which soon was decorated with the most beautiful furnishings from the best houses of the town.

But it was not enough for her to have the archbishop of Toledo under her roof; others must know of it. The secret was choking her, so she eased her frustration by sharing it with some of her fellow gossips who told others, and soon the whole town shared the secret. Immediately everyone clubbed together to provide His Eminence with meals

[8]   I can not find any confirmation of this supposed quotation.

[9]   The great number of priests, monks, and other churchmen among the prisoners brought into France proved a major embarrassment. Devout Catholics were shocked to see them captive, though they included some of the cruelest Spanish irregulars. They refused to work, claiming treatment as officers.

[10]   Central France (a pre-Revolution province).

worthy of his exalted station. They also paid him homage in the form of a well-filled purse, so that he could extend charities to other Spanish prisoners. The rogue refused it for quite a while, finally deigning to accept it, but only as a loan. He had the role of Tartuffe[11] by heart: he even carried his impudence so far as to say mass privately in his room, and it was no small favor to be admitted that holy ceremony. The hostess was triumphant; she had become a leader in the town's society; the other devotees treated her with great respect. Her happiness bordered on delirium.

These happy times lasted three months. The authorities knew what was going on, but — believing that the swindler really was the archbishop of Toledo, and seeing nothing that might threaten the local law and order — did nothing about it. One day a new column of Spanish prisoners arrived; one of them, a colonel, had letters of recommendation to the assistant prefect, who invited him to dinner. During the dessert, the latter said to the colonel: "We have a Spaniard of the highest distinction here in our town."

"What is his name?"

"The archbishop of Toledo."

"Why, that's my uncle!"

"You don't say! You can see him right away."

"That's more than I'd hoped for, and yet I don't understand how my uncle could be here. I haven't heard that he had been captured."

"However, he is here."

"Well it's been six months since I last heard from him and a lot can happen in that time. My regiment was in Catalonia, and things move fast when there's a war going on."[12]

"Would you like to see him now?"

"Gladly. Let's go."

The colonel and the assistant prefect came into the drawing room where the "archbishop," in a violet robe, seated in a splendid armchair, was giving audience to all the imbeciles of the area. The officer came up to him and quickly saw he was not the uncle he had expected. "Villain," he told him, "you have had the insolence to assume a respectable name to swindle these honest people, but your act is over. Gentlemen, ladies, the archbishop of Toledo is my uncle, and this man is an imposter." And the colonel ended his speech with a vigorous whack to His Eminence's cheek. The rogue did not lose his head; with a saintly expression he cried out, "If someone strikes you, turn your other cheek to him! Happy those whom the world humiliates, for the Lord shall glorify them." Everyone, male and female, who formed the swindler's "Court" began screaming in outrage against the colonel. They attacked him, some of the most furious opened the windows to pitch him into the street by the shortest route, but the assistant prefect somehow managed to extricate him and to get him to safety amid the cries and uproar that swelled up in the streets. The soldiers of the garrison and the gendarmes turned out to put down the riot; the Spanish colonel was gotten away during the night under strong escort, and the next morning all the dupes were really astonished to learn that their "Archbishop" had vanished along with their silver.

It usually is a misfortune for an officer to be taken prisoner; however one of my friends found it very pleasant. His case was so very rare that I mention it as an exception. Monsieur K___ was being herded by cossacks through the Russian snows, when the

11 A religious hypocrite and confidence man in Moliere's 1664 comedy of that name.
12 Toledo is in central Spain, Catalonia is in the far northeast.

Grand Duke Constantine[13] rode through the column of French prisoners. By chance, he spoke to that officer, who answered him sensibly; a conversation began and the prince took a fancy to him. Then and there Constantine ordered that K___, with one of his comrades, be taken to a nearby chateau, where, until the war ended, they were treated like princes by the grand duke's people.

In 1814 they returned to Paris by post. Constantine protected them, got them assigned to regiments, heaped them with favors, was a witness to their marriages and a godfather to their children. Certainly that prince's death was not more regretted by the Russians[14] than by two French families.

Sometimes it happens that individuals in the two opposing armies help each other in adversity; for, in fact, combat soldiers kill one another without hatred. During an armistice we often visited the enemy's cantonments, and, while ready to gobble us up at the first alarm, they were always willing to do us a favor if the opportunity offered.

Before the 1809 Austrian campaign, the French army occupied the principality of Bayreuth; the Austrian army was camped along their Bohemian frontier. War had not yet been declared, but everyone knew that it would come with the springtime. We visited the Austrian officers in the area around Egra;[15] those gentlemen returned our visits. We dined together, champagne flowed freely, and everything went splendidly. Just before the armies began to move, we had a last rendezvous and all of us pledged ourselves over the blue flames of a bowl of punch to render each other all possible assistance if any of us became prisoners of war. Each of us wrote the names and addresses of all our friendly enemies in his notebook, and we went our separate ways. That pledge was scrupulously kept. Fifteen days later, at the battle of Ratisbon, both sides captured members of our association. They were well recommended to friends in those towns in France and Austria through which they would pass and where they would be held; they were loaned money (everyone thereafter helping to repay that debt of honor); and thus individuals mitigated the misfortunes caused by their governments.

As for myself, I was never made prisoner of war except in time of peace. Those two words seems to clash, so I shall explain. After the armistice which followed the battle of Bautzen[17] our army, composed of provisional regiments, grouped into provisional divisions, was immediately reorganized. A regiment might have one battalion at Dresden, another at Magdeburg, a third at Hamburg; these battalions, hastily raised after the return from Russia, had been sent off to the most important sectors as soon as they were formed.[18] Thus almost all colonels commanded three battalions, each from a different regiment. That was a faulty organization, but it did not keep us from winning the battles of Lutzen, Wurschen,[19] and Bautzen.

As soon as it was possible, all these fractions of the army moved out to join their regimental headquarters. It was like a swarm of bees in flight, and soon each one reached its destination. We were on the road the day after the armistice took effect and, since we had to cross a countryside devastated by both armies, I was ordered to precede

---

[13] Constantine Pavlovich, younger brother of Alexander I; noted as dashing, but erratic and not too bright.

[14] I have seen no evidence of any regret whatever!

[15] City at the western tip of Bohemia, also spelt as Eger; now known as Cheb.

[16] Now Regensburg. In central Bavaria, on the Danube River.

[17] 20-21 May 1813.

[18] See *Swords*, p. 216

[19] By Wurschen, Blaze apparently means the first day's fighting at Bautzen.

our division to arrange for food and shelter. On the third day, close to the little town of Sagan, I rode through a forest, thinking myself perfectly safe because of the armistice. It was a beautiful morning in June; I rode with loose reins, building castles in Spain — when all at once I was surrounded by a dozen cossacks, and I saw as many lances pointed at my chest. What can one man do against twelve? Surrender, isn't that it? That's what I hastened to do, as gracefully as possible. I certainly would have been a hero if I had killed all twelve. What a stirring tale of saber strokes could I have written today! It's really too bad! The next chance I get, I shall conduct myself better.

In an instant I was disarmed and stripped by five or six of the most expert valets you could find. I tried to explain the situation, but nobody understood me. The cossacks told me by signs that I must follow them, and I departed with a really impressive escort, and without the slightest worry over meeting highwaymen. We rode for two hours through the woods to a village where my captors' regiment was camped. These polite cossacks were operating as partisans in the rear of our army.

They took me to their colonel, Prince Galitzin, and I found a man of very good breeding, speaking French as well as you and I. "Good!" I said to myself, "He'll listen to reason, and I'll not end up in Siberia." I protested that his soldiers had made me a prisoner contrary to law of nations, that an armistice had been signed between the two armies three days previously, and that I counted on the honesty of a Russian colonel to let me continue on my way.

"That which you tell me, monsieur, is doubtlessly true, but I can not be certain, so I have the right to doubt it. However, if I receive an official announcement I give you my word of honor that you will be released."

"Very well, colonel, but your soldiers have taken my purse, my watch, my portmanteau, my epaulets —"

"Don't worry. You'll get them all back."

"But it would probably be better to collect all of them yourself, so as to have them available if I have told you the truth."

"I'll take care of it."

"This would be the best moment to do so, for soon my property will have changed owners. Besides, what do you risk in returning it to me right now? If I have lied, your soldiers can take it back because in that case I shall be your prisoner."

"I'll be responsible for everything; don't let it worry you the least bit. You shall have lunch with us; come and eat."

I lunched. I dined. The colonel and his officers were friendly and treated me with much respect. We talked about war, politics, the theater, literature, and the like; all went very smoothly. During the night, an orderly brought news of the armistice. At daybreak the next morning I was awakened by four big bearded fellows who made signs that I should follow them. My horse was ready; they indicated that I should mount up. One of them handed me my saber and wished me "bon voyage." I vainly tried to get them to comprehend that I wanted to speak to the colonel, or at least some officer; they hoisted me into my saddle, one of them took hold of my reins, and all five of us went off at the gallop. When we were near the main road my escort about-faced and I found myself all alone.[20]

---

[20] Blaze may have been the victim of a typical Russian charade. Cossacks, officers and men alike, frequently ignored armistices, the latter often playing highwaymen in their off-duty hours. Galitzin undoubtedly took his cut of Blaze's property.

However the division had arrived and had found neither food nor lodging. A hungry belly may not have ears, but it certainly does have a tongue. I was cursed from one end of the column to the other. General P___ was so furious when I reached him that he could not articulate one word. He had many things to say that, if "prison," "arrest," and "destitution"[21] did escape from his mouth, they were lost amid a deluge of interjections. I let him pour out his anger without interruption and when he had finished, I told him my story. For proof, I displayed my shoulders without epaulets, my horse without a portmanteau, my pocket and my fob without either purse or watch — and the general began laughing. "It's extremely fortunate," I told him, "that I got off so easily."

[21] Separation from the service under dishonorable conditions; no pension, decorations, and any titles revoked.

IN THIS ILLUSTRATION, IT IS THE COSSACK TAKEN PRISONER (JOB)

XVII
Military Executions

Military laws are very severe. They have to be — otherwise how would a general control 100,000 men, all of whom, personally, are as strong as he is. A simple misdemeanor, which in civilian life would cost the guilty man only a few days in prison, imposed by the court of petty sessions,[1] can mean a death sentence for the soldier. The least violence toward a superior, the least thing stolen in enemy country, can kill a man. This latter case is punished only by fits and starts; when there are no rations to distribute, the soldiers are allowed to forage as they please for fifteen days or three weeks. But as soon as some wagonloads of bread or biscuit arrive, an order of the day forbids any sort of pillage, and the first poor devil caught doing it has to pay for everyone's sins. I have seen one of these petty thieves shot for taking a pair of boots from a peasant — but the big thieves of the large financial enterprises never suffer the slightest punishment Sometimes the Emperor made them disgorge their ill-gotten gains, but he never shot them.

Military executions are for the small fry. The laws resemble cobwebs: the gnats are caught, the bumblebees break through. Just before the battle of Wagram, twelve employees[2] of the ration service were caught in the act of selling the Imperial Guard's rations. Several hours later they were executed.

"I hope that example will not be lost on you." I said to a certain *Riz-pain-sel*[3] of my acquaintance. "It's a good lesson. Take it to heart."

"Bah," he replied. "Didn't you see several of your friends killed during that last battle?"

"Yes, but how does that —?"

"Will that keep you from fighting tomorrow?"

"There's a difference!"

"I don't see any."

"So much the worse for you."

These pompous ration service personnel were really the curse of the army. While its military element fought or bivouacked in the mud, these gentlemen flaunted themselves in neighboring towns, chasing the ladies, while storing up the flour collected [from the countryside] by requisition. Probably some of it stuck to their hands for in general they were rolling in money they didn't know what to do with. You know the proverb on the embarrassment of riches; I have very often recollected its truth when applied to some of these gentlemen. They could send only small amounts of money back to France by the army postal system. If the sum was too large, someone would have become suspicious. The Ministry of War, calculating that it was impossible to save 10,000 francs a year out of a salary of 2,000 francs, would have broken the thief. They dared not leave

---

[1]   Roughly equivalent to our justice of the peace.

[2]   The bottom grade of Army administrative personnel.

[3]   "Rice-Bread-Salt." Blaze's Note: "The soldiers gave that name to the personnel of the ration service because they issued rice, bread, and salt to them; they also called them 'celery.'"

their hoard in their rooms, for eventually their doors would be broken in or their locks picked. To keep it constantly with them was painful and inconvenient. Poor unfortunates! All of them followed that last method. I have seen some whose waist belt was enormously heavy, whose coats were cuirasses of gold coins, sewn between the cloth and the lining.

Differing from the Paris loan-sharks who make young men sign a note for twice the sum they actually loan them, these administrative officials would offer officers whose parents were well-to-do a bonus of thirty to forty francs for every 100 loaned them; they were bargain-counter bankers. Officers whom I knew received 1,500 francs in gold for a letter of exchange for 1,000 francs, payable in six months in France. The essential thing for these officials was to hide their fortune; that bonus was of no great importance to them; they could make it up in three days.

It was a happy day for the soldiers when they caught a *riz-pain-sel* in an awkward position. If he had to pass a column, jeers of all sorts showered on him like snowflakes. I have seen some who didn't know how to hide themselves from that flood of mockery. Some tried to laugh it off, and that was best, for you can not out-shout a whole regiment.

One day at Kloster-Neuberg, an illustrious and celebrated abbey four leagues from Vienna, the immense wine cellars had been seized for distribution to the troops at the rate of one liter per man. A *fourrier* tasted the wine and found it weak.

"Look here, monsieur store-keeper, you're giving us water."

"What, water! You can see for yourself that it's wine."

"Wine that's been thoroughly baptized.[4] We *fourriers* ourselves would be blamed for that operation. We should not be the ones to risk punishment for it."

"*Fourriers* are never satisfied."

"Because you always satisfy yourselves first. Just remember that we're camped on the banks of the Danube. I refuse to accept this issue. I'm not going to have my detail breaking their backs just to carry water along the riverside."

"But all of you taste it now, and you will see who is right, the *fourrier* or I."

The head of a cask was staved in, and a dipper inserted. What came up? — A live fish, as frisky as his fellows in the nearby river.[5] There was one big howl against the storekeeper; the soldiers rushed him, and the officer in charge of the distribution had the greatest difficulty in getting him out of their hands.

We have nothing in France that can compare to the abbeys of Melk, Raygern, and Kloster-Neuberg. Their immense wine cellars have sufficed to quench the thirst of the French army for whole months on several occasions. I do not believe that the Paris markets have more wine than these abbeys possess, to the greatest glory of God. You'd think, when you see the wine cellars of those sanctuaries of godliness, that their owners couldn't have time for any other occupation than filling them—and then emptying them again.

> *"God lavishes his blessings*
> *On those who vow to be His own."*

Dufresny[6] said to Louis XIV: "I never look at the Louvre without saying to myself, Super monument of the power of our greatest kings, you would be perfect if you had

---

4   Soldier slang for diluting wine with water.
5   This same unfortunate discovery led to the wrecking of the Last Chance Saloon in Billings, Montana, in my extreme childhood. Only afterwards was it discovered that a playful cowboy customer was responsible for slipping minnows into the beer barrels.
6   Charles R. Dufresny (1648-1724), French writer and satirist.

been giveN to one of the orders of mendicant friars,[7] to hold their meetings and house their general."

The road from Vienna to Kloster-Neuberg runs along the right [south] bank of the Danube; the Austrians held the left bank where they had emplaced batteries at various places. Every Frenchman who passed that way was certain to be the target of all their cannon.

This uproar practically never had any unpleasant results; we called it "shooting at sparrows." But the Germans[8] were so methodical that they always did it, apparently as an act of conscience. I made the trip to Kloster-Neuberg twice and, both going and coming, I had a hundred cannon fired at me. My life certainly wasn't worth all that expense and noise.

The Germans are exact and methodical in small things as they are in important ones. For example, the mayors have long-bladed scissors to cut the paper on which billeting orders were printed, two to a sheet; they would cut and recut them until they were square. One of these gentlemen could not, he said, give me a billet because he had mislaid his scissors. I pointed out that a penknife or kitchen knife would do as well. Impossible, he replied — it was never done that way. Thereupon I picked up one of the sheets and tore it in half. The good man was really upset; he grumbled between his teeth and took at least a quarter-of-an-hour to complete my order. If the injury was serious, his vengeance was equally so, for I was never so badly lodged as I was that day.

One of my friends was very angry with certain important people who had returned to France with the restoration of Louis XVIII: "They only seem to know one word — *formerly* we did this, *formerly* no one did that, we are no longer the men we *formerly* were. I'd like to be king for twenty-four hours: I'd have them all shot."

"Bah," I told him, "You're becoming very spiteful."

"They would sill have the audacity to reply, 'Monsieur, *formerly* one didn't shoot—' Never mind — stand him over there, bandage his eyes, and let's get on with it."

The man who first though to associate glory with the military profession was certainly no fool. Without that motivation, nobody would enter it; it is surprising that they do so even with that reward. Let us suppose that a man like ourselves, sat on the moon, and that someone told him: "Behold 100,000 men; they are going to fight under the command of a single individual for reasons they do not understand and for which not one of them gives a damn. Some were brought there by force, others because they like it, but all of them will risk all possible dangers out of self respect. They will be killed, possibly crippled, or mutilated — which often is worse than death. They will endure every hardship, fatigue, and kind of bad weather. If one of these men disobeys his commander, he will be killed; what's more, his comrades will be his executioners. While these 100,000 men leave their country to pick a fight with their neighbors, those who remain behind in their native land must labor to feed and clothe them and especially to make up for the vast waste for which war is always a pretext. The 100,000 men return, wounded, crippled by rheumatism, and in rags — and for a reward they can admire the statue of their general in a public square.

---

[7]   The Augustines, Carmelites, and Dominicans, which began as wandering beggar (mendicant) priests, but later became wealthy and fond of luxury.

[8]   The French considered the Austrians proper to be "Germans" — something that a good many northern Germans did not.

What would the man in the moon say? He would laugh in your face, maintaining that such things are not possible. Whole populations would tell him that nevertheless it is true. Forced to believe that, he would think that the general is an immensely strong man, of whom everyone is frightened. But what would he say when he saw a man covered with decorations, but often physically weaker than the least of the camp followers. He would say — I guess he would say, that the inhabitants of earth are fools, and that their rulers are not too stupid.

Having seen so many brave soldiers mutually working themselves to death for nothing, I have sometimes told myself that there is really something curious about a man; his total disregard for his own life under certain circumstances. Why then do these men — who yesterday grumbled, ranted, and swore over executing a very simple order, requiring them at most to march one or two leagues out of their way — do not grumble today when they're about to play for their lives at double-or-nothing. Because we consider dishonor far from grumbling and close to cowardice. Who was the first to set these standards? He was the man with the heaviest fist: he beat the others; he wanted to be honored. It is very agreeable to be honored, said the others. We have been beaten; now let us beat our neighbors and force them in turn to respect us.

Some Arab tale, [I can't recall which] tells of a prince who possessed a marvelous ring which made him invisible when he turned it. What would happen, I ask, on a day of battle if each of us — French, Prussian or Russian — had such a ring on his finger? I'm very certain that everyone would have turned their ring as soon as they heard the first cannon shot. I am there because you are there, and you know where I am and what I'm supposed to be doing — but the devil take it if I'll stay if you don't know it.

When you fight at night you seldom have much difficulty; to begin with, because you can't see anything; and also because no one can see you. Do you think that the brave Bianchelli who led the assault at Tarragona, would have shown such bravery if he had not been certain that the eyes of the whole army were on him?

A regiment is on the march; they talk, they laugh loudly, someone sings a merry ballad; it's a constant blaze of buffoonery. An aide-de-camp arrives and speaks with the colonel who orders a halt to load muskets. Soon the march resumes, but there is no more joking, nobody says anything, everyone is quietly thinking about what is going to happen; behold the man alone with himself. Then the enemy appears. Everyone yells, "Forward!" Everyone wants to advance at the run; behold the man in contact with other men. Do you want to do that? Me too! Do you want to charge? O.K., I'll get there before you — but if you'd just as soon sit down, I'll ask for nothing better than to lie down.

I have said that the gnats get caught in the spider's web. During the retreat from Portugal,[9] General D___ had a poor devil shot for having eaten a cluster of grapes. "How horrible," say some. "That's impossible," say others. To which I respond that it is true; what's more, it was the right thing to do. Dysentery was ravaging the army; the soldiers were dying by dozens. It was forbidden under pain of death, to eat grapes, that fruit being the sole cause of that disease. The first soldier surprised doing so served as an example for all the rest. A court-martial went into session beside the road; a quarter-hour afterwards, the poor devil no longer existed.

What was the result? No one ate any more grapes; men recovered their health. The death of one man saved several thousand. The commanding general had acted

---

[9]   Probably Massena's retreat in early 1811.

correctly. As the Romans said on critical occasions, "Fear the consuls."[10] Whether or not D___ had the right to give that order does not matter; everyone approved that extreme severity because it probably saved half the army. If those fine masters of portentous wordage had been there[11] they would certainly have had a wonderful opportunity to display their loquacity. They would have won a pardon for the poor devil — and killed the body to save a finger. The death of that grape-eater was necessary for the good of us all; it was essential that everyone saw that that order of the day was not an empty threat; as soon as they understood that, the disease ended by the removal of its cause.

If someone had been as prompt to apply the laws to the large-scale thieves, the war in Spain would not have lasted as long. How many images of saints in gold or silver, how many pyx chests and chalices, were melted down into ingots to be later exchanged for Paris mansions? How many diamonds and rubies, after having ornamented the pompous and poetical ceremonies of the Roman Catholic Church for centuries, have been all amazed to find themselves on the bare throat of a dancer of the Paris Opera?

Nearly all of the magnificent paintings which decorated Spanish churches have taken the road into France; today they grace the galleries of the prosperous families of our capital. Today you will seldom see them in Spain; they show you the empty space where they once hung, filled up with a shabby black serge drape. Only bad paintings of *autos-da-fe*[12] painted by the Inquisition's daubers, remain.

If we had shot a few of our patrons of the fine arts, who protected their thefts so carefully in their strongly escorted wagons, the war would not have become a national one, but that would have required that those gentlemen have themselves shot.[13]

These robberies were the cause of the war to the death which the Spaniards waged against us. Thousands of soldiers were murdered[14] because certain persons pillaged churches and convents. The priests and monks, seeing all that they had amassed for several centuries carried off in one day, excited the people everywhere to arise in insurrection.[15] They proclaimed it the holiest of duties, they damned to the eternal flames anyone who did not take up arms against their common enemy, and promised all the joys of paradise to those who died fighting. In a country where the word of any man in a monk's cowl or a priest's cassock was always accepted as truth, such a crusade — preached with a crucifix in one hand and a dagger in their other — must produce the most horrible results. The marvels of the siege of Saragossa should not have surprised us.[16]

But what I have always disapproved, and what has always been a great vexation to me, is the severity with which we punish pillaging one day after having tacitly allowed it for a month. From the moment the order prohibiting it is published, woe to the man who

10 The two chief magistrates of the Roman Republic.
11 Blaze could practically be describing our own legal profession, especially its "civil rights" contingent!
12 The sentencing and/or burning of condemned heretics.
13 Probably the biggest thief was Marshal Soult, who commanded in southern Spain.
14 Blaze says "hanged," but the Spanish usually showed more imagination.
15 This is all true, but there is also the fact that Joseph Napoleon's government proposed closing monasteries; faced with the disagreeable prospect of having to work for a living, their inmates preferred to fight.
16 Saragossa held out during sieges in June-July, 1808 and December 1808-February 1809, Lannes finally methodically took the city apart. The resistance *was* fanatical, but much embroidered in Spanish/English mythology.

does not obey it; the next day he no longer exists. We arrived at Wismar, the soldiers went marauding through the neighboring villages, a peasant was killed. Suddenly the pillagers were rounded up; 200 were put under arrest and imprisoned in a church. General L___ at once named a court-martial to judge the assassin, who was to be shot before the division moved the next morning.

One of my friends, appointed judge-advocate of the court, went into the church, followed by all the peasants. None of them could identify the guilty soldier, who probably had escaped the round-up. His mission ended there, since no one could be accused. He went to the general and explained the situation.

"Never mind, monsieur," said L___ who was busy with his supper, "Take care of things. That crime must be punished."

"Certainly, sir. But whom do we punish?"

"That's your business."

"All the peasants agree that the killer had red epaulets, so he is a grenadier. We have forty locked up — I have separated them from the rest — but no one recognizes any of them as the guilty man."

"Put the names of all those grenadiers [on separate slips of paper] in a bag, have them each draw one. The first one to draw his own name will be shot tomorrow."

"My general, I cannot do such a thing."

"I order you to."

"I refuse."

The general rose from his table in a fury, calling for the corporal of the guard. "Give me your sword!"

"There it is."

"Lock the captain up."

The judge-advocate was marched away. But the next morning "Philip Sober"[17] returned his sword, and nobody was shot.

During the Bautzen campaign, a voltigeur of my regiment was executed for having stolen a woman's black apron to make a cravat out of it.

The officers of his company entreated and beseeched General P___ to postpone the execution until they could ask the Emperor for a pardon. All that was fruitless; the poor devil must die. While the troops were getting into position for the execution, some soldiers found a baby hare. Riding up, the general saw and demanded the animal.

"Oh, but it's cute! Oh, how pretty! It would be wrong to kill it; it's so young."

To prevent the little hare from being trampled by the soldiers, the general galloped off, deposited the animal in a safe place, and then calmly returned to see his voltigeur shot.

---

17 Blaze here refers to a story of Philip II, King of Macedon and father of Alexander the Great: while dozing/drunk he sentenced an officer, who thereafter appealed to Philip "awake"/ "sober" and was pardoned.

There was something strangely incongruous, to an observer, that this man, in his embroidered coat, would ride through the rye to find a place of safety for his baby hare — he who only a short time earlier had remained insensitive to the tears of an old captain pleading for a veteran voltigeur. I have known here and there a good many of these people whom nature has endowed with truly exquisite sensibilities.

A military execution is a terrifying spectacle. I have never seen a civil execution; I know of the guillotine only through pictures, but quite often my duty has fixed me opposite some unlucky fellow who was about to be shot. I don't know how fast his pulse was beating, but certainly it did not beat faster than mine.

The troops from a square with only three sides — the fourth is left vacant for the passage of musket balls. All available troops take part, which is certainly a good idea — if you're going to make a terrible example, you should at least make it useful for those who aren't being shot. The condemned soldier arrives, accompanied by a priest.[18] Immediately the drums beat the *aux champs*, keeping it up until he is in the center of the square. Then they beat a *ban*.[19] The judge-advocate reads the sentence, the drummers close the *ban*, the condemned is made to kneel, and his eyes are bandaged. Twelve corporals, commanded by a sergeant-major, then shoot the unfortunate at a range of ten paces.

To diminish, if that is possible, the condemned man's agony, commands to the firing squad are silent, the sergeant-major making them with his cane. In case the man is not killed outright, as sometimes happens, a reserve squad of four men stands ready to finish him off, firing point-blank.

It is with a heavy heart that I describe these horrors; sad memories of them haunt me. The poor unfortunates whom I have seen kneeling at that fatal moment all pass before my eyes like ghosts.[20] At all these executions, if they take place near a town, some fine ladies never fail to appear. Despite their so-delicate nerves, they work their way into a good place from which they can see everything perfectly — and if you killed a chicken in their presence the next day, the sight would make them sick.

After the execution, all the troops present are marched past the body and back to their barracks. Everyone talks about it for three days, and soon it is forgotten.

I have seen several of these unfortunates die with admirable composure. In 1817 we were assembled for that sad ceremony on the plan of Grenelle.[21] The culprit was on his knees, but arose and asked permission to say goodbye to his company. Since that would only prolong everyone's distress, his request was refused. He knelt again, but promptly stood up, saying that he wished to satisfy a minor need. "You will not refuse me," he said, "for this will be the last time." The operation took at least two long minutes; once it was completed, he knelt, replace the bandage over his eyes, and —

I have seen some who harangued the regiment, who gave the command to fire themselves, without the least hint of emotion. But the man who, in such a case, showed

---

[18] Seldom during 1792-1814.
[19] Blaze's Note: "A *ban* is a certain drum beat which precedes ["opens"] and follows ["closes"] any proclamation."
[20] Since, especially in time of peace, the death penalty was imposed chiefly for serious crimes — murder, rape, forcing a safeguard, mutiny — Blaze's maunderings here seem about on par with General P___'s "sensibilities."
[21] Just outside Paris.

THE EXECUTION OF MALET AND HIS ACCOMPLICES ON OCTOBER 23, 1812

the most astonishing courage was Malet.[22] Brought out to the plain of Grenelle with thirteen of his accomplices, he demanded — as chief of the conspirators — permission to give the order to fire.

"Carry ... arms!" he shouted in a voice of thunder. "That's sloppy — try again. Everyone! Support ... arms!"

"Carry ... arms! Good, very good, Squad ... ready arms! Aim. Fire!" All fell, except Malet who still stood. "And then me, sacred Name of God! Reserve squad, forward! Good. Carry ... arms! Squad ... ready arms! Aim. Fire!"

---

[22] General Charles-Francois de Malet (1754-1812). Of noble birth; entered service as a "musketeer" of the Royal Guard. Commissioned as a captain, 1789. Turned Republican; general during Revolution. Probably mentally unbalanced. Involved in a plot in 1809; forced to retire. While Napoleon was in Russia, master-minded an elaborate conspiracy that momentarily got control of Paris.

XVIII
Retirement

"Haven't you ever wanted to be a soldier?" I said one day to Father Barberi, who was the first to initiate me into the mysteries of declension and conjugation, the merry science of the participle, and the pleasant combinations of gerundive and supine.

"Oh! I certainly have wished to be one, and still would like to, if I could choose my position."

"And which one would you prefer?"

"Frankly, I have always wanted to be a retired major general."

During the thirty years that an officer serves, he is always thinking of that time when — having retired — he will be free from all duties and can do as he pleases, plant his cabbages or have them planted.[1] When that time comes, when he settles down in his little hometown, he ordinarily is bored. Every day of his former life had been full of events and incidents; now, it takes on an appalling sameness. He is lucky if he has settled in a garrison town. In that case, the daily guard mount, the arrival of a regiment, a large-scale maneuver are happy events, which he never misses. There are more retired officers in Metz, Lille, Valenciennes, and Strasbourg than elsewhere. Those who have no families and have no particular preference as to where they live, chose a fortress city since there they can at least see others doing what they once did themselves. So Virgil describes the heroes in the Elysian Fields,[2] breaking their horses and readying their weapons for combat.

A retired officer is easy to recognize To begin with, his face is entirely different from those of a lawyer or a doctor; it is bronzed and stern; its features are strongly marked. His speech is short and emphatic. If the retired officer still has occasion to give orders, his meaning is unmistakable; he obeys orders, and he sees that they are obeyed, because it is essential that he obey and that he be obeyed; it is a basic requirement of his existence. He is kind, but his children tremble before him; if he is speaking, they'd better keep quiet. He is old, but his back is still straight; he walks straight-legged; if he is lame, if he has only one leg, if that missing leg is replaced by a piece of wood, it does not matter — you still will hear the regular, cadenced military step. If I may make use of the most unflattering comparison, just as you always can recognize a galley-slave[3] who has escaped from prison by the way in which he drags the leg to which his chain was riveted, an old soldier is easily identified by the way he holds his head. The former always retains the habits he learned in the squalor of the prison; in his mind, he still is at Brest or Rochefort. The second, proud of his long service, of his wounds, and his ribbon,[4] remembers Marengo, Austerlitz and Wagram.

---

[1] "To plant cabbages" is old French slang for "retiring into private life."

[2] The classical Greek version of heaven, reserved for an elite clientele — most went to Hades.

[3] The term was still used, though these convicts were then employed only at hard labor, especially around naval bases such as Brest and Rochefort.

[4] Of the Legion of Honor.

Even in civilian clothes, the retired officer retains something of his old regiment. His black cravat shows a white edging; the buttons of his waistcoat are from an old uniform; he often wears his old uniform trousers. When at home, he always dons his old fatigue cap; his dressing gown is an old overcoat, cut six inches shorter. He never says, "Clean that up," but "Police that up." If he takes his wife to see a maneuver (most retired officers are married), his attention is absorbed by the commands he hears given; he sees the mistakes and points them out to the people around him. If the troops begin to move in his direction, he never fails to say, "Let's get out of here, my dear; they want to come this way."

Arrange an appointment with a retired officer, and he will always be the first to arrive; military punctuality is never forgotten. He never says, "I'll come see you after twelve o'clock," but "after guard mount." The words "guard mount," "drill," and "maneuver," are incrusted in his brain. To him, his old regiment was the finest in the army. Start him on that subject, and you will hear some wonderful things. That esprit de corps that unites 2,000 men around the same single flag comes from the noblest sentiments, tinged perhaps with a slight portion of pride — but then, what can you do without pride?

An officer often counts up his years of service, his campaigns, and his wounds; he knows the law on retirement and its supplementary tables by heart. He is always calculating when he will get that long awaited promotion, which naturally will increase his retired pay. Laborie did nothing else all day long; his head was always struggling with the calculations needed to establish the exact total of the money he had on hand, plus his back pay. The whole sum, wisely invested, would increase his income after he retired. Every day he could tell you, within two hours, the time still had to serve.

"What day of the month do we possess?" He would say to me every morning.

"It's the 20th." (You can be sure that Laborie knew that better than I did.)

"Good. Tomorrow's the 21st."

"Necessarily."

"After tomorrow, the 22nd; Sunday the 23rd. That day will pass quickly; we'll have an inspection."

"And a full-dress parade, so we won't get out of the habit."

"Monday, the 24th. All week long we'll come and go; then comes the end of the month."

"I agree with you that it will come!"

"I am already due ten month's pay; that will make eleven. At 114 francs (I'm not counting what they'll deduct for the band) that will make 1,254 francs,[5] and there's 660 francs which I have in my purse (and right there and then he would display them, "roll call" he termed it), so I command 1,914 francs. I've also twenty francs in cash, but I won't count them in. If they'll give me the maximum of retired pay, that will be fine, for I'll go rejoin Babet."

The day we commenced a new month, Laborie would ask me the date sooner than usual. He gloried in adding the 114 francs due him on the 30th to what he had. My worthy lieutenant did not like those months with thirty-one days and had a particular liking for February, especially when it was not leap year.

---

[5] Pay often was badly in arrears during the latter years of the Empire, but old sweats like Laborie seldom seemed to have worried much. Note that it was customary for each officer to "contribute" one day's pay each month to support the regimental band.

"When I retire, I'll settle in Brittany — living is cheap there and there's good hunting," said one. "It's Burgundy, where they drink good wine, for me," said another. "And I'm for Provence; the weather's always good in spite of the mistral; or maybe because of the mistral."[6] A few cannonballs often upset these fine plans, but that didn't stop the survivors from building new castles in Spain the next day.

Laborie always talked of rejoining Babet: you would think that the honest man was in love with his wife, but when they were together they spent all their time arguing. The woman was shrewish and stingy; to have peace in the family, Laborie turned his pay over to her, keeping back only what he absolutely needed for personal expenses.[7]

We often poked fun at him about his docility.

"If you were in my place," he would reply, "we'd see how well you'd do." One day, to cure him of his extreme complaisance, we decided to trick him into a real quarrel with Babet. Seizing the moment when he had gone out, we went to call on his wife.

"We'd like to speak to Monsieur Laborie."

"He is at the barracks, gentlemen."

"That's really too bad, for we wanted to speak to him right away."

"About what?"

"Oh, nothing — nothing."

"But, really —"

"It's his personal business. He might possibly be angry with us if we told you."

"Why is that, gentlemen? My husband tells me everything, and I want to know all about this."

"He doubtless will tell you, but I'm afraid he'd want to tell you all about it himself."

"It is absolutely necessary that I know what you want to tell my husband."

Then we pretended to discuss it amongst ourselves Should we tell her? Or shouldn't we? After several minutes of pretended consideration. "We don't risk anything in telling madam all about it," I said to the scapegraces who accompanied me, "because the secret can't be kept much longer. Once she has the monkey, she'll know all about it."

"What monkey?"

"A monkey your husband wanted to buy. It's a really fine animal. The dealer wanted 200 francs at first; Monsieur Laborie offered him 150. For a long time the dealer refused to accept his offer, but today he has agreed. We were going to give your husband the good news. It's a real bargain, and certainly not expensive."

"Ah! My husband wants to have a monkey?"

"A charming monkey, a real jewel."

"Well! Let him show up with his monkey! I'll take care of the dealer and the purchaser — I'll arrange them —"

"But madam, think —"

"I think that because of you he's already bought a flute, and that it is you who really gave him that idea. I still have the flute. If anyone wants it, I'll sell it cheaply."

"I assure you that 150 francs is not much money —"

The dame slammed the door in our faces. But when the husband returned, it was something else again. For a quarter-of-an-hour she wept and threatened, while saying that he was ruining them to buy monkeys. Making no sense of that, the poor man

---

[6] A wind out of the north, dry and cold. It blew all the time I was on post-WIA recuperation leave. The Outer Hebrides would have been more comfortable.

[7] Then how did he happen to have 660 francs in his purse?

thought his wife had lost her mind, and said so. Then from threats they went to blows, and we were barbarians enough to laugh. I must admit that we were really rascals in those days.

I have forgotten to tell you the story of that flute, which Madam Babet accused me of having persuaded her husband to purchase. I was the truly innocent cause of that extraordinary expenditure — judge for yourself.

In the camp at Tilsit, Laborie and I shared the same hut. Alone with him, I had the habit of singing every now and then, but softly and for my own pleasure.

One day there was an auction of the effects of several officers killed during that campaign. Among those items was a flute, which Laborie saw fit to buy. All his comrades laughingly asked what he intended to do with an instrument he did not know how to play, if he were going to take music lessons, and like pleasantries. "Follow me," he said, "and we'll all have a laugh."

I was lying on my bed, reading while I awaited the time for drill, when I saw Laborie enter with thirty officers of all grades. The hut could not hold all of them, so half had to wait outside the door. I promptly stood up, trying to comprehend the reason for such a mass of visitors, when Laborie placed himself in the middle of the crowd and made this superb speech: "Gentlemen, I am curious to know if my second lieutenant, who has called me a Gascon[8] often enough, is not himself more of a one than I am. We're going to see what you can do," he continued, thrusting the flute at me. "You sing all the time when we're together here; you must believe that I consider you a good musician. Well, *if you are, let's hear you play this!*"

"I never told you that I understood music, or that I could play the flute."

"I'm certain of that," shouted Laborie triumphantly. "Every time you start singing, I'll give you the flute to play. It cost me thirty francs, but I'd have been happy to buy it if it cost me 200."

In the pursuit of glory you win many things: the gout and medals, a pension and rheumatism. "Ouch! My leg; the weather is changing; Oh, my arm; the barometer is falling."[9] Also frozen feet, one limb missing, a musketball lodged between two bones where the surgeon cannot extract it. Do I say one ball? It might be two or ten. I have known good soldiers whose skin resembled a skimmer and who carried enough lead in their bodies to go hunting the day the season opened. What hazards there are in this world — some men are wounded every time they go into action; others always come out of it safe and sound.

All those bivouacs in the rain and snow, all those privations, all those fatigues endured when you are young — you pay for them when you are old, after you have retired. Because you have already suffered, you must suffer again — which doesn't seem entirely fair. The pay is less, but — to even things up — your needs are doubled.

Sometimes a retired officer utilizes his free time for honorable work; in that case he passes from strict necessity to an honorable competency. There are plenty of old campaigners in merchants' accounting houses and in governmental offices. The precision which they bring to their new duties is the same as that with which they formerly executed their orders. The retired officer does everything conscientiously; he

[8] In contemporary French slang, this meant a braggart, possibly also a swaggerer. It has come into English as "gasconade."

[9] As Kipling put it, "Dry scars that ache of winter-nights."

is generally a good husband and a good father—a little brusque, a little surly, but honest and worthy.

If there are those who work to keep themselves busy and to increase their income, there are many who do nothing and don't want to do anything. They are bored from morning to night; they roam around the barracks and often they are inclined to request permission to command a period of drill. Thus a shopkeeper, retired from business, doesn't know what to do from the moment he no longer has customers to talk to.

Others retire in the country. They take care of their gardens and hunt as much as they can. They do well; I have no fault to find with them. I have known those who never accept employment from anyone, at any wage. After obeying for thirty years, they delight in that sweet thought that they are their own masters; they do not have to ask anyone's permission to go, come, eat, or sleep, and that they are free to do as they wish.

A captain of cavalry, who was about to retire, made an unusual proposal to the oldest trumpeter in his regiment.

"My friend, I'm about to retire in the country. I have a small house, some acres of farmland, and my pension. With all that, I hope to live at my ease. If you wish to accompany me, we shall plant cabbages and eat them together."

Retired Officers watch soldiers at drill (Job)

"If I wish! I know that's exactly what I wish."

"Very well. I shall arrange for your discharge, but I make one condition."

"Which?"

"You perform in the country with me the same service you do in the regiment. You will sound reveille, roll call, stable call, drill call, guard mount, and all the rest."

"Captain, I shall sound all you wish."

Our men left the service and installed themselves in a simple house where the captain was delighted to be his own commanding officer and to do as he wished. At certain hours the trumpeter — after having blown his warlike instrument — would come all out-of-breath into the officer's room.

"Well, what is that?"

"Captain, the regiment is mounting up."

"That's very well for the regiment; if I were there I'd be doing the same. In my place, I do as I wish, and I make fun of the regiment."

That honest captain did not exactly say, "I make fun of." He used a more colorful expression, but I do not choose to employ it here. Those dignified cavalry officers are always cursing; we infantrymen are much more reserved. The captain got up late; sometimes he didn't get up at all. He smoked his pipe, watched the cabbages grow, and laughed up his sleeve as he listened to the trumpeter periodically sound his harmonious solos.

"Well, what was that one?"

"My captain, large-scale maneuvers today."

"I make fun of it."

"The weather is fine."

"So much the better, my friend. I make fun of it too."

"Guard mount."

"Good."

"Stable call."

"Excellent."

"Inspection."

"Better and better."

"Dismounted drill."

"After that?"

"Mounted drill."

"I'll look forward to it."

"And then tomorrow the marshal reviews us."

"Very early in the morning I'm sure, by Jove!" And then he burst into laughter.

"Well, tell him that I make fun of him — and I'm going to bed."

As for myself, benevolent reader, to thank you for the patience that you have shown in following me through all my babbling, I will tell you very confidentially that I somewhat resemble that worthy captain. I have no trumpeter at my orders, which frequently irks me, but, in ample compensation the cabbages which I plant grow in Chennevieres-sur-Marne. From the upper end of that village I have the pleasure of hearing the drums, the trumpets, and even the cannon of Vincennes. "Keep up your courage, my friends," I tell them, now and then. "Beat, blow, shoot, thunder — I make fun of it — and I'm going to bed."

Appendix

As a student entomologist, I learned to be careful with new specimens - they might have a sting in their tail!

So it has been with Blaze's military service.

This book has him retiring in 1819 as a captain. However another edition of *Vie Militaire*[1] states that he did so in 1830 as a *chef de bataillon*, after having been wounded in Paris street fighting against the July Revolution of that year. (It also stated that he had successfully employed one aspect of his military skills in 1818 to conquer a rich widow.)

Then, at the last moment — with this book cocked, locked, and headed for printing — Pierre Piffaretti, a good friend of many years, succeeded in locating Blaze's statement of service in the archives of the *Service Historique de l'Armée de Terre* at Vincennes. It is short, succinct - and ends in a sting.

NOMS DE BAPTÊME ET DE FAMILLE.	DETAIL DES SERVICES.	DATES.			CAMPAGNES ET BLESSURES.	NOMINATION dans un autre corps, RETRAITE OU MORT.
		Jours.	Mois.	Années.		
Jean Joseph Louis Elzéard Blaze	Né à *Paraillou*, Arrondissement d'Avignon, Département de *Vaucluse*. Entré aux Chasseurs à pied de la garde impériale le ... nommé sous-lieutenant au 108e Régiment lieutenant le Capitaine le	13. 11 11 8 3	8bre 9bre Avril Juin août	1788 1806 1807 1809 1811.	a fait la Campagne de 1807, de 1809 d'Allemagne, 1811 et 1812 en Espagne, 1813 à la défense de Hambourg	Nommé aide de Camp du Général *Kellermann* le 1er 9bre 1811. Rentré le 1er Mai 1813. Déserté à Harbourg le 25 avril 1814

OBSERVATIONS.   DATES.

215

Statement of Service

Jean Joseph Louis Elzeard Blaze[2]

Born 18 October 1788 at Cavaillon, *arrondissement* of Avignon, Department of Vaucluse.

Entered the *chasseurs à pied*[3] of the Guard, 15 September 1806.

Commissioned *sous* (second) lieutenant, 108th Regiment of Line Infantry, 11 April 1807.

Served in the campaign of 1807 (Friedland).

Promoted to (first) lieutenant 8 June 1809.

Served in the campaign of 1809 (Wagram).

Promoted to captain 3 August 1811.

Served in Spain 1811-1813.

Detached as aide de camp to General (illegible) 1 December 1811.

Returned (apparently to regimental duty) 1 May 1813

Took part in the defense of Hamburg, *from which he deserted 25 April 1814.*[4]

(A letter in his dossier notes that he was still alive and receiving a pension as of 2 October 1823.)[5]

---

[1]   Sent to me by my Anglo-Swedish friend, Paul B. Austin, it was published sometime between 1872 and 1913 by *Libraire Henry du Parc of Paris*, with the subtitle *Morals and Customs of the Garrison, the Bivouacs, and the Barracks*. It omits considerable material, including chapter I and XI, but it is heavily salted with new *"adventures galantes,"* at least one of which — that Blaze "cuddled" a Prussian mistress for a month without realizing she only had one arm — seems decidedly odd.

[2]   As written here, his name looks more like "Blase."

[3]   In this book Blaze says his velite service was with the far more prestigious *chasseurs à cheval*. Clerical error, or did Blaze remember it "with advantages"?

[4]   Though Marshal Davout, who had received no official notice of Napoleon's abdication on 11 April, was carrying on cautious negotiations with the Russian commander (General Bennigsen, a thoroughly untrustworthy incompetent) at this time, outpost fighting was still going on briskly until 29 April, and the French did not begin evacuating Hamburg until 27 May. Blaze therefore deserted his comrades in the face of the enemy — a thoroughly contemptible action which no subsequent peacetime service under the Bourbons could extenuate.

[5]   Louis XVIII's government would have regarded this desertion as a virtuous act. From some passages of this book, it seems likely that he served under the Bourbons for at least a few years after 1814/1815. It really would be interesting to know what he did during the Hundred Days!